STONE TOOLS IN HUMAN EVOLUTION: BEHAVIORAL DIFFERENCES AMONG TECHNOLOGICAL PRIMATES

In *Stone Tools in Human Evolution* John Shea argues that over the past three million years hominins' technological strategies shifted from occasional tool use, much like that seen among living non-human primates, to a uniquely human pattern of obligatory tool use. Examining how the lithic archaeological record changed over the course of human evolution, he compares tool use by living humans and non-human primates, and predicts how the archaeological stone tool evidence should have changed as distinctively human behaviors evolved. Those behaviors include using cutting tools, logistical mobility (carrying things), language and symbolic artifacts, geographic dispersal and diaspora, and residential sedentism (living in the same place for prolonged periods). Shea then tests those predictions by analyzing the archaeological lithic record from 6500 years ago to 3.5 million years ago.

John J. Shea is Professor of Anthropology at Stony Brook University. He is the author of *Stone Tools in the Paleolithic and Neolithic Near East: A Guide* (2013), and co-editor of *Out of Africa 1: The First Hominin Colonization of Eurasia* (2010). Shea is also an expert flintknapper whose demonstrations of stone tool production and other "ancestral technology" skills appear in numerous television documentaries and in the United States National Museum of Natural History in Washington, D.C., as well as in the American Museum of Natural History in New York City.

STONE TOOLS IN HUMAN EVOLUTION

Behavioral Differences among Technological Primates

JOHN J. SHEA

Anthropology Department
Stony Brook University

CAMBRIDGE
UNIVERSITY PRESS

CAMBRIDGE
UNIVERSITY PRESS

One Liberty Plaza, 20th Floor, New York, NY 10006, USA

Cambridge University Press is part of the University of Cambridge.

It furthers the University's mission by disseminating knowledge in the pursuit of education, learning, and research at the highest international levels of excellence.

www.cambridge.org
Information on this title: www.cambridge.org/9781107123090

First published 2017

Printed in the United States of America by Sheridan Books, Inc.

A catalogue record for this publication is available from the British Library

Library of Congress Cataloguing-in-Publication data
Shea, John J. (John Joseph) author.
Stone tools in human evolution : behavioral differences among technological primates / John J. Shea, Anthropology Department, Stony Brook University.
Cambridge, United Kingdom : Cambridge University Press is part of the University of Cambridge, [2017] | Includes bibliographical references and index.
LCCN 2016028973 | ISBN 9781107123090 | ISBN 9781107554931 (paperback)
LCSH: Tools, Prehistoric. | Stone implements. | Human evolution. | Social evolution.
LCC GN799.T6 S54 2017 | DDC 930.1/2–dc23
LC record available at https://lccn.loc.gov/2016028973

ISBN 978-1-107-12309-0 Hardback
ISBN 978-1-107-55493-1 Paperback

For Pat, Bianca, and Boudicca

CONTENTS

FIGURES

TABLES

BOXES

PREFACE

Stone tools are potentially rich sources of information about the evolution of human behavior, but archaeologists squander that potential. Countless books and papers try to convince other paleoanthropologists of stone tools' relevance to major issues in human evolution, but time and again when archaeologists read papers about stone tools at scientific meetings, their colleagues check email, peruse the meeting program, or head for the restrooms or the bar. College textbooks on human evolution barely mention the lithic (stone tool) evidence. In my own archaeology classes, I spend less and less time lecturing about stone tools each year.

This is a shame. No other line of evidence has such a wide perspective on the evolution of human behavior. Our ancestors and other hominins left stone tools everywhere they lived. Because non-human primates also use stone tools, stone tool use is a logical focal point for comparisons of human vs. non-human primate behavior. Behavior varies, and human behavior varies more than that of any other animal. Stone tools outnumber hominin fossils by multiple orders of magnitude. Each fossil preserves time-averaged evidence for lifetime behavior. Each stone artifact is a snapshot of human behavior at one moment. Stone tools' durability and widespread occurrence make them almost uniquely well suited for research on the evolution of human behavioral variability.

I decided to write this book while I was attending a scientific meeting about European and Asian stone tools dating to around 30,000–40,000 years ago. Earlier archaeologists had grouped these tools together into a single "Aurignacian Industry." My colleagues were debating whether regional differences among these tools were sufficient to justify calling them different names. For archaeologists, calling groups of stone tools by different names implies that they represent different groups of people. Archaeologists had long linked the Aurignacian Industry to *Homo sapiens*' dispersal into Europe; so, knowing whether it represented one, two, or even more distinct groups of people could shed light on how humans dispersed from Africa into Eurasia.

The meeting had been going on for hours when I realized we were wasting our time. We were treating stone tools as if they were emblems of prehistoric social identities, like the plastic name tags we were wearing. Hypotheses about those identities can only be proven wrong by interviewing extinct humans themselves. Stone tools are not people; they are residues of behavior. Their variation and their variability arise from differences in humans' and ancestral hominins' strategies for solving problems requiring sharp cutting edges, piercing tools, abrasive surfaces, and rigid percussors. Anything more than this, any claim to greater knowledge based on the stone tool evidence, requires theoretical justification. The most credible such "middle-range" theoretical justifications are hypotheses grounded in observations of contemporary human and non-human primate behavior. This approach to explaining the past, "uniformitarianism," originated in geology, but it is now a guiding principle in all historical sciences. The least credible hypotheses are those derived from the archaeological record itself. One cannot use the same evidence to test an hypothesis as that which inspired the hypothesis in the first place. All too often, however, and with the Aurignacian in particular, the archaeological record is both wellspring and proving ground for hypotheses about stone tool variation. In a word, archaeologists err by equating the patterning of the stone tool evidence with the processes that created it.

It would be convenient if the Aurignacian and other named stone tool industries corresponded to social and cultural differences among prehistoric humans; but there is no reason to assume they do and compelling reasons to think they do not. The word "Aurignacian" first appears in the archaeological literature more than a century ago. Archaeologists applied this term and others like it to stone tools excavated from caves, rockshelters, and other sites throughout western Eurasia. In deciding how to organize these artifacts into higher-order groupings, such as artifact-types and industries, early archaeologists relied on their intuition. This intuitive approach created many problems, if only because intuition varies. Comparisons of stone tools from the same levels of sites collected decades apart routinely reveal variation due to differences in earlier archaeologists' intuitive choices about which artifacts were important enough to keep. Worse still, efforts to investigate older collections with newly developed analytical methods often fail to take such "selective curation" into account. Debates about the nature of particular artifact-types and stone tool industries, exhortations to recognize new ones, and attempts to redefine established ones, swell the archaeological literature of all continents from the oldest phases of prehistory to recent times.

In theory, these lithic "systematics" help archaeologists explain human biological and cultural evolution using concepts analogous to those used to explain historical events. In practice, they do no such thing. "Anthropogenic" narratives (hypotheses about human evolution presented as narratives) and "prehistory" can be satisfying explanations of the facts we know at any given moment. But inductively generated explanations lack predictive power. Every new discovery comes as a surprise, a "game changer" in the argot of "press-release science." Consequently, archaeologists constantly tinker with these narratives and their component elements in order to accommodate newly discovered evidence. Such constant tinkering makes these narratives ever more complex and less comprehensible to non-archaeologists.

Discontent with traditional archaeological approaches to stone tool analysis runs deep, but there is also a lot of complacency, even a bit of fatalism, about prospects for change. Invoking Gabriel de Mortillet, the French researcher who identified many of the stone tool industries we still recognize today, archaeologist Lawrence Straus recently despaired, "We are all prisoners of de Mortillet!" But does this make any sense? Is there any other science whose ways of organizing evidence have remained fundamentally the same for more than a century? Do physical anthropologists analyze DNA in order to redefine human races? Are cultural anthropologists still searching for primitive cultures? Archaeologists revere the past, but we misplace our reverence when we apply it to concepts developed in the infancy of prehistoric research. All prisoners want to be free.

Told that I was writing a book about stone tools' role in human evolution, a colleague remarked, "If anyone can write that book, you can; after all, you're a flintknapper." I was flattered. I do make and use stone tools and practice other ancestral skills. But, the questions this book asks and the hypotheses it proposes do not arise from my making and using stone tools. I wrote this book as a paleoanthropologist who uses archaeological methods to answer evolutionary questions. Stone tools, properly studied, have tremendous potential to change our views about human evolution. Traditional archaeological approaches to the lithic evidence prevent us from realizing that potential.

Archaeologists need to see alternative paths for connecting the stone tool evidence to major issues in human evolution. Physical anthropologists and geneticists need to see these other paths too. Many of them think narrative prehistory is all stone tool analysis has to offer human origins research. *Stone Tools in Human Evolution* explores a new path. It uses a comparative analytical approach to assess how the evolution of behavioral differences between humans and non-human primates influenced the stone tool evidence at various inflection points over the last 3.5 million years. *Stone Tools in Human Evolution* develops an hypothesis about how hominin strategies for making and using stone tools changed from an ancestral pattern of occasional stone tool use, one much like that seen among living non-human primates, to a situationally variable mixture of occasional, habitual, and obligatory stone tool use, a condition in which all humans lived until recently.

Students, physical anthropologists, and archaeologists will each get something different from this book. *Stone Tools in Human Evolution* will help students identify and understand the "big questions," the questions all of us involved in human origins research care about. Physical anthropologists will find in it a possible path to "consilience," that rare occasion when research in separate fields leads to new integrative syntheses that are more than the sum of their parts. How better to test hypotheses about the origins of behavioral differences between humans and non-human primates originating from analyses of genes, fossils, and behavior than with a virtually indestructible archaeological lithic record? Archaeologists will be surprised that *Stone Tools in Human Evolution* does not use age-stages or named stone tool industries, and uses only a handful of named lithic artifact-types. I do this to make an important point. These terms and concepts are so deeply embedded in archaeological method and theory that the impossibility of reforming them is itself a major barrier to more anthropologically engaged stone tool analysis. *Stone Tools in Human Evolution* shows not only that we do not need these things, but also that paleoanthropology is better off without them.

ACKNOWLEDGMENTS

This book profited from discussions with many colleagues, including John Fleagle, Philip Lieberman, Ian Wallace, and Daniel Lieberman. For helping me fill the gaps in my knowledge about the archaeological evidence from various regions and time periods, I thank Dan Adler, Ofer Bar-Yosef, Nicholas Conard, Metin Eren, Peter Hiscock, John Hoffecker, David Meltzer, Alan Simmons, Nicola Stern, Lawrence Straus, Gil Tostevin, Katheryn Twiss, and Evan Wilson. For the photograph in Figure 2.1, I thank Tetsuro Matsuzawa of the Kyoto University Primate Research Institute. For procuring publications I needed for my research, I thank Stony Brook University's Interlibrary Loan staff, Donna Sammis, Jay Levenson, Diane Englot, and Hanne Tracey. For reading the proposal for this book, I thank Grant McCall, Gil Tostevin, and two anonymous reviewers. I thank Asya Graf and Beatrice Rehl of Cambridge University Press for their editorial guidance and Christina Sarigiannidou and Julene Knox for assistance in production. For support and encouragement during the writing, I thank Nancy Franklin and my wife, Patricia Crawford. I alone am responsible for opinions expressed and any errors.

CHAPTER 1

INTRODUCTION

> What we observe is not nature itself, but nature exposed to our method of questioning.
>
> Werner Heisenberg (1958) *Physics and Philosophy: The Revolution in Modern Science*

This is a book about questions. Many archaeological books and scientific papers ask what stone tools can tell us about human evolution. Others ask what the evidence for human evolution can tell us about stone tools. These are both good questions, but they each suffer the same weakness. They want to use the inferred qualities of one unknown thing to explain the inferred qualities of another unknown thing. This book asks different kinds of questions. It asks how something we can observe today explains something else we can observe today. Specifically, it asks how behavioral differences between humans and other primates explain changes in the archaeological stone tool evidence. This is a very different sort of question from the ones archaeologists have been asking, and unsuccessfully trying to answer, with the stone tool evidence. This chapter argues that many of the archaeologists' difficulties connecting the stone tool evidence to major issues in human evolution stem from asking the wrong questions and from inappropriately projecting qualities of recent human tool use back into remote antiquity.

LITTLE QUESTIONS VS. BIG QUESTIONS

For the last three million years hominins (bipedal primates) littered the Earth with stone tools. This lithic evidence adds richness and detail to our understanding of human evolution beyond what fossils and genes alone can tell us. Fossils are rare and fragile, and genes speak mainly about ancestry. Stone tools are common, nearly indestructible, and preserved no matter what their authors' evolutionary fates. To understand stone tools' place in human evolution, we have to ask "big" questions, questions central to human origins research. All too often, archaeologists ask "little" quasi-historical questions, such as who made which sets of lithic artifacts and how prehistoric tool makers were related to one another culturally. There is nothing objectively wrong with such little questions. Properly investigated, they are worthy of attention. Culture history is no less a part of our evolutionary heritage than our opposable thumb is. But, culture history questions are not "big" questions. Archaeologists are the only people who ask such questions, and few people other than archaeologists care about the answers to them. By focusing so much of our energies on culture historical questions, archaeologists neglect more evolutionarily important and anthropologically interesting issues (Shea 2011c).

Anthropology's two big questions are (1) how are humans different from other animals and (2) why do humans differ from one another? Everything anthropologists do is ultimately in the service of those two questions. Paleoanthropology investigates the origins of these differences, and the stone tool evidence is directly relevant to both of them. Humans and non-human primates differ in the extent to which we make and use stone tools, how we use them, and in the kinds of tools we make. The most adept non-human primate tool users are our nearest living non-human relatives, chimpanzees (*Pan troglodytes*) and bonobos (*P. paniscus*). Behavioral differences between humans and these apes are obvious starting points for research on behavioral variation among "technological primates." All humans were stone tool users until a few thousand years ago – yesterday on an evolutionary timescale. If there are deep and transcendent principles governing human cultural and behavioral variability, they ought to be discoverable in the stone tool evidence.

Stone Tools in Human Evolution investigates the lithic evidence for the evolution of behavioral differences between humans and non-human primates in comparative, analytical, and strategic perspectives. The behavioral differences on which it focuses include the following:

- Cutting tools (Chapter 4): Non-human primates use stone tools as percussors. Humans also use stone tools to cut, pierce, and divide things.
- Logistical mobility (Chapter 5): Non-human primates bring consumers (themselves) to resources. Humans also transport resources to consumers.
- Language and symbolic artifacts (Chapter 6): Non-human primates communicate by gestures and vocalizations. Humans also use language and symbolic artifacts.
- Dispersal and diaspora (Chapter 7): Non-human primates live in the tropics and warmer temperate latitudes. Humans live in a global diaspora.
- Residential sedentism (Chapter 8): Non-human primates move daily. Humans reside in the same places for periods ranging from days to their entire lives.

Chapters 4–8 evaluate how these differences affect human and non-human primate stone tool use today, and they predict how the stone tool evidence should have changed as the distinctively human behavior pattern evolved. Each chapter tests these predictions by examining lithic assemblages from the period when fossil, genetic, and other non-lithic evidence suggest the characteristically human behavior appeared. These are not the only important behavioral differences between humans and non-human primates, but they are enough to show a new path to better integrating the stone tool evidence into human origins research.

To test predictions about changes in the stone tool evidence, this book employs data from lithic assemblages dating from around 6000 years ago (6 Ka, Ka = × 1000 years) to more than 3,000,000 years ago (3 Ma, Ma = × 1,000,000 years). In selecting these assemblages, I chose ones from sites generally viewed as representative of the evidence from given regions and time periods. I assessed their representativeness from their being named in recent published syntheses of particular time periods and from correspondence with colleagues. I winnowed a list of several hundred assemblages to a manageable 250 by applying four further selection criteria. Assemblages had to have been published in peer-reviewed books or journals and in languages in which I am fluent (English, French, and German). Their archaeological contexts had to be reasonably well dated, and their descriptions of the lithic evidence sufficiently detailed to allow me to reorganize it in the framework this book uses for describing variation in how stone tools were made. Some less-well-known assemblages were selected in order to achieve a degree of geographic representativeness. No assemblages were added after the fact to alter the results of any statistical tests or to support predictions that were previously unsupported.

This book differs from previous books about stone tools and human evolution in several important ways.

First, *Stone Tools in Human Evolution* does not try to tell a story about human evolution. Stories, or "narrative explanations," are cultural universals as old as history itself, and probably much, much older. Early paleoanthropologists expressed their hypotheses about human evolution in narrative frameworks, and the practice continues to this day (Landau 1991). Narratives force one to arrange complex evolutionary processes into simple linear chains of cause and effect. All evolutionary narratives of human origins begin with the oldest evidence, evidence about which geological attrition alone guarantees we know the least. Interpretive errors made at the beginning of such a narrative make all subsequent interpretations in that narrative wrong too. Narrative explanations for events that took place over geological/evolutionary timescales are intrinsically likely to be wrong.

Second, *Stone Tools in Human Evolution* does not speculate on evolutionary relationships among the various hominins associated with stone tools. This book does not reject hypotheses that evolutionary divergences among hominins influenced the stone tool evidence (Foley 1987, Mithen 1996), but neither does it invoke evolutionary relationships to explain the variation in the lithic record. Instead, it seeks explanations for prehistoric lithic variation in terms of behaviors whose influences on stone tool production and use can be empirically verified by ethnography, ethology, and experimentation.

Third, *Stone Tools in Human Evolution* speculates minimally about how cognitive changes in hominin evolution might have influenced lithic variation. There are almost certainly important linkages between human cognitive evolution and change/variability in the stone tool evidence. However, "cognitive archaeology" today offers divergent views about the nature of these changes (Mithen 1996, Stout et al. 2015). As with phylogeny, there are so many competing hypotheses about changes in hominin cognition that discussing all or even a fraction of them would overshadow those parts of the book devoted to less controversial behavioral differences between humans and non-human primates.

Fourth, *Stone Tools in Human Evolution* is neither a technical manual about how to analyze lithic artifacts from archaeological sites nor a guide to how to make and use stone tools (for such works, see Whittaker 1994, Inizan et al. 1999, Odell 2004, Andrefsky 2005, Patten 2009, Shea 2015a). It is intended as a "course book," a book to accompany the main text for college-level courses in human evolution. While I hope archaeologists will find it interesting, it is really addressed more to biological anthropologists who are skeptical about stone tools' value in human origins research.

Finally, as noted in the Preface, *Stone Tools in Human Evolution* does not use many traditional archaeological terms for time periods, stone tool industries, or artifact-types. The evolution of behavioral differences between humans and non-human primates was not a part of nineteenth- and early twentieth-century archaeologists' research agendas. We should not expect their ways of organizing the archaeological lithic record to be helpful in investigating this subject. Late nineteenth- and early twentieth-century archaeologists devised these terms and concepts as aids to sorting stone tool assemblages in time, or "chronostratigraphy" (e.g., de Mortillet 1883). Decades later, other archaeologists repurposed them, largely unmodified, as aids to writing Stone Age "culture history" (e.g., Bordes 1968). It is not impossible that these artifact-types might work well in their new purposes; but, this is something archaeologists *hope* to be true, not something they *know* to be true (Shea 2014). Much of the progress archaeologists have made in understanding the lithic evidence for Pleistocene hominin behavioral variability they have accomplished in spite of these traditional ways of describing the stone tool evidence, rather than by recourse to them (e.g., Binford 1983, Potts 1988, Boëda, Geneste, and Meignen 1990, Rolland and Dibble 1990, Kuhn 1993, Shea 2010; for a recent review, see McCall 2014).

We need terms to describe stone tool production and stone tools themselves. For this purpose Chapter 3 introduces Modes A–I. Modes A–I is a framework based on observed tool making behaviors among humans and non-human primates (Shea 2013a). Using Modes A–I allows simple and straightforward comparisons of evidence from different regions and time periods. To explain why this book requires a break with traditional archaeological approaches to the lithic record, the next section discusses how archaeologists' difficulties with stone tools arose in the first place.

WHY ARCHAEOLOGISTS MISUNDERSTAND STONE TOOLS

What would one make of an artifact of extraterrestrial origin? If it was made of metal, one could confidently infer those who made it controlled heat, but hypotheses based on analogies with our own technologies would be more risky. If it was elongated and pointed at one end, one might conclude that it was a weapon. But might it not be an art object or a telecommunications device? (The 1951 science fiction film *The Day the Earth Stood Still* showed such uncertainty leading to near-disastrous "first contact" with an extraterrestrial emissary.) We humans share far more evolutionary history with earlier hominins than we would with an extraterrestrial; so, our surmises about prehistoric stone tools ought not be as wide of the mark as those involving alien technology. Nevertheless, many misunderstandings about stone tools arose and persist because early archaeologists interpreted prehistoric lithic artifacts through the lens of familiar technology.

European archaeologists recognized stone tools as prehistoric artifacts in the late eighteenth and early nineteenth centuries (Grayson 1986). Like geologists and paleontologists, early archaeologists interpreted these artifacts using principles derived from observing the world in which they lived. Early archaeologists lived in industrial states, and their hypotheses about prehistoric stone tools reflected analogies with Industrial Era technology. "Flintknapper" or "knapper," terms now used for stone tool producers in general, originally referred to craft specialists who mass-produced gunflints (Skertchly 1879). The names archaeologists gave to stone tools, such as burin (French for chisel), pick, and scraper, were originally terms for metal implements. Archaeologists thought prehistoric lithic technology was organized as a simple linear process, much like that involved in the mass-production of nails, pottery, or gunflints. Raw materials were gathered from "quarries" and transported in bulk to "factory sites" where craftsmen shaped "finished artifacts" that were dispersed to consumers (Clarke 1935) (Figure 1.1). They envisioned chronologically sequential changes among stone tools as substitutions in much the same way that technological change occurs in industrial societies, with older and obsolete technologies replaced by "new and improved" ones (e.g., horse-drawn carriages by automobiles, whale oil candles by electric lights).

The mismatch between this "Industrial Model" and how pre-industrial and non-industrial societies made and used stone tools is increasingly obvious.

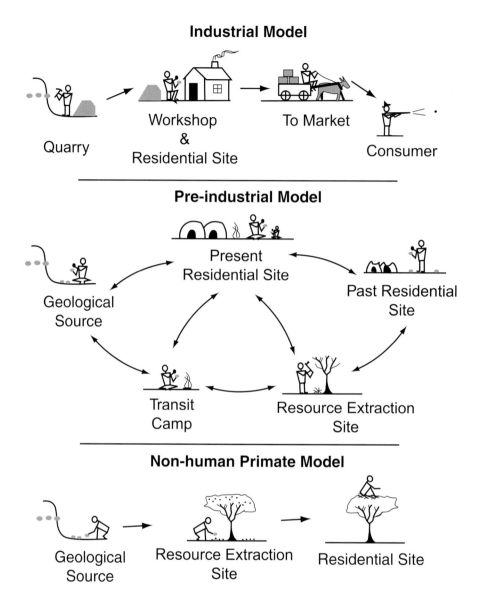

Figure 1.1 Industrial vs. pre-industrial and non-human primate models of stone tool production. Industrial Era flintknapping (above) was a linear process in which raw material procurement, tool production, use, and discard occurred separately from one another. Pre-industrial stone tool production by mobile populations was complex and non-linear (below). Raw material procurement, tool production, use, and discard could occur separately or commingled with one another. Non-human primate stone tool use is also a linear process in which tool materials are moved from places where they occur to places where they are needed.

Pre-industrial societies organized stone tool production, use, and discard as non-linear networks dispersed across landscapes (e.g., Gould 1980, Holdaway and Douglas 2012). These networks were especially complex among hunter-gatherer populations who frequently relocated their habitation sites, groups with high "residential mobility." Among such residentially mobile humans, relationships between artifact designs, stone tool functions, and cultural identities were complex and contingent over time and space. Multiple lines of evidence suggest earlier hominins were at least as residentially mobile as recent human hunter-gatherers, if not even more so. It follows that we should expect similar, if not even greater, qualities of technological and functional variability in those hominins' lithic archaeological record.

Humans are not the only stone-tool-using primates. Field studies and experimental research show that our nearest living non-human primate relatives, chimpanzees and bonobos, exhibit a wide range of stone-tool-using activities. Archaeological investigations of non-human primate tool use, or "primate archaeology" (or, more precisely, archaeological primatology) are increasingly popular (Haslam et al. 2009). These studies enrich our understanding of human evolution, but one must use them cautiously.

First, living non-human primates are not ancestral hominins. That chimpanzees crack open nuts with stone tools does not mean earlier hominins did so, too.

Second, descriptions of non-human primate tools borrow terms in common usage for human tools, such as "hammerstones," "anvils," and "spears." All tools used by non-human primates are morphologically, measurably, and functionally distinct from tools made and used by humans.

Finally, reports of non-human tool use tend to emphasize similarities with human behavior. Similarities can be interesting, but they may reflect common ancestry, convergent evolution, or simply perceived analogies. In evolution, differences are more important than similarities.

Earlier hominin stone tool use was probably not identical either to non-human primate stone tool use or to ethnographic stone tool use. Wild-living primates do not make stone cutting tools like those found in prehistoric archaeological sites. Complex patterned variation like that seen among ethnographic stone tools graces only the latest phases of prehistory. Prehistoric hominin stone tool use likely combined evolutionarily "primitive" (i.e., ancestral) behaviors as well as "derived" (newly evolved) ones. Determining which combinations of such ancestral and derived behaviors were in place at any given point in human evolution requires us to explore the reasons why there are differences between human and non-human primate stone tool use. If we can determine why, for example, humans do something with stone tools while other primates do not, such as attaching stone tools to handles ("hafting"), then we can make predictions and test hypotheses about where and when in prehistory we should find evidence for hafting. Admittedly, hafting might have originated in activities no longer undertaken by living humans, but our hypotheses have to come from somewhere, and the best such sources are those we can observe directly.

The merits of a comparative analytical approach seem so obvious they beg the question of why early archaeologists did not use studies of living stone-tool-using peoples and non-human primates as sources of hypotheses about prehistoric stone tool use. Some nineteenth- and early twentieth-century archaeologists actually did look to the ethnographic evidence for inspiration, but they had limited resources at their disposal (Lubbock 1865). Museum collections housed artifacts gathered by explorers and colonial officials, but few of these artifacts were accompanied by detailed information about how they were made and used. A few gunflint knappers still practiced their craft in Europe, but traveling to observe stone tool production and use in non-industrial settings was dangerous and difficult. During the late nineteenth and early twentieth centuries, stone tools were still being made and used in Africa, Asia, Australia, New Guinea, the Pacific Islands, and in the Americas. At the time, however, indigenous populations in many of these regions were struggling against European and American colonial powers. A visiting archaeologist seeking stone tool makers stood a good chance of being killed in the process. Some early ethnographers (cultural anthropologists) encountered stone-tool-using people, but few made detailed studies of this fast-vanishing technology. Anthropologists of that era were mainly interested in recording languages, kinship systems, and other phenomena that they thought predicted variation in human behavior. Few ethnographers had much professional training in archaeology or experience describing lithic technology.

Most ethnographic accounts of stone tool production and use were written by explorers, missionaries, and colonial administrators, but only rarely by anthropologists or archaeologists. Some of these accounts are good and remain useful, but nearly all of them are "normative." That is, they focus on "typical" patterns of stone tool production and use, on central tendencies and modalities, rather than on other dimensions of variation and sources of variability. Such normative descriptions of lithic evidence were not unique to ethnography. Most terms archaeologists used to describe prehistoric stone tool evidence were normative ones, too (Taylor 1948, Binford 1962), and they remain so to this day (Clark and Riel-Salvatore 2006). During the 1970s archaeologists began undertaking "ethnoarchaeological" studies of recent human material culture and site formation processes, but by this point in time few ethnographic groups were still habitually making and using stone tools. Ironically, ethnographic lithic technology declined just as "craft/hobby flintknapping" began to grow in North America and Europe (Whittaker and Stafford 1999).

Early archaeologists did not draw on studies of non-human primate stone tool use as models for earlier hominin behavior largely because they were unaware non-human primates used stone tools. Experiments with captive chimpanzees had shown that they could be taught to use tools and that they could solve problems with tools creatively (Köhler 1925). However, traveling to African apes' equatorial habitats during the late nineteenth and early twentieth centuries was even more dangerous than visits to ethnographic stone-tool-using humans.

Primatologists only reported tool use by wild-living non-human primates in the 1960s and stone tool use more recently than that. Most detailed studies of chimpanzee and other non-human primate tool use have only been published in the last several decades (McGrew 1992, Boesch-Aschermann and Boesch 1994, Haslam et al. 2009).

We still do not know as much as we might wish about pre-industrial human and non-human primate stone tool use. But, as Chapter 2 shows, we can use what we know to construct a more realistic alternative to the Industrial Model of lithic technology, a "Pre-Industrial Model" from which we can deduce testable predictions about prehistoric stone tool production and use.

CHAPTER 2

HOW WE KNOW WHAT WE THINK WE KNOW ABOUT STONE TOOLS

> Of each thing, ask what is it in itself, in its own constitution? What is its substance and material, and how did it come to be? What does it do in the world, and how long does it persist?
>
> Marcus Aurelius Antonius (AD 167 *Meditations* 8.11)

This chapter explores the sources of our current knowledge about stone tools, namely ethnographic and ethological observations, experimental archaeology, and contextual clues from the archaeological record. These sources allow us to develop a "Pre-Industrial Model" of human/hominin stone tool use. Contrasts between this Pre-Industrial Model and observations of non-human primate tool use allow testable predictions (hypotheses) about changes and variability in hominin stone tool production and use.

SOURCES OF INFORMATION ABOUT LITHIC TECHNOLOGY

Most of what archaeologists think we know about prehistoric stone tool technology is based on either actualistic or contextual information. Actualistic information comes from ethnoarchaeology, experimental archaeology, and any circumstances in which stone tool production, use, and discard have actually been observed. Contextual information is archaeological evidence interpreted according to generally accepted principles of geology, biology, chemistry, and other scientific disciplines.

Actualistic Information

Ethnoarchaeology: Ethnoarchaeology observes how living humans create an archaeological record. Most systematic ethnoarchaeological studies of stone tool technology involve people who otherwise use metal tools, or people who are lithic craft specialists, producing stone knives, axes, and grinding stones (Binford 1986, Toth, Clark, and Ligabue 1992, Searcy 2011). There are relatively few ethnoarchaeological studies of people who habitually make and use stone tools as routine parts of their daily lives. Ethnoarchaeological accounts of stone tool production and use are unevenly distributed around the world. The most detailed accounts of stone tool use by hunter-gatherers are from Australia (Hayden 1979, Gould 1971, 1980; for recent overviews, see Holdaway and Douglas 2012, McCall 2012). Stone tool use by horticulturalists, pastoralists, and former hunter-gatherers is more widely documented in Africa, Southeast Asia, and the Americas (Nelson 1916, White 1968, Gallagher 1977, Miller 1979, Clark and Kurashina 1981, Brandt and Weedman 1997, Weedman 2006).

Experimental Archaeology: "Experimental archaeology" describes a wide range of activities from contrived mechanical experiments to more holistic "experiential" activities. Experiments can often demonstrate *probable* sources of variability (Eren et al. 2016), while experiential activities more typically suggest *possible* sources of variation (Shea 2015a). Many rocks used to make knapped stone tools fracture conchoidally, and mechanical experiments have investigated this property (for a review, see Dibble and Rezek 2009, Lin et al. 2013). The mechanics of groundstone technology have been less extensively researched, possibly due to the wide range of rocks shaped by abrasion (Dubreuil and Savage 2014). Hobby/craft knappers have documented experiential approaches to investigating rock fracture (Johnson 1978, Whittaker 1994) to such an extent that archaeologists use their terms for stone tool production rather than terms from fracture mechanics (Crabtree 1972, Inizan et al. 1999). Other experiential activities include teaching stone tool production and use to others and using stone tools for various purposes (Shea 2015b). Some of these tool use experiments focus on identifying microwear patterns diagnostic of certain activities (Keeley 1980, Odell 1981). Others aim for subjective assessments of how well stone tools with different qualities perform in one or another task (e.g., Jones 1981, Schick and Toth 1993: 147–186, Shea, Davis, and Brown 2001, Shea, Brown, and Davis 2002). Still other experiments simulate trampling and geological sources of damage in order to develop criteria for recognizing their effects in the archaeological record (e.g., McBrearty et al. 1998, Pargeter and Bradfield 2012).

Contextual Information

Contextual information is inferred from the archaeological record. Such information includes stratigraphic associations, artifact-refitting patterns, stone tool cut-marks, microwear, and residues. Because contextual information is based on inferences rather than direct observations, it has to be used cautiously.

Stratigraphic Associations: Stone tools occur together with other artifacts and ecofacts (natural objects), and these associations can inspire hypotheses about the motivations of prehistoric tool makers. Yet, such spatial and stratigraphic associations can also be misleading, or at least interpretively complex (Schiffer 1987). The geological "principle of association" holds that artifacts enclosed in the same sediment were buried at the same time in a broad sense, but this does not mean they were buried simultaneously or as the result of the same activity. Tools in the same archaeological assemblage may have been deposited days, weeks, months, years, even centuries apart from one another. The most common targets of archaeological excavations – caves/rockshelters and landforms near water sources – are perennial magnets for human occupation. If humans are in the vicinity, they reside there. Assemblages from such sites likely combine the traces of multiple occupations near to one another in time. More valuable sources of insights come from small sites where sediments were deposited quickly, and in which the possibility of multiple separate human/hominin occupations is low. Because such "mini-sites" lack the archaeological visibility of larger lithic accumulations, they form a tiny fraction of the global record for hominin stone tool use.

Artifact Refitting: Matching fracture surfaces on stone tools can allow one to reconstruct how artifacts were shaped and detached from one another, but not all such matches provide the same information. Fractures caused during core reduction and artifact shaping (refits) and edge resharpening (modifications) shed light on tool production and maintenance. Fragments separated by other causes (breaks) may reflect trampling, soil compaction, and other depositional processes, even excavation-related damage. Spatial analysis of artifact refitting patterns can provide insights into toolmaking strategies as well as about site formation processes (for overviews, see Cziesla 1990, Laughlin and Kelly 2010). Refitting studies frequently assume that all flakes struck from a particular rock were detached near to one another in time, by the same person, or at least by members of the same co-residential community. This is not necessarily true. The ethnographic record offers up numerous accounts of stone tools being made from artifacts found eroding from abandoned habitations and archaeological sites.

Stone-tool Cut-marks and Percussion Damage: After stone tools, vertebrate fossils are the second most common things found at prehistoric archaeological sites. Some of these fossils preserve cut-marks and fractures caused by stone tool use (Shipman 1981, Blumenschine and Pobiner 2007). Sites with exceptional preservation can also preserve wood with wear traces from stone tool use. Such discoveries are revolutionizing archaeologists' views about earlier hominin technological strategies (e.g., Conard et al. 2015). Needless to say, however, such evidence suffers from the problem of "false negative" findings. The absence of preserved bone, wood, cordage, and other organic artifacts does not necessarily indicate hominins overlooked these materials' potential value as tools.

Microwear: Microwear (fractures, abrasion, and polish) on stone tool edges and surfaces furnishes clues about the use of particular stone tools, about the parts of the tools that were used, the motions employed, and the nature of the worked materials (for reviews, see Semenov 1964, Shea 1992, Odell 2004: 152). Activities involving high loading forces, prolonged use, and work on relatively hard materials leave more distinctive wear traces than tasks involving low loading forces, brief use, and cutting softer materials. Microwear traces are relatively small-scale phenomena that can be altered by post-depositional mechanical wear, such as flowing water, soil movement, trampling, and other factors (Shea and Klenck 1993, Levi-Sala 1996).

Residues: Organic residues, including blood, hair, starch particles, and inorganic substances, such as red ochre (iron oxide), can sometimes be detected on stone tool edges and surfaces. The principal challenge in interpreting this evidence lies in differentiating between residues bonded to the tool surface as the result of cutting; residues from handles, fibers, and mastic use to attach tools to handles; and residues from sediments enclosing the tools. Though archaeologists have gained considerable expertise in visual identifications of residues, many such residues are ambiguous, and interpreting them can require physical or chemical analysis (for a recent review, see Monnier, Ladwig, and Porter 2012).

A PRE-INDUSTRIAL MODEL OF LITHIC TECHNOLOGY

Insights from actualistic and contextual sources allow one to construct a model for lithic technology, one that differs from early archaeologists' Industrial Model. This "Pre-Industrial Model" contrasts with its Industrial counterpart in recognizing a greater range of variability in stone tool production, use, and discard (Table 2.1). Inasmuch as this model pulls together evidence from both historical and present-day (ethnographic) sources, it is discussed below using the "ethnographic present" tense.

Pre-industrial Stone Tool Production

Pre-industrial humans' choices of lithic raw material are governed by a combination of practical mechanical considerations such as ease of access, fracture properties, hardness, and silica content (Binford 1980, Gould 1980). Nevertheless, subjective qualities, such as aesthetics or perceived symbolic associations, play roles as well. Lithic raw material procurement is frequently "embedded" in daily foraging tasks carried out within a few kilometers of habitation sites. The most common lithic raw materials at any archaeological site are usually those available in the immediate geological substrate or within a 10–30 km radius of the site. Quarrying operations ("direct procurement") occur, too, but these usually involve small work parties or individuals visiting

TABLE 2.1. *Industrial, pre-industrial, and non-human primate models of stone tool use*

Activity	Industrial Model	Pre-industrial Model	Non-human Primate Model
Raw material procurement	Quarried and transported in-bulk to production sites	Mixed strategies of quarrying, embedded procurement, recycling	Aggregates of individually transported objects
Agency	Adults	Adults (males >females), children (?)	Mainly females and children
Transmission	Formal apprenticeship	Imitation and directed learning	Imitation
Production methods	Standardized	Some stereotyped production, but little standardization, much variability	Tools used without modification
Artifact designs	Size varies, but form and function are strongly correlated	Size varies, and form–function correlations are variable	Large tools, whose form and function are strongly correlated
Context of production	At special-purpose workshops at or near habitation sites	Not necessarily correlated with habitation sites	Not applicable
Artifact repair	Yes, typically by specialists	Yes, but variable, context-dependent	No
Artifact discard	Distant from production sites	Variable, both near and far from production sites, habitation sites, resource extraction sites	At location where used to extract food resources
Change through time	Substitution	Addition	Little/no change? (Inadequate evidence)

a geological source. At such sources, people replace worn-out tools on the spot and reduce raw rock into small, efficiently transportable packages. Sedentary groups supplying long-term residential sites sometimes undertake in-bulk quarrying operations. Abandoned habitation sites and archaeological sites are also used as sources of tool materials. Lithic materials are also procured socially, through exchanges among individuals. Such exchanges range from straightforward commercial transactions involving producers, consumers, and middlemen to more complex ones guided by symbolic/supernatural motivations. Many individuals deploy more than one such raw material procurement strategy simultaneously.

Unlike Industrial Era factory work, ethnographic flintknapping occurs on an irregular schedule, either as tools are needed or during "down-time" between other activities. Most ethnographic tool makers use more than one distinct way of obtaining cutting edges. Indeed, stone tools continued to be made and used thousands of years after the appearance of metallurgy in the Near East and in Africa (Rosen 1997, Mitchell 2002). To this day, some indigenous populations in Africa, Asia, and Australia continue to use stone tools alongside metal ones.

While there are instances of craft specialization in the ethnographic record, much stone tool production involves non-specialists. In ethnographic literature, adult males do most of the tool making, but this may reflect reporting bias by adult male ethnographers (but see Gould 1980). There is no reason to assume prehistoric stone tool production or use was invariably organized along gender lines (Gero 1991, Arthur 2010). For evidence of prehistoric stone tool use by women, one need look no further than Exodus 4: 25–26,

> Now it came about at the lodging place on the way that the Lord met (Moses) and sought to put him to death. Then Zipporah took a flint and cut off her son's foreskin and threw it at Moses' feet, and she said, "You are indeed a bridegroom of blood to me." So He let him alone.

There are few detailed ethnographic accounts of children making or using stone tools, but it is reasonable to suppose prehistoric children did so, either for their own tool needs or in learning by imitating adult activities (Shea 2006a). Only recent post-Industrial parents systemically keep children away from sharp implements "for their own good."

Ethnographic flintknapping can be either highly stereotyped or widely variable, but there is little standardization. Even when ethnographic knappers work toward the production of similar artifacts, complex patterns of similarities and differences emerge (Binford 1986, Toth et al. 1992). The same variability can be seen in the work of craft/hobby flintknappers, some of whom can identify one another's work by simple visual inspection of the artifacts (Whittaker 2004).

Pre-industrial Stone Tool Use

Ethnographic humans use stone tools as projectile armatures, as tools for butchery, pulverizing seeds and nuts, carpentry, hide-working, flintknapping, carving stone, bone, and other hard materials, and for symbolic/ritual purposes (e.g., scarification, bloodletting). Though ethnographic documentation for stone tool use in some of these activities is actually rather sparse, many tasks performed today with metal tools were undoubtedly done in earlier times using stone tools. This being said, there are at least three activities for which ethnographic humans use metal tools for which there is little ethnographic or archaeological evidence of stone tool use. These activities include immediate pre-oral food processing (cutting food into small pieces immediately prior to eating them), digging in soil, and as weapon armatures for fishing. Inuit and other Arctic peoples used abraded-edge cutting knives (*ulus*) to cut up food prior to ingesting it, but other than this, the ethnographic record offers few other examples of stone tools (or indeed metal ones either) specifically dedicated to this activity. Wear traces and plant and animal tissues preserved on archaeological stone tools suggest simple flakes may have been used for these tasks, but it is also possible that much pre-oral food processing with stone tools was so brief that it left little detectable archaeological evidence. A few stone tools from North American contexts preserve "hoe polish" from tilling silty sediments (Witthoft 1967), but such wear traces are otherwise rare. That so few stone tools are used to dig in soil or as tips for fishing spears probably reflects the fact that these tasks involve high risks of tool breakage due to collisions with rocks in the geological substrate.

Nearly every major category of stone tool that has either been subjected to microwear and/or residue analysis or whose use has been observed ethnographically exhibits functional variability (Odell 2004). Mobility also affects form–function relationships (Binford 1979, Parry and Kelly 1987). Transported stone implements are often design compromises, tools that perform adequately in the wide range of tasks their owners might encounter while on the move. Sedentary populations maintained larger and more functionally specialized toolkits.

Some findings from ethnoarchaeology contradict common archaeological assumptions about retouch and stone tool use. For example, archaeologists often equate retouch (small fractures along tool edges) with evidence of use. Ethnographic humans routinely use tools without putting such edge damage on them. They also retouch tools that they do not end up using. Predictably, many retouched archaeological stone tools preserve no traces of microwear or residues. Most archaeologists assume that unretouched flakes/flake fragments shorter than 2–3 cm in any dimension were too small to have been used as cutting implements, but ethnographic stone cutting tools include many such small unretouched artifacts.

Pre-industrial Stone Tool Discard

Stone tools are sharp. Understandably, much ethnographic stone tool production takes place away from high-foot-traffic areas in habitation sites. When lithic production happens at residential sites it can be accompanied by in-bulk removal and re-deposition of lithic artifacts away from living spaces (Gallagher 1977). Thus, archaeological sites where residues of stone tool production occur in great quantities may not have been habitation sites at all, but rather workshops or dumping areas located some distance from where people were actually living at the time. Juxtaposed concentrations of flintknapping debris and habitation traces (hearths, architecture) may reflect reuse of former habitation sites as impromptu stone tool procurement/production sites.

Ethnographic stone tool discard behavior varies widely and in response to several circumstances. Where raw materials are abundant, the threshold for discarding them is often relatively low. That is, tools are discarded with minimal effort to retouch or resharpen them. Where raw materials are scarce, tools are often heavily resharpened, but this can vary widely, too. Because of the considerable amount of time and energy needed to remove and replace tools attached to handles, these artifacts are often heavily retouched and resharpened (Binford 1979, Keeley 1982). Hand-held tools are often discarded as soon as their cutting edges become perceptibly dull.

NON-HUMAN PRIMATE STONE TOOL USE

Chimpanzees, bonobos, gorillas, orangutans, and macaques (*Macaca*), as well as more phylogenetically distant monkeys (e.g., capuchin monkeys *Cebus* spp.) use tools in the wild (Panger et al. 2003, Haslam et al. 2009, Toth and Schick 2009). For research on the stone tool evidence, however, chimpanzees and bonobos are most directly relevant due to their morphological similarity to humans. Table 2.1 summarizes some of the ways in which stone tool use by these non-human primates differs from both Industrial and Pre-Industrial models of human stone tool use.

Non-human Primate Raw Material Procurement and Stone Tool Production

Non-human primate raw material procurement involves transporting rocks from localities where they are available on the surface to places where they are used. Tool materials are neither excavated from bedrock deposits nor pre-shaped for transportation.

Wild-living non-human primates use stone in its natural form. They select stones for use as tools based on size, shape, and compositional criteria, but raw material choice is largely governed by the local geological substrate. Chimpanzees have been observed transporting stones several kilometers (Boesch and Boesch 1984a), but these are extreme examples for that species. They rarely carry stones more than a few hundred meters.

Two captive bonobos have been taught to make and use stone cutting tools in laboratory settings (Toth et al. 1993), but spontaneous and systematic flaked stone cutting tool production has not been observed among apes living outside captivity.

Non-human Primate Stone Tool Use

The overwhelming majority of observations of non-human primate stone tool use report hand-held stone percussors being used to crack open nuts (Haslam et al. 2009) (Figure 2.1). These artifacts are relatively larger in comparison to their users' body size than the stone tools humans use for similar tasks. Monkeys

Figure 2.1 Chimpanzee stone tool use. (Photograph provided by Tetsuro Matsuzawa of the Kyoto University Primate Research Center, used with permission.)

also use stone tools to fracture the shells of crabs and molluscs as well as to dig in sediment. Neither edges nor abrasive stone surfaces are used to modify other materials. Non-human primates may bring stone tools into juxtaposition with one another, but they do not attach them to other non-lithic materials as multi-component tools. Nut-cracking stones are rarely repurposed for other tasks.

Adult females chimpanzees and their dependent offspring use stone tools more often than adult males (Boesch and Boesch 1984b). Juveniles learn techniques for cracking nuts with stone tools mainly by observing and imitating adults over prolonged periods (i.e., years).

Non-human Primate Stone Tool Discard

In those cases where stone tools have broken during use, non-human primates may continue to use them, but they do not attempt to restore their function-ality by further physical modification. Non-human primates usually abandon stone tools where they are used. Consequently, after many individual episodes of stone transport, use, and deposition large accretional accumulations of stones can appear at non-human primate tool use locations (Mercader, Panger, and Boesch 2002).

Why Compare Human vs. Non-human Primate Lithic Technology?

Anthropologists have long viewed non-human primate behavior as a model for the behavior of human ancestors (Kinzey 1986), but doing this risks ignoring significant evolutionary differences between extant primates and extinct homi-nins as well as differences in their habitats (Potts 1987). Just as comparing human vs. non-human primate anatomy inspires hypotheses about sources of morphological variation among hominin fossils, comparing differences in human vs. non-human stone tool use can help us develop hypotheses about how evolutionarily derived human behaviors influenced variation in the stone tool record. Before we can make these comparisons and generate the hypoth-eses that can be tested with prehistoric lithic evidence, we need to change some of the ways archaeologists describe that evidence. These changes are outlined in the next chapter.

CHAPTER 3

DESCRIBING STONE TOOLS

Always make sure your observations can be evaluated separately from your inferences.

Arthur Jelinek (personal communication, 1980)

This chapter critically examines the ways archaeologists describe stone tools. Many of archaeologists' terms for stone tools institutionalize assumptions of the Industrial Model. Some essential terms can be retained, if used mindfully. Inessential terms and those that conceal more than they reveal about hominin behavioral variability can be discarded. In their place, this chapter introduces Modes A–I, a framework devised specifically to describe changes in the stone tool evidence associated with major shifts in hominin evolution.

ESSENTIAL TERMS AND CONCEPTS

Many traditional archaeological terms for lithic raw materials, artifacts, groups of artifacts, and some abstract concepts about stone tool variability remain useful. These, we can retain with minor modifications. Because their meanings vary and often go unstated in professional archaeological literature, however, these meanings need to be clarified here at the outset. Conventions for illustrating stone tools also vary widely. Box 1 describes the approach this book uses to depict stone tools.

Lithic Raw Materials

For the most part, archaeologists describe the rocks of which stone tools are made using the same terms employed by geologists (Table 3.1). They sometimes subjectively rate certain rocks as either "high-quality" or "low-quality" based on their perceived fracture properties and silica content. Such ratings can be problematical. Crystal quartz, for example, is often rated as low-quality because of its somewhat unpredictable fracture properties. Nevertheless,

TABLE 3.1. *Lithic raw materials commonly used to make stone tools*

Formation process	Rock types
Igneous	Obsidian (volcanic glass)
	Basalt (non-vesicular varieties)
	Rhyolite (welded tuff)
	Felsite (porphyritic rhyolite)
Sedimentary	Chert/Flint
	Shale
	Chalcedony
	Jasper
	Limestone
Metamorphic	Quartzite (recrystallized sandstone)
Mineral	Quartz
Artificial materials	Glass
	Ceramics

prehistoric knappers routinely used quartz to make stone tools identical in all other respects to artifacts made of other rock types. Obsidian (volcanic glass) is almost universally regarded as a high-quality material, but because it is brittle, it is a poor choice for tools engaged in forceful tasks, such as heavy-duty woodworking. Uncommon materials in a lithic assemblage are sometimes described as "exotic," thereby implying distant origins, even though the actual source of the rock is unknown. Stone tool sources are fixed in space and not infinite. What may appear to be uncommon local materials in archaeological assemblages could be rocks whose near-surface exposures have been depleted or concealed by recent geological processes (Minichillo 2006).

Artifacts and Groups of Artifacts

Artifacts are objects whose shape and/or composition are largely the result of human activity. Ecofacts are objects whose shape/composition are determined by non-human agencies and that have been deposited together with artifacts and other traces of human activity. Assemblages are groups of artifacts and ecofacts that share stratigraphic association, such as coming from the same site or the same level of a multi-component site (Clarke 1978). Most lithic assemblages contain flakes, cores, retouched pieces, and hammerstones, as well as a variable number of named artifact types (Figure 3.1 and Glossary).

Flakes: Flakes are the relatively flat and sharp-edged objects detached from rocks by fracture. By convention, the relatively flat and freshly fractured surface of a flake is its "ventral" surface. Most flakes' ventral surfaces feature a convexity, the "bulb of percussion," located adjacent to the point of fracture initiation. The "dorsal" surface is the side of the flake that was formerly the exterior surface

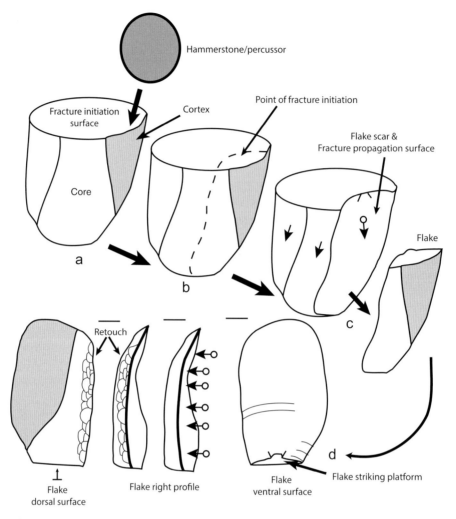

Figure 3.1 Basic terms for stone tools and lithic artifact production. a. Cores and percussors, b. fracture initiation and propagation, c. fracture termination and flake detachment, d. retouch.

of the core. Dorsal surfaces are usually convex, and they feature areas weathered prior to flake detachment ("cortex") as well as ridges and scars from previous flake removals. The striking platform is the part of the flake between the point of fracture initiation and the dorsal surface. An edge, usually 90 degrees or less in cross-section, divides the striking platform from the dorsal surface.

Archaeologists distinguish blades, prismatic blades, bladelets, and microblades from other flakes. Blades are rectangular flakes and elongated triangular flakes whose length is greater than or equal to twice their width. "Prismatic" blades also feature straight lateral edges and parallel dorsal flake scars. Bladelets/microblades are prismatic blades less than 50 mm long and narrower than 12 mm wide. Blades are thought to be somewhat more difficult to make than flakes, and, for this reason, some archaeologists view variation among blades as more informative about tool maker abilities than variation among other flakes.

The French term *débitage* (waste) is often used as a collective term for flakes and flake fragments longer than 2–3 cm. Lithic artifacts shorter than 2–3 cm are called "debris."

Cores, Core Reduction: Cores are rocks that feature relatively large (>20 mm long) fracture scars on their surfaces. Many cores also preserve use-related damage and residues from use as cutting implements and/or as hammerstones. "Worked edge" refers to ridges on a core on which fractures are initiated and from which flakes are detached. For any given flake removal, the working edge is divisible into two surfaces. The fracture initiation surface is the side of the edge on which a fracture is initiated by a percussor. The fracture propagation surface is the side of the edge under which a fracture spreads ("propagates") before emerging to the surface ("terminating"). "Core reduction" is the act of detaching a series of flakes from a core.

The archaeological literature has many alternative terms for flakes that have been used as cores. This work refers to them as "cores-on-flakes."

Retouched Artifacts/Pieces: "Retouched artifacts" or "retouched pieces" are flakes and flake fragments that have had a series of smaller fractures detached from their edge (retouch). Cores that have retouched edges are often called "core-tools." How large and continuous along an edge these fractures must be in order to be recognized as retouch varies among individual archaeologists and archaeological research traditions. Continuous damage running for a centimeter along an edge and extending more than 2–3 mm onto either side of an edge is almost universally recognized as retouch. Archaeologists interpret discontinuous and less invasive edge damage more variably.

Hammerstones/Percussors: Hammerstones, or "percussors," are rocks used to initiate fractures in cores and retouched tools. Most hammerstones are rounded pebbles or cobbles, but prehistoric knappers also used angular rocks, cores, flakes, and retouched artifacts as percussors. Traditional typologies differ in how they describe such "ad hoc" percussors.

Abstract Concepts

More abstract concepts used to describe lithic variation include artifact-types, operational chains, shaping vs. flake production (*façonnage* vs. *débitage*), curation, discard thresholds, typology vs. technology, and function vs. style. This book uses these terms minimally, but, even so, they require clarification.

Artifact-types: An artifact-type describes a group of tools whose shared patterns of retouch, size, and shape allow them to be distinguished from other artifacts (Clarke 1978). Most named artifact-types are either cores or retouched pieces. Their names usually include a site or stone tool industry (see below, p. 27) and a term indicating some aspect of its morphology. For example, the

"Clovis fluted point," an artifact found in Early Holocene contexts in North and Central America incorporates a site name (Clovis, New Mexico) and terms that describe its morphology, "point" (an elongated and bifacially flaked core with converging edges at its distal end) and "fluted" (invasive basal thinning). Compendia of recognized artifact-types, or "typologies," vary widely within and between regions and among archaeological research traditions.

Operational Chain/Reduction Sequence: Operational chain (from the French *chaîne opératoire*) refers to two things: (1) the sequences of transformations that occur to materials, stone or otherwise, from raw material procurement, through manufacturing and use, to discard (Lemmonier 1992), and (2) inductively generated archaeological models for how prehistoric humans made stone tools (Sellet 1993). The term "reduction sequence" is roughly synonymous with operational chain, though somewhat more specific to core reduction/tool production (Shott 2003).

Shaping vs. Flake Production (*Façonnage* vs. *Débitage*): In describing core reduction strategies, some archaeologists differentiate shaping (aka *façonnage* in French) from flake production (*débitage*) (Inizan et al. 1999). Shaping is core reduction that imposes a particular shape on an artifact that is not intrinsic to that material. Flake production generates flakes intended for use as tools in their own right and whose size/shape are largely predictable from raw material properties. These concepts pose no deep theoretical difficulties as long as one recognizes that shaping and flake production are endpoints on a continuum, and that they can occur simultaneously. Flakes detached while shaping a core-tool can be intended for use as tools. Shaping is a necessary step in the preparation of cores intended to produce flakes. *Façonnage/débitage* only create problems when archaeologists use them as a dichotomous way of classifying operational chains and core reduction strategies.

Curation, Expedient Tools, and Discard Thresholds: "Curation" describes strategies for prolonging tool utility by transport, reuse, and/or resharpening (Nash 1996, Odell 1996, Shott 1996). Curation and its opposite, expedient (least-effort) tool production/use, are useful terms for describing qualities of technological strategies. They become problematical when archaeologists use the terms to describe categories of stone tools. Retouched artifacts and hierarchical cores are often described as "curated" and contrasted with expedient unretouched flakes and non-hierarchical cores. Yet, retouch can be done to impose a shape on a tool, to shape the tool's edge for a particular mode of use, or to aid in prehension or hafting. It can also be done to resharpen an edge that has become dull. Tools can be transported without being retouched and *vice versa*.

"Discard threshold" refers to the point at which costs for retaining an artifact exceed the benefits for doing so. Discard threshold is a useful concept, but it is employed inconsistently in the archaeological literature. Following the medical concept of a "pain threshold," a low discard threshold refers to minimal artifact curation/early abandonment, whereas a high discard threshold refers to prolonged artifact curation/delayed abandonment.

Technology/Typology and Function/Style: Archaeologists often use paired contrasting concepts, technology vs. typology and function vs. style, to describe differences among stone tools reflecting variation in prehistoric tool maker activities and social identities, respectively (Bordes and de Sonneville-Bordes 1970, Sackett 1982). Technological variation reflects differences in manufacturing techniques, and it is thought to mainly reflect ecological/economic adaptation. Typological variation registers differences in artifact morphology, such as tool shape and the distribution of retouch. These qualities are thought to reflect cultural differences among tool makers. Function refers to variation reflecting either intended or actual tool use. Style describes lithic artifact design variation arising from differences in the social identities of the tool makers.

INESSENTIAL TERMS AND CONCEPTS

Most published works about human evolution organize the stone tool evidence in terms of age-stages, industries, and technocomplexes (Figure 3.2). These concepts are the sources of many difficulties connecting the stone tool variation to other evidence for human evolution.

Age-stages

Age-stages are long periods of time demarcated by the occurrence of particular kinds of stone tools. Lubbock (1865) made the earliest such division of a previously undifferentiated Stone Age into an older "Paleolithic" Period, during which stone tools were shaped by fracture alone, and a younger "Neolithic" Period, during which stone tools were also shaped by abrasion. Later archaeologists subdivided the Paleolithic into Lower, Middle, and Upper Paleolithic Periods and added a "Mesolithic/Epipaleolithic" Period between the Upper Paleolithic and the Neolithic (see Appendix: Traditional Archaeological Age-stages and Industries). Changes from one age-stage to another are variously described as "transitions" or "revolutions," depending on the perceived speed and scope of the changes.

Archaeologists initially developed age-stages as aids to chronostratigraphy, but nearly all the lithic artifact-types that mark particular age-stages are now known to occur in more than one age-stage. Age-stages are often treated as universal, but the most widely used (Lower, Middle, and Upper Paleolithic, Mesolithic, and Neolithic) are based on the evidence from Europe and the Mediterranean Basin. With greater distance from these regions, it becomes increasingly difficult to organize the archaeological record in terms of these

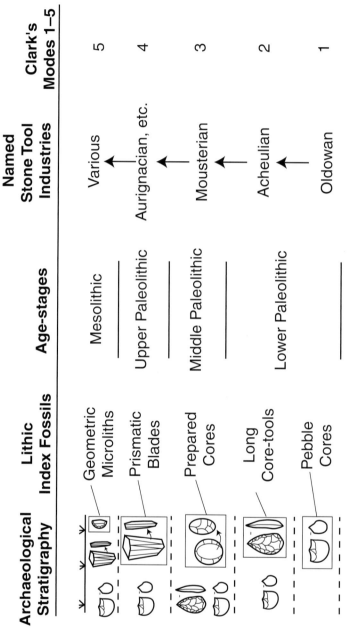

Figure 3.2 Index fossils, age-stages, industries, and technocomplexes.

age-stages, as they were originally defined. Alternative age-stage frameworks developed in Sub-Saharan Africa, Asia, Australia, and the Americas suffer from similar problems of mismatches caused by geographic variation in the archaeological evidence.

Age-stages were useful in the initial chronological ordering of archaeological assemblages, but they have largely been displaced from this role by advances in geochronology. This book refers to time in terms of geological periods, the present Holocene Epoch (<12.5 Ka) and the Pleistocene Epoch (>12.5 Ka to 2.5 Ma), subdivided as necessary. Unlike age-stages, geological periods have formal definitions based on changes in rock composition and fossils. They are unaffected by geographic variation in the archaeological record.

Stone Tool Industries

Stone tool industries are groups of artifact assemblages with similar inventories of named artifact-types. Industries are identified inductively and usually given formal names after a key site or region where they are well-documented (de Mortillet 1883). For example, the Aurignacian Industry (see Preface) takes its name from a town, Aurignac, in the Haute-Garonne region of France, where caves containing the distinctive stone tools attributed to this industry were first identified. Late Pleistocene and Holocene stone tool industries are sometimes described as "cultures" or "complexes" if their diagnostic characteristics include non-lithic evidence, such as distinctive ceramics, architecture, or art. Archaeologists often treat named stone tool industries as if they correspond to self-conscious social groups of prehistoric humans but there are at least three good reasons to not do this. First, many industries are distributed at geographic and chronological scales far greater than any historic or ethnographic human cultures. Second, older industries are associated with fossils of multiple hominin species. Finally, industries from recent time periods are often only weakly correlated with variation in ceramics, architecture, and art, evidence generally viewed as more sensitive to cultural differences than stone tools are.

Technocomplexes

Technocomplexes (also known as "industrial complexes") group together assemblages with similar technologies but variable typological characteristics (Clarke 1978). Some archaeologists name technocomplexes more or less along the same lines as stone tool industries. For example, the Oldowan Industry of Olduvai Gorge (Tanzania) becomes the Oldowan Technocomplex when it refers to lithic assemblages of comparable antiquity and similar technological properties outside of Olduvai Gorge or eastern Africa.

Since the 1970s many archaeologists have used Grahame Clark's (1977) Modes 1–6 as a way of describing technocomplex-level variation (e.g., Foley and Lahr 1997, Barham and Mitchell 2008, Gamble 2013). Mode 1 refers to pebble cores and flaked tools. Mode 2 features handaxes and other large bifacial core-tools. Mode 3 assemblages contain flakes struck from Levallois prepared cores. Mode 4 shows evidence of punch-struck prismatic blades retouched into endscrapers, burins, backed blades, and points. Mode 5 assemblages contain retouched microliths and other lithic components of composite tools. Though little used, Mode 6 indicates groundstone tool production. Assemblages and industries are assigned to one or another of these modes based on which of the most "advanced" ways of making stone tools is represented among them. Whether a particular way of making stone tools is "advanced" (i.e., derived in evolutionary terms) is based on the chronological order in which different ways of making stone tools appear in the European archaeological record. Modes 1–6 are really little more than traditional European age-stages expressed as numbers.

By focusing solely only on technology, technocomplexes provide archaeologists with a coarse-grained picture of hominin behavioral variability. For example, a group of assemblages featuring evidence of prismatic blade production would be classified as "Mode 4" regardless of variation among artifacts referable to Modes 1–3 in those same assemblages. Technocomplexes are thought to correspond to broad patterns of adaptation involving stone tools. Yet, many of them span entire continents for hundred of thousands of years or more, and they exhibit little or no correlation with paleoecological variables or the hominin fossil record.

Better Off Without Them?

Age-stages, industries, and technocomplexes all suffer from the same four problems. They are not based on prior theory linking lithic variability to variation in human behavior. They are formulated intuitively and inductively, by looking at the chronological and geographic patterning of the archaeological stone tool evidence and then equating that pattern with the process that created it. They use one term to summarize multivariate stone tool variability (i.e., they are "homotaxial"). Finally, they are defined using variable criteria. Some are defined in terms of the presence or absence of artifact-types, others on artifact relative frequencies, still others on inferred qualities, such as operational chains. Still others take geographic and chronological variables into account. Age-stages, technocomplexes, and industries conceal more than they reveal about lithic variation. Archaeologists have made numerous efforts to reformulate and to redefine these concepts, but these efforts seem scarcely worth the trouble. As this book will show, one can relate the lithic evidence to major issues in human evolution quite well without them.

A NEW DESCRIPTIVE FRAMEWORK

With what should we replace age-stages, industries, and technocomplexes? Any new framework has to focus on different ways of making stone artifacts. Inferences about stone tool function remain too difficult to refute to be the basis for such a taxonomic framework (Bordes 1969). It cannot be based on the archaeological record of just one geographic region. No region contains a full record of the full range of things hominins have done with stone tools over the last three million years or more. This framework should be neither holistic nor homotaxial. Stone tool production is a phenomenon better characterized by multiple variables simultaneously. The distinctions this framework makes have to be justifiable in terms of prior theory, not derived inductively from the archaeological record nor conjured up intuitively from the archaeological imagination.

Modes A–I

A newly proposed framework, Modes A–I, fulfills all of these criteria (Shea 2013a). Modes A–I refer to different ways of modifying stone observed among humans and non-human primates, as well as ways reconstructed from archaeological evidence. Modes A–G involve controlled conchoidal fracture. Modes H and I involve abrasion (Figures 3.3–3.4). Distinguishing between fracture and abrasion is justifiable in that they are fundamentally different mechanical processes with contrasting energetic costs and benefits. One can knap a stone cutting edge from brittle rock in seconds, but the edge will dull quickly. Making an abraded-edge cutting tool can take hours, but its edge can be resharpened with minimal loss of mass, and the tool can remain useful for years.

Among modes involving fracture, this framework distinguishes between non-hierarchical and hierarchical core reduction strategies. In non-hierarchical core reduction (Modes A–C, and E), opposite sides of a working edge have flakes struck from them in more or less the same way and/or interchangeably. In hierarchical core reduction (Modes F–G) there are systematic differences in how opposite sides of the same edges are treated. Discriminating between hierarchical cores and non-hierarchical cores is justifiable in that detaching flakes from a hierarchical core requires a knapper to adhere to a predetermined arrangement of core surfaces and a procedural template for using them, while reducing a non-hierarchical core does not. Cores knapped by captive bonobos are non-hierarchical. Most novice knappers begin by making non-hierarchical cores then add hierarchical core reduction to their repertoire later on (Shea 2015a). These observations suggest that reducing hierarchical cores requires more skill, or at least greater impulse control, than reducing non-hierarchical cores.

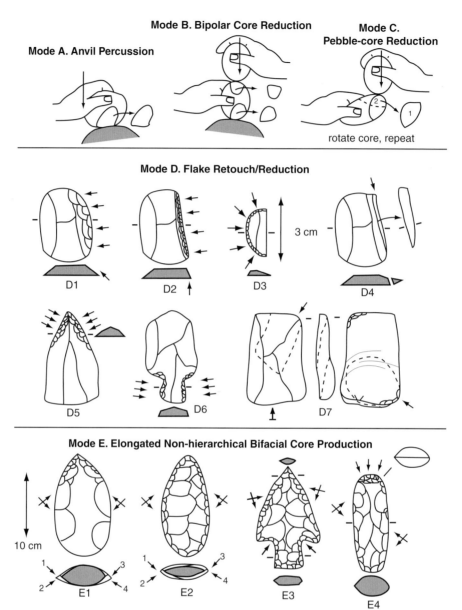

Figure 3.3 Modes A–E.

Some modes are divided into "submodes" (indicated by Arabic numerals). These indicate variation that archaeologists think reflects behaviorally significant differences among tool making strategies (Table 3.2). For clarity, this book refers to Modes A–I and their Submodes mainly by terms in common usage in archaeological literature. In a few cases where older terms are problematical, new and more concise ones have been introduced.

Anvil percussion (Mode A) involves creating a fracture by throwing or striking a core against a hard substrate. When this strategy results in one or

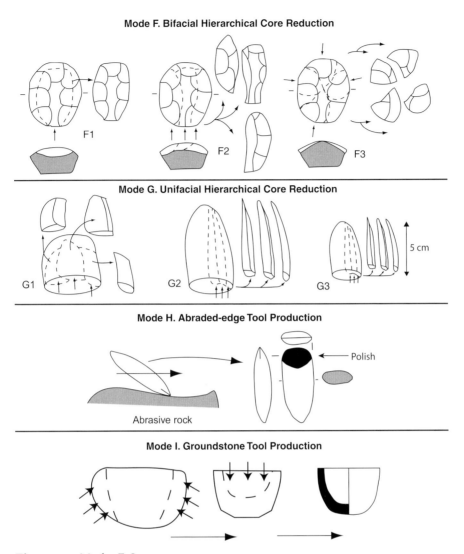

Figure 3.4 Modes F–I.

more large (>3 cm long) flakes, the moving artifact is called a "tested stone." When repetitive striking results in multiple, overlapping, and incompletely propagated fractures (comminution) in the core and/or fractures in the rock against which it was struck, the core is called a "hammerstone" or a "percussor." Common archaeological synonyms for hammerstones/percussors include anvils, pitted stones, pounded pieces, spheroids, and subspheroids.

Bipolar core reduction (Mode B) creates fractures by striking the uppermost surface of a core or flake that is resting on a hard substrate. This strategy results in both large-scale shear fractures and comminution. Mode B's most diagnostic products include bipolar cores and (if flake landmarks are visible) "scaled pieces." This work uses the term "bipolar core" for both such artifacts.

TABLE 3.2. *Modes A–I, and terms for their products*

Modes	Terms used in this book for artifacts resulting from particular modes/submodes	Common archaeological terms used for artifacts resulting from particular modes/submodes
A. Anvil percussion	Stone percussor	Tested stone, hammerstone, anvil, pitted stone, pounded piece, spheroid, and subspheroid
B. Bipolar core reduction	Bipolar core	Bipolar core, scaled piece
C. Pebble core reduction	Pebble core	Chopper, discoid, protobiface, polyhedron
D. Flake retouch/ reduction	Retouched flake fragment	Retouched tool
D1. Orthogonal retouch	Scraper/notch/denticulate (SND)	Scraper, notch, denticulate
D2. Macrolithic backing/ truncation	Backed/truncated piece	Backed knife, truncation/truncated piece
D3. Microlithic backing/ truncation	Microlith	Microlith, small backed and/or truncated piece
D4. Burination	Burin	Burin, burin spall
D5. Convergent distal retouch	Point	Point, awl, retouched triangular flake, perforator, various named point types
D6. Concave proximal retouch	Tanged piece	Tanged piece
D7. Flake core reduction	Core-on-flake	Core-on-flake, truncated-facetted piece, "carinated" piece
E. Elongated non-hierarchical bifacial core-tool production	Elongated bifacial core-tool	See below
E1. Long core-tool (LCT) production	Long core-tool (LCT)	Handaxe, pick, cleaver, bifacial knife, bifacial "preform" or "roughout"
E2. Thinned biface production	Thinned biface	Bifacial knife, lanceolate point, foliate point, cache blade (Americas only)
E3. Tanged biface production	Tanged biface	Projectile point, spear point, knife, drill
E4. Celt production	Celt	Flaked-stone axe, adze, chisel
F. Bifacial hierarchical core (BHC) reduction	Bifacial hierarchical core (BHC)	Levallois core
F1. Preferential BHC reduction	Preferential BHC	Preferential Levallois core

(continued)

TABLE 3.2. *(continued)*

Modes	Terms used in this book for artifacts resulting from particular modes/submodes	Common archaeological terms used for artifacts resulting from particular modes/submodes
F2. Recurrent laminar BHC reduction	Recurrent laminar BHC	Recurrent laminar Levallois core, Levallois blade core
F3. Recurrent radial/centripetal BHC reduction	Recurrent radial/centripetal BHC	Levallois discoidal core, various other discoidal cores
G. Unifacial hierarchical core reduction	Unifacial hierarchical core	
G1. Platform core reduction	Platform core	Platform core, core-scraper, heavy-duty scraper
G2. Blade core reduction	Blade core	Prismatic blade cores, blade, prismatic blade
G3. Microblade core reduction	Microblade core	Bladelet core, microblade core, bladelet, microblade
H. Abraded-edge tool production	Abraded-edge tool	Edge-ground/abraded/polished celts, knives, and scraping tool
I. Groundstone tool production	Groundstone tool	Mortar, pestle, quern, handstone, perforated stone, stone vessel

Pebble core reduction (Mode C) involves sequential non-hierarchical flake removals from clasts (rounded rocks), flakes/flake fragments, or angular rock fragments. This work uses the term "pebble core" in the broad sense, for these cores can be made on cobbles or boulders, too. Common synonyms for pebble cores include choppers, discoids, polyhedrons, and protobifaces/elongated discoids.

Flake retouch (Mode D) detaches flakes from the edge of a flake or flake fragment. This retouch can be either hierarchical or non-hierarchical. Traditional archaeological typologies feature dozens of named retouched artifacts, but seven submodes are adequate for this book's purposes.

Orthogonal retouch (Submode D1) removes a series of flakes continuously along the edge of a flake/flake fragment in such a way that the resulting edge is relatively acute in cross-section ($<70°$). This work refers to orthogonal retouch's characteristic products collectively as scrapers, notches, and denticulates (SNDs).

Submodes D2 and D3 both refer to backing/truncation, retouch along an edge that results in edges that are relatively steep in cross-section ($<70°$). Macrolithic backing/truncation (Submode D2) results in artifacts longer than 3 cm, or "backed/truncated pieces." Microlithic backing/truncation (Submode D3) results in artifacts less than or equal to 3 cm long, artifacts to which this book refers as "microliths."

Burination (Submode D4) creates fractures that propagate roughly perpendicular to a flake's ventral surface, in effect, removing a long portion of the flake's edge. Artifacts on which such fractures have been created are called "burins" (French for "chisels"). A flake detached by burination is called a "burin spall." When a burin spall is detached in such a way that it propagates at a low angle to the flake core's ventral surface and/or transversely to its long axis, archaeologists call the resulting burin spall by the French terms, *tranchet* or *chanfrein*.

Submodes D5 and D6 both refer to retouch that imposes a particular shape on either the distal or proximal end of a flake. Convergent distal retouch (Submode D5) creates retouched edges at the distal end of a flake that converge sharply with one another. Archaeologists refer to the products of convergent distal retouch as "points," "perforators," or "awls." This work calls them "points." Concave proximal retouch (Submode D6) creates one or more symmetrically positioned concavities near the proximal end of a flake, ostensibly as aids to hafting. Because the area around these concavities is traditionally described as a "tang," this work refers to products of Submode D6 as "tanged pieces."

Flake core reduction (Submode D7) detaches relatively large flakes (>2 cm long) from flake fragments. Often these flake fragments/cores-on-flakes have been backed and/or truncated, and their retouched edges are used as striking platforms.

Elongated non-hierarchical bifacial core-tool production (Mode E) involves non-hierarchical flake detachments from an elongated core (length > width) in such a way that flakes propagate roughly perpendicularly to the core's long axis. This work refers to artifacts modified in this way as "elongated bifacial core-tools." The theoretical justification for distinguishing elongated bifacial core reduction from pebble core reduction is that elongation increases the risk of lateral fracture (i.e., fracture perpendicular to the long axis). Traditional archaeological typologies offer up dozens of named types of elongated bifacial core-tools, but for this work, four submodes suffice.

Long core-tool (LCT) production (Submode E1) creates bifacial cores with width/thickness ratios usually less than 3 to 1. This thickness is mainly the result of flakes struck from the core edge not propagating far across the core surface. Most LCTs are 10–20 cm long, but smaller and larger examples occur in many assemblages. Common archaeological terms for LCTs include handaxe, pick, cleaver, bifacial knife, and large cutting tool. In recent contexts these artifacts are often called "preforms" or "roughouts," names that imply they were discarded early on in a longer operational chain rather than being intended tool forms.

In thinned biface production (Submode E2), flakes struck from the edges of the core propagate relatively far across the core surface, reducing the core's thickness with minimal reduction in its circumference. The "biface thinning flakes" detached in this way are broad and thin with irregular shapes. Their striking platforms are relatively wide in relation to their thickness. Their striking platforms and ventral surfaces intersect at relatively high angles (>90–100°). Thinned bifaces usually have width/thickness ratios greater than 3 to 1. Common synonyms for thinned bifaces include bifacial knife, lanceolate point, foliate point, and "cache blade" (a term used mainly in the Americas).

Tanged biface production (Submode E3) is essentially the same as proximal concavity retouch (Submode D6, see above) but applied to an elongated bifacial core. Traditional archaeological terms for tanged bifaces, tanged pieces and points overlap with one another in complex ways. Many tanged elongated bifacial cores also feature convergent distal retouch. This work calls these artifacts "tanged points."

Celt production (Submode E4) involves knapping a sharp cutting edge at the distal end of an elongated bifacial core. "Celt" is the most common archaeological term for these core-tools. Celts' steeply retouched lateral edges give these artifacts relatively low width/thickness ratios, usually 2 to 1 or less. Common synonyms for celts include "axes," "adzes," and "chisels." Some abraded-edge tools are also called celts, but this work distinguishes between the two.

Bifacial hierarchical core (BHC) reduction strategies (Mode F) detach relatively short flakes from one side of an edge and longer flakes from the other side of that same edge. The shorter flakes set up convexities that concentrate force from the hammerstone on a small area, creating longer flakes from the flake detachment surface than would otherwise result. Archaeologists use a variety of terms for the cores and flakes produced by bifacial hierarchical core reduction. The most common adjective applied to them is "Levallois," after a Parisian suburb where examples of such artifacts were first excavated and identified in the nineteenth century. This work distinguishes three submodes of BHC reduction. Preferential BHC reduction (Submode F1) detaches a single relatively large flake from the fracture propagation surface. In recurrent laminar BHC reduction (Submode F2) an overlapping series of large flakes are detached parallel to one another from the fracture propagation surface. In recurrent radial/centripetal BHC reduction (Submode F3) an overlapping series of flake scars converge with one another from multiple points around the circumference of the flake detachment surface.

Unifacial hierarchical core reduction (Mode G) entails a stable hierarchy of fracture initiation and fracture propagation surfaces in which the fracture initiation surface is roughly planar and maintained at nearly a right angle to the fracture propagation surface by small-scale retouch, abrasion, or the occasional removal of larger "tablet" flakes that undercut the fracture initiation surface. Because their striking platform surfaces require minimal modification between successive flake removals, unifacial hierarchical core reduction can

Box 1 *Lithic Artifact Illustration*

Stone tools do not photograph well. Sometimes the problem is translucency; other times their topographic complexity. Instead, archaeologists often illustrate stone tools using line drawings. As in the author's previous work (Shea 2013b: 25–27), *Stone Tools*

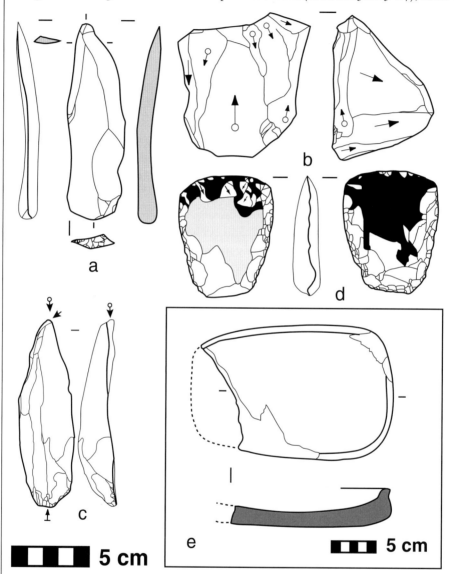

Figure 3.5 Illustration conventions used in this book. a. Unretouched flake showing plan, lateral, and proximal profiles, cross-sections and point of fracture initiation, b. core showing scar directionality, c. burin showing use of arrows to indicate inferred direction of flake removals, d. celt showing use of stippling to indicate cortical surface, black shading to indicate polished surface, e. quern (groundstone artifact) showing plan and section views. Note differences in scale. Source: Shea (2013b).

Box 1 (*Cont.*)

in Human Evolution follows common conventions for orienting and illustrating stone artifacts (Addington 1986) (see Figure 3.5).

In arranging flakes and retouched flakes in a drawing, the striking platform is in the proximal position. The point of fracture initiation is indicated either by a drawing of the striking platform or by a short arrow with a bar at its base. The dorsal side is uppermost. The ventral side is not illustrated unless it has retouch scars on it and if these scar patterns differ from those on the dorsal side. A dash line between drawings indicates different views of the same artifact. Archaeologists use a variety of schemes for positioning drawings of the same object next to one another. The drawings in this book follow the "American" convention, one that involves the minimum movement of the object (i.e., right profile *view* positioned to the right of the artifact) (Aprahamian 2001). Cross-section views are shaded gray, and short lines positioned around the edges of the main tool drawing indicate their locations.

Simple lines and shading indicate flake scar boundaries on flakes, retouched tools and cores. Many artists use radial lines to indicate contour and flake scar direction. This creates a cluttered drawing that does not resemble an actual stone tool. To convey three-dimensional shape, this book uses sections and profile drawings. When necessary (chiefly with cores) arrows indicate flake scar directionality. If the flake scars are too small to place an arrow on them, one places the arrows adjacent to the artifact, next to the point of fracture origin. An arrow with a ring at its base indicates a flake scar with a visible point of fracture initiation. Arrows lacking this ring indicate scar directionality inferred from other surface features. Weathered surfaces (cortex) are lightly shaded. Surfaces of flaked stone artifacts that have been ground and polished are shaded black. Groundstone tools are shown stippled in plan/profile and black in cross-section, more or less using the same conventions for illustrating ceramics.

allow more efficient exploitation of core volume for flake production than BHCs (but see Eren, Greenspan, and Sampson 2008). Any such increased efficiency, however, comes at the cost of increased risk that a bending fracture will occur during fracture propagation. When this happens, a knapper must undertake considerable and raw-material-costly efforts to "rejuvenate" (i.e., restore to functionality) the core's fracture propagation surface. Because these costs increase with greater fracture propagation surface elongation, this work distinguishes the reduction of relatively short platform cores from relatively elongated blade cores of differing sizes. A platform core (Submode G1) is more or less hemispherical, and the flakes detached from it are relatively short (length $<2 \times$ width). Blade cores (Submode G2) are elongated cores greater than 5 cm long from which blades are detached parallel to one another. Bladelet/

microblade cores (Submode G3) are 5 cm or less in length, and reducing them creates blades/flakes less than 1 cm wide.

Abraded-edge tool production (Mode H) creates a cutting edge by abrasion on one or both intersecting surfaces. The most common and widespread abraded-edge tools are celts with a mechanically "polished" cutting edge, but recent stone-tool-using humans also manufacture abraded-edge knives, weapon armatures, and other tools.

Groundstone tool production (Mode I) creates convex, planar, or concave surfaces, and/or perforations on artifacts by cycles of percussion and abrasion ("pecking and grinding"). The most common and widespread groundstone tools are seed-pulverizing tools, but vessels, perforated tools, and other artifacts occur in many ethnographic and archaeological contexts. Because Modes A–I focuses on tool production rather than use, Mode I does not include "grind-stones," otherwise unmodified artifacts identified solely on the basis of use-related abrasion (polish, striations) or percussion.

Modes A–I is not exhaustive. Some strategies for making stone tools combine different modes. For example, blade production using an indirect percussor (a "punch") combines aspects of Modes B and G. There are also strategies for modifying stone tools that Modes A–I does not register, such as exposure to fire (thermal alteration/heat treatment). This framework does not distinguish among particular techniques for initiating fracture (i.e., hard vs. soft hammer percussion, pressure flaking). Nor does it catalog the many operational chains by which each of Modes A–I could be accomplished. This book uses Modes A–I for two reasons. It does so first and foremost so that its observations and interpretations can be evaluated separately from one another. Traditional archaeological accounts of the stone tool evidence often skip this essential scientific practice. Second, it uses Modes A–I for consistency, and such consistency has considerable benefits. Rather than wasting time attempting to reconcile irreconcilable differences in how different archaeological research traditions describe the same lithic artifacts, it can move directly to the stone tool evidence for human evolution, as it does in the next chapter.

CHAPTER 4

STONE CUTTING TOOLS

Grandmother, what big teeth you have got.
  Andrew Lang (1891) "Little Red Riding Hood" in *The Blue Fairy Book*

For humans, stone tools are essentially artificial teeth and fingernails (Schick and Toth 1993). Non-human primates use stone tools as percussors to gain access to food. To shape sticks and other materials into tools, they use their teeth and fingernails. Humans also use stone tools to cut things and to shape tools out of other media. This chapter examines how using lithic tools as artificial teeth/nails affects hominin stone tool production and use. Humans' stone tools differ from those of non-human primates in featuring sharp cutting edges and in wide size/shape variability. The earliest such stone cutting tools occur at African sites younger than 3.5 Ma. Early hominins used these tools to obtain food, for pre-oral food processing, and to make tools out of other materials.

STONE TOOLS AS ARTIFICIAL TEETH/NAILS

Humans and our nearest primate relatives are omnivores and generalist feeders. Each species eats seeds, fruits, nuts, leaves, roots, as well as both vertebrate and invertebrate animals. Although we humans consume many of the same kinds of foods as non-human primates, we differ from them in how we use stone tools as aids to food processing. Non-human primates use their teeth to separate food particles from their sources and to shape sticks into tools. Humans use stone tools for these and other purposes.

The Anatomy of Artificial Teeth/Nails

Many of the differences in how humans and non-human primates make and use stone tools reflect differences in our teeth and hands.

Teeth: Human and non-human primate molar teeth contrast with one another in their crown topography, enamel thickness, and in other subtle ways, but the differences in our incisors and canines, our "anterior" teeth, are obvious (Lieberman 2011) (Figure 4.1). Humans' incisors and canines are all about the same size. Maxillary and mandibular canines/incisors contact one another on a relatively level occlusal plane. Non-human primate incisors project forward away from the occlusal plane and their canines project above and below it. A gap (diastema) between their canines and premolars allows their canine teeth to interlock with one another when their mouths are closed and to self-sharpen as they slide against one another.

On apes' heads, the temporalis and masseter muscles that power chewing are relatively large and anchored on prominent ridges on the top and sides of the skull. These features, together with their large, projecting anterior teeth, allow non-human primates to tear through the hard rinds of tropical fruit, a staple of their diets. They also allow apes to use their teeth to shape tools out of wood and as weapons in interpersonal combat. Male apes hunt and fight more often than females, and, predictably, male apes' canines are larger. Humans' relatively small teeth and smooth, rounded skull do not allow us to do these things well. No humans systematically shape wood or other implements with their teeth, and few of us use our teeth as weapons other than as a last resort in close-quarters hand-to-hand combat. Human male vs. female canines are about the same size.

Hands: Differences between human and non-human primate hands influence the kinds of artificial subsistence aids they can devise (Figure 4.2). Apes have relatively long fingers, an elongated palm, and a small thumb. These features are all aids to climbing, and they are retained even among apes that spend considerable time on the ground and that use their forelimbs to walk quadrupedally, such as gorillas. Human hands, in contrast, have short fingers, a relatively short and roughly square palm, and a long, robust thumb. Our thumbs are attached to a thick *opponens pollicis* muscle that is either weakly developed (vestigial) or absent among non-human primates (Susman 1994). These features do not prevent humans from climbing trees, rock faces, or other surfaces, but they do preclude our matching apes' speed and agility in arboreal locomotion.

These differences in hand shape influence apes' and humans' abilities to devise lithic subsistence aids. Both humans and apes can use a "power" grip, in which they grasp an object between the tips of fingers and the palm. Chimpanzee nut-cracking stones and stone percussors used by bonobos are held in this way. When chimpanzees and bonobos use small tools requiring precise movements, they typically grasp the object between their thumb and the side of their first finger. Apes' small thumbs constrain them from "precision" grasping, in which an object is held between the tip of the thumb and the tips of either one or two fingers (Marzke 1997, 2013). Effective flintknapping and much cutting tool use require precision gripping. This gripping power is especially important for butchery tools, whose surfaces can become lubricated with blood and fat, making them both

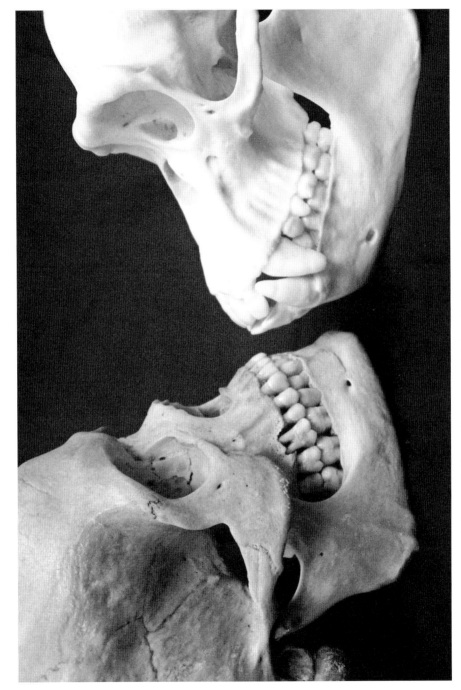

Figure 4.1 Contrasts in male human (left) vs. chimpanzee (right) teeth. Photograph by author.

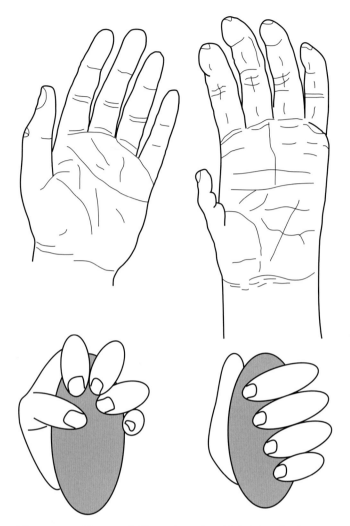

Figure 4.2 Human (left) vs. bonobo (right) hands shown with fingers extended (above) and gripping a stone percussor (below).

difficult and painful to grasp during forceful cutting. Some bonobos can knap stone tools in spite of these limitations, but there remain profound differences between how these apes make and use stone tools and how humans do so (see Box 2).

Lacking a powerful precision grip ought not to be an obstacle to using stone tools to pulverize food such as seeds by percussion or grinding, but non-human primates do not use stone tools in these ways.

Differences in Human vs. Non-human Primate Lithic Subsistence Aids

Differences in how humans and non-human primates use stone tools as subsistence aids allow three predictions about how the stone tool evidence ought to have changed when hominins began to devise lithic cutting tools (see Table 4.1).

TABLE 4.1. *Differences between non-human primate and ethnographic human stone tool use related to the use of stone cutting tools*

Characteristic of stone tool use	Non-human primates	Ethnographic humans
Stone tool size, morphology	Relatively large percussors	Percussors and cutting tools, both relatively large and small
Stone cutting tools used for pre-oral food processing	No	Butchery, processing of nuts, seeds, roots, tubers, fruit, vegetables, leaves
Stone cutting tools used to manufacture subsistence aids out of other materials, such as wood and bone	No	Yes

Systematic Production of Relatively Small Stone Cutting Tools: Stone tools made and used by humans differ from those used by non-human primates in being relatively small, and in featuring cutting edges. Stone percussors used by apes and monkeys are relatively large compared to the body size of the animals using them. (Scaled up to human size, some chimpanzee nut-cracking stones would weigh several kilograms.) Stone cutting tools made by humans vary widely in size, but most of those used for cutting tasks while held directly in the hand are relatively small, usually less than 10 cm long. Humans also make and use very large stone cutting tools, but small stone cutting tools are the most evolutionarily derived component of hominin lithic technology.

Humans and non-human primates both use tools to extract food from sources that are hidden from view or embedded in the tissues of other living organisms. These subsistence aids include tools for perforating and for fracturing. Only humans make stone cutting tools. These tools differ from those used by non-human primates in having been shaped by fracture and by featuring sharp functional cutting edges. Chimpanzees and other primates occasionally fracture rocks in the course of using them as percussors, but they do not use the resulting edges to cut things. When non-human primates use stone tools to segment sticks and other linear materials, they do so by percussion.

Stone Cutting Tools Used for Pre-oral Food Processing: Most humans who made stone cutting tools used them for pre-oral food processing, that is, to modify food particles before ingesting them. Such pre-oral processing has three advantages. First, it separates edible portions of food items, such as meat and fat, from inedible portions, such as hide and bone. This can be a crucial consideration for food procured from large animal carcasses, which expose consumers to predation. Second, it can reduce time and energy otherwise spent chewing tough foods (Zink and Lieberman 2016). An individual chimpanzee can require eleven hours to consume the meat from a single red colobus monkey (Goodall 1986). Individual humans using stone cutting tools can butcher, cook, and consume animals much larger than this in an hour or two. Finally, and most fundamentally, dividing food up into smaller pieces increases its surface to mass ratio, making it more efficiently digestible.

Stone Cutting Tools Used to Manufacture Tools: Non-human primates shape wooden tools with their teeth and fingernails, but they do not use stone tools to shape artifacts out of other media. All stone-tool-using ethnographic human societies use lithic artifacts to shape implements out of stone, wood, bone, and other materials. In industrial societies and among craft specialists in non-industrial societies, stone tools are often embedded in specialized devices with multiple parts. In less formal settings, relatively large flakes and core-tools are used while held directly in the hand for woodworking and similar tasks.

What Is Not Predicted: In framing predictions for an archaeological record involving lithic cutting tools, one should not repeat early archaeologists' mistake of projecting all features of ethnographic stone cutting tool use back into the prehistoric past. This chapter and those that follow base their predictions on aspects of human stone tool production/use that are universal and plausibly detectable. For example, aesthetic qualities guide many but not all ethnographic raw material choices. Unfortunately, archaeologists have not yet developed methods for detecting such aesthetically guided selection practices among prehistoric stone tools. Including aesthetically guided raw material choice as a prediction would needlessly inflate the number of mismatches and ambiguous findings.

Predictions for the Archaeological Record

Contrasts between human and non-human primate stone tool use suggest that an archaeological record created by hominins using stone cutting tools ought to differ from patterns of stone tool use by living apes and earlier hominins in the following ways:

1. Systematic production of small stone cutting tools.
2. Stone cutting tools used for pre-oral food processing.
3. Stone cutting tools used to manufacture tools out of other materials.

THE PLIO-PLEISTOCENE EVIDENCE

On strictly morphological grounds, the Plio-Pleistocene hominins, *Australopithecus, Paranthropus*, and early *Homo* are the most likely candidates for the earliest hominin stone-toolmakers. Species of these genera lived between 1.7 and 3.5 Ma, during the final Pliocene and early Pleistocene geological epochs. All of these hominins share the crucial morphological features that distinguish humans from our nearest primate relatives who use stone tools. They were all bipedal,

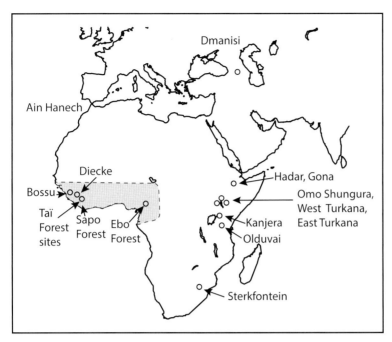

Figure 4.3 Locations of important Plio-Pleistocene sites, modern-day chimpanzee habitats (shaded area) and stone tool use sites.

more than 1.0–1.5 m tall, with reduced anterior dentition, small canine teeth, relatively short fingers, and large, powerful thumbs (Lieberman 2013). All appear to have been sexually dimorphic, with males ranging between 32 and 50 kg and females between 24 and 31 kg (Grabowski et al. 2015). The paleoanthropological record prior to 1.7 Ma includes sites from Africa and Eurasia (Figure 4.3). For recent overviews of this evidence, see Plummer (2004), Barham and Mitchell (2008: 59–107), Fleagle and Grine (2014), and Alemseged (2014). Toth and Schick (2006), and Braun (2014) specifically review the Plio-Pleistocene lithic evidence. For extensive descriptions and illustrations of stone tools from Plio-Pleistocene contexts, see M. Leakey (1971) and Isaac and Isaac (1997).

African Plio-Pleistocene sites are concentrated in southern, eastern, and northwestern regions of that continent, and these sites' characteristics vary between these regions. The best-documented Plio-Pleistocene sites in southern Africa are "caves" (mainly sinkholes and karst fissures). Eastern African sites are open-air localities, formerly the edges of lakes, rivers, and streams now eroding from the walls of the Rift Valley. Northwest African sites are mostly open-air sites concentrated along the shore of the Mediterranean Sea in beach terraces uplifted by tectonic activity. Outside of Africa, the oldest generally accepted paleoanthropological site is Dmanisi (Georgia) dated to 1.8 Ma (Gabunia et al. 2001). There are many sites from Europe and Asia claimed to date before 1.8 Ma or older, but many of these sites suffer from uncertainties about dating and/or the artifactual status of their stone "tools" (Fleagle et al. 2010). Sites from this period are dated by radiopotassium, uranium-series assays, and by stratigraphic correlation with the record for shifts in the Earth's magnetic polarity (magnetostratigraphy) or with dated sequences of fossils (biostratigraphy).

Paleoenvironment

The Plio-Pleistocene period encompasses an important climatic transition. As shown in the oxygen-isotope record of marine sediment cores, global temperatures had been cooling since mid-Miocene times (ca. 12 Ma) (Zachos et al. 2001). Throughout much of Africa and temperate-tropical Eurasia, this cooling caused extensive forests to give way to grasslands. Around 2.5 Ma, the cooling trend accelerated, and it was accompanied by an increase in climatic variability. These changes in climate increased the availability of plant underground storage organs (roots and tubers) and large animal carcasses, food sources humans exploit uniquely among living primates. In arid habitats, plant underground storage organs grow largest along seasonal watercourses (Sept 1994). The expansion of grasslands likely increased the proportion of the landscape in which such roots and tubers could be found. Grasslands also encourage sociality among both predators and their prey, among the former for defense and among the latter for foraging efficiency. Solitary predators, such as leopards, rarely attack prey animals much larger than themselves, but social predators such as lions and hyena do this routinely (Van Valkenburgh 2001). Ancestors of Africa's and Asia's larger social predators, such as lions, hyenas, and wolves, first appear in Plio-Pleistocene times (Turner and Antón 2004). Like their modern-day counterparts, these larger social predators probably generated sizeable animal carcasses that early hominins could have scavenged as food sources (Blumenschine 1986). Even today, in many parts of Africa, one can find herbivore carcasses that leopards have placed in trees in order to put them out of reach of lions and hyenas (Cavallo and Blumenschine 1989). Some of the roughly circular patches in which lithic artifacts occur at some Plio-Pleistocene sites might have resulted from hominins procuring food from these "meat trees" and consuming their strange fruit in the shade.

Hominins

Fossils of *Australopithecus*, *Paranthropus*, and *Homo* are each broadly contemporaneous with the earliest stone tools (Table 4.2 and Figure 4.4) (Klein 2009, Anton, Potts, and Aiello 2014). Fossils of all three genera occur at Plio-Pleistocene sites in eastern and southern Africa. These fossils' isotopic composition and wear patterns on their teeth suggest considerable overlap in their diets (Ungar and Sponheimer 2011). All appear to have been generalist feeders. Plio-Pleistocene hominins' mandibles are thicker and their molar teeth relatively large compared to those of living humans and those of earlier hominins and fossil apes. These features

TABLE 4.2. *Plio-Pleistocene hominins*

Genus	Species	Date range (Ma)	Estimated brain size (cm^3)	Estimated body mass (kg)
Australopithecus	*A. garhi*	1.8–3.9	400–560	25–50
	A. afarensis			
	A. africanus			
	A. sediba			
Paranthropus	*P. robustus*	<1.4–2.8	410–550	24–45
	P. boisei			
	P. aethiopicus			
Early *Homo*	*H. habilis*	1.3–2.7	500–800	27–38
	H. rudolfensis			

Source: Lieberman (2013), Grabowski et al. (2015).

indicate mechanically challenging diets that should have provided incentives for making stone cutting tools.

Plio-Pleistocene Stone Tools

The Plio-Pleistocene stone tool evidence is best documented in eastern and southern Africa. Table 4.3 summarizes the lithic evidence from selected Plio-Pleistocene sites in terms of Modes A–I, juxtaposing them with ethnological and archaeological evidence for chimpanzee stone tool use.

Early stone artifacts include stone percussors, bipolar cores, pebble cores, platform cores, and retouched pieces (Figure 4.5). A few assemblages preserve long core-tools (LCTs), though these are less distinct from pebble cores than LCTs from more recent contexts. All these artifact categories grade into one another. Many of the differences among them reflect the shape of the rock at the start of core reduction/retouch, the mechanical properties of different rock types, and the amount of flakes detached from them (Toth 1985, Harmand 2007). There was some preferential selection of fine-grained lithic raw materials with better fracture properties, such as quartz or chert, but many early stone artifacts are made of coarse-grained rocks, such as basalt and quartzite. Early stone tools range widely in size but surface to volume ratios are consistently low. They are, in a word, "chunky." Many assemblages feature large cores and retouched pieces (>10 cm long) as well as cores and flakes less than 2 cm long.

Retouched pieces are uncommon among assemblages older than 1.7 Ma. In recent years, archaeologists have grown more rigorous in differentiating retouch from incidental edge damage. Predictably, recent excavations report fewer such retouched flakes than older excavations in the same areas (de la Torre and Mora 2005, Domínguez-Rodrigo, Barba, and Egeland 2007). Edge damage on cores suggests some may have been used as cutting tools. Thus far,

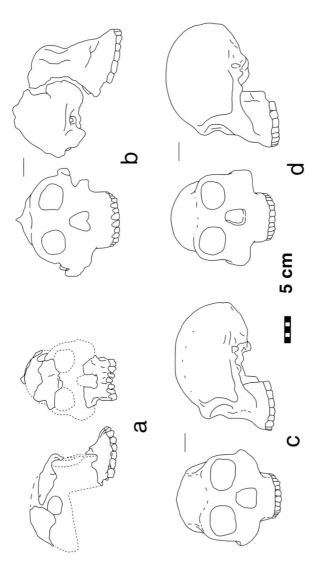

Figure 4.4 Plio–Pleistocene hominin fossil crania. a. *Australopithecus garhi* (Bouri BOU-vP121/130), b. *Paranthropus boisei* (Olduvai 5), c. *Homo habilis* (reconstruction of KNM ER 1813), d. *H. rudolfensis* (reconstruction of KNM ER 1470). Scale is approximate.

5 cm

TABLE 4.3. *Representation of Modes A–I among Plio-Pleistocene lithic assemblages, and chimpanzee nut-cracking sites*

Sample	Date (Ma)	A	B	C	D1	D2	D4	D5	E1	G1	Reference
Plio-Pleistocene sites											
Lomekwi 3	3.3	+									1
Gona (Busidima Formation)	2.5–2.6		+	+	+					+	2
West Turkana Kokiseli 2	2.6										3
Hadar AL 894 Afar	2.6			+							4
Omo Shungura Formation Member F	2.2–2.4	+	+	+							5
West Turkana Lokalalei 1	2.3–2.4			+							6
West Turkana Lokalalei 2C	2.3–2.4	+	+	+	+	+				+	7
Sterkfontein Mbr. 5	1.9–2.0	+	+	+	+					r	8
Kanjera	2.0	+	+	+	+						9
Olduvai Gorge Bed I	1.9	+	+		+		+				10
East Turkana/Koobi Fora KBS Tuff Complex	1.6–1.8	+	+	+	+	+				+	11
Konso KGA6-A1 Locus C	1.6–1.8	+		+	+	+	+		+		12
Ain Hanech	1.8	+		+	+	+	+	+			13
Dmanisi	1.8	+		+							14
Olduvai Lower Bed II	1.7	+	+	+	+	+	+	+	+	+	10
Chimpanzee Sites											
Noulu (Taï Forest, IC)	2–4 Ka	+									15
Panda 100 (Taï Forest, IC)	2–4 Ka	+									15

(continued)

TABLE 4.3. (*continued*)

Sample	Date	A	B	C	D1	D2	D4	D5	E1	G1	Reference
Sacoglotis B (Taï Forest, IC)	1 Ka	+									15
Bossu (G)	P	+									16
Diecke (G)	P	+									16
Sapo Forest (L)	P	+									17
Taï Forest (IC)	P	+									18
Ebo Forest (C)	P	+									19

KEY: Column Headings: A. Anvil percussion, B. Bipolar core reduction, C. Pebble core reduction, D1. Scraper retouch, D2. Macrolithic backing/truncation, D4. Burination, D5. Convergent distal retouch, E1. Long core-tool production, G1. Platform core reduction. Symbols: + = present, r = reported as "rare." Dates for chimpanzee sites are either Ka or "p" = present/<100 years ago. Locations for chimpanzee sites: G = Guinea, IC = Ivory Coast, L = Liberia, C = Cameroon.

References: 1. Harmand et al. (2015), 2. Semaw, Rogers, and Stout (2009), 3. Roche et al. (2003), 4. Hovers (2009a), 5. Delagnes et al. (2011), de la Torre (2004), 6. Kibunjia (1994), 7. Delagnes and Roche (2005), 8. Kuman and Field (2009), 9. Plummer et al. (1999), 10. Leakey (1971), 11. Isaac and Isaac (1997), 12. Beyene et al. (2013), 13. Sahnouni (2006), 14. Baena et al. (2010), 15. Mercader et al. (2007), 16. Carvalho et al. (2008), 17. Anderson, Williamson, and Carter (1983), 18. Boesch and Boesch (1982), 19. Morgan and Abwe (2006).

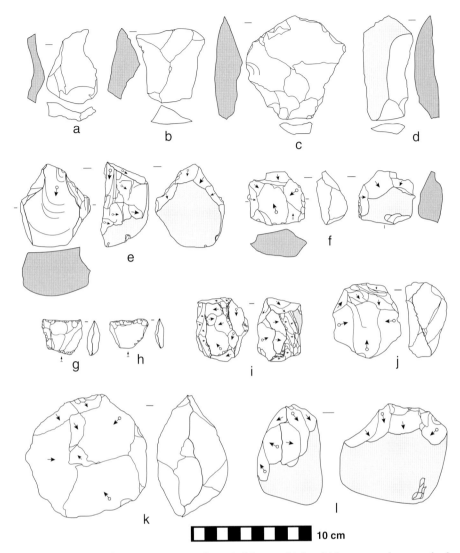

Figure 4.5 Plio-Pleistocene stone tools. a–d. flakes, e–f, i–l. pebble cores, g–h. retouched flakes fragments. Sources: East Turkana (Kenya) KBS Formation Sites FxJj1, 3, 10 (a–f), Olduvai Gorge (Tanzania) Site DK, Bed I (g–l). Redrawn after Isaac et al. (1997), Leakey (1971).

however, microwear traces referable to cutting have only been identified on retouched pieces and unretouched flakes (Keeley and Toth 1981, Lemorini et al. 2014). The surfaces of many Plio-Pleistocene stone tools show pitting and scarring indicating they were used for pounding hard materials (Mora and de la Torre 2005). This damage may reflect food processing, perhaps pulverizing roots or leaves, flintknapping, or some combination of both. It is not beyond the realm of possibility that some of this damage reflects hominins' making noise for some social display purpose or for signaling to one another through dense vegetation or at night.

STONE CUTTING TOOLS: PREDICTIONS EVALUATED

Lithic assemblages resulting from chimpanzee tool use preserve evidence for stone percussors only. Plio-Pleistocene assemblages preserve evidence for these as well as for several different modes of cutting tools (Table 4.4).

Matches with Predictions

The Plio-Pleistocene stone tool evidence matches all three predictions related to the use of lithic cutting tools.

Systematic Production of Small Stone Cutting Tools: Some Plio-Pleistocene stone tools, such as those from Lomekwi 3 (West Turkana, Kenya) are relatively large (Harmand et al. 2015), but every known Plio-Pleistocene lithic assemblage contains relatively small (<10 cm long) flakes and cores that would not stand out among stone tools knapped by ethnographic humans. Rocks with higher silica content and superior fracture properties were transported up to 12 km, further than less siliceous rocks (Plummer 2004). These observations show Plio-Pleistocene small cutting tool production was a planned, systematic activity. Neither Plio-Pleistocene nor older contexts have thus far furnished evidence for percussor-only lithic assemblages like those created by chimpanzees.

Stone Cutting Tools Used for Pre-oral Food Processing: Stone tool cut-marks on vertebrate fossils and lithic microwear patterns both indicate pre-oral food processing. The oldest stone tool cut-marks date to 3.4 Ma from Dikika (Ethiopia) (McPherron et al. 2010). Similar evidence has been found on vertebrate fossils from all the major Plio-Pleistocene site complexes, including Olduvai Gorge (Tanzania), West and East Turkana (Kenya), as well as in various of the South African cave sites (Blumenschine and Pobiner 2007). Microwear traces on stone tools from East Turkana are interpreted as damage from cutting animal hides and from cutting soft plant matter (presumably food)

TABLE 4.4. *Summary of occurrences of Modes A–I in recent chimpanzee vs. Plio-Pleistocene contexts*

Modes/Submodes	Chimpanzee (n = 8)	Plio-Pleistocene (n = 14)
A. Anvil percussion	8	9
B. Bipolar core reduction	0	6
C. Pebble core reduction	0	10
D1. Scraper retouch	0	8
D2. Macrolithic backing/truncation	0	4
D4. Burination	0	3
D5. Convergent distal retouch	0	2
E1. Long core-tool production	0	2
G1. Platform core reduction	0	5

(Keeley and Toth 1981). Striations and polish on stone tools from Olduvai Gorge are interpreted as having been caused by scraping tubers' woody outer surfaces (Lemorini et al. 2014).

Stone Cutting Tools Used to Manufacture Tools From Other Materials: Plio-Pleistocene contexts preserve no actual wooden artifacts, but microwear traces from woodworking occur on some Plio–Pleistocene flakes (Keeley and Toth 1981). Fossil bone fragments with traces of artificial abrasive wear on them appear at several South African sites (Brain and Shipman 1993). Most of these wear traces appear to be damage from digging in soil. A few such bone tools from Swartkrans (South Africa) show abrasion facets and striations consistent with their having been shaped prior to use (d'Errico and Backwell 2003).

Major Interpretive Issues

Some of the major interpretive issues surrounding traditional approaches to the Plio-Pleistocene lithic evidence concern the tasks for which hominins used the earliest stone cutting tools and stone tools' attribution to specific hominins.

Subsistence or Tool Making?: Archaeologists often link the origins of stone cutting tools to increased hominin carnivory (Stanford and Bunn 2001). Stone tool cut-mark evidence from 3.5 Ma onwards clearly shows some early hominins were using stone tools to obtain food from large animal carcasses in ways that living non-human primates do not (Blumenschine and Pobiner 2007). However, this does not mean that butchery was either the first, only, or most important activity for which early hominins used stone tools. Recent humans use stone tools to make implements out of wood and other media, and Plio-Pleistocene hominins seem to have done so, too. The strongest argument for viewing carnivory as a more likely prime mover for the inception of distinctively hominin stone tool production is that while both humans and non-human primates use stone tools as subsistence aids, only humans use stone tools to make tools out of other materials. Thus, using stone cutting tools to make other non-stone tools is plausibly the more evolutionarily derived (i.e., new) behavior.

Attribution to *Homo*: Paleoanthropologists have long viewed early *Homo* as the most likely maker of Plio-Pleistocene stone tools (Leakey, Tobias, and Napier 1964). This attribution follows from a longstanding theory that sees brain enlargement as the prime mover in human evolution (Bowler 1986). Yet, stone tools were made and used at least a million years before the first appearance of *Homo*, around 2.2–2.4 Ma. Moreover, relatively small-brained bonobos have been taught to knap stone tools. Australopithecine and paranthropine hand bone morphology suggest both possessed a capacity for precision gripping (Susman 1998, Rolian and Gordon 2013). There is no objective evidence-based reason to exclude any Plio-Pleistocene hominin from being a stone-toolmaker. If we view stone tools as "artificial teeth," then any hominin with small canines would have had a motive to knap stone cutting tools. While it is possible only one hominin lineage employed such niche-widening tools between 3.5 and 1.7 Ma, nothing in the stone tool evidence supports this hypothesis to the exclusion of alternatives invoking multiple hominin tool makers.

Trying to identify "the" stone-toolmaker among Plio-Pleistocene hominins by looking for relatively large brains and reduced canine teeth overlooks the fact that using stone tools for pre-oral food processing and other tasks ought to have changed the skulls and teeth of toolmaker(s). The reduced prognathism and musculo-skeletal chewing features archaeologists see as incentives for using stone tools might actually be consequences of stone tool use. Experimental studies show that cutting food up and/or pulverizing it before eating it greatly reduces the amount of time and energy spent chewing (Zink and Lieberman 2016). Seeing these changes in Plio-Pleistocene hominin crania may actually tell us that hominins had been using stone tools for pre-oral food processing for a very long time previously. It is also worth reflecting that much as Darwin and other early paleoanthropologists viewed hominin bipedalism as "liberating the hands" for tool use, by reducing the amount of time spent chewing, using stone cutting tools could have "liberated the mouth" for the evolution of another distinctively human behavior, spoken language.

Contrasts with Traditional Approaches

Traditional archaeological approaches to the Plio-Pleistocene lithic evidence suffer from many of the problems already reviewed in Chapter 3. In his earliest synthesis of this evidence, Louis Leakey (1936) used terms for artifact-types and industries imported directly from Europe (e.g., Chellean, Acheulian). In the mid-1960s, Mary Leakey (1966) coined a new term, the Oldowan Industry, that has since become a catch-all term for Plio-Pleistocene lithic assemblages. One obvious disadvantage with assigning all Plio-Pleistocene stone tools to the Oldowan is that it encourages the assumption that all occurrences of these artifacts are meaningfully connected to one another in terms of the identity of the hominin tool makers and the activities undertaken with Oldowan tools. Neither of these assumptions is necessarily true. Indeed, given the nearly two million years over which Oldowan assemblages are distributed, the likelihood that these inferences are correct seems exceedingly low. Additional Plio-Pleistocene stone tools industries, such as the "Pre-Oldowan" and the "Lomekwian," are said to differ technologically from Oldowan assemblages (Semaw et al. 2003, de Lumley, Barsky, and Cauche 2009, Harmand et al. 2015), but whether these differences reflect evolutionarily significant behavioral differences remains an open question. Like all named stone tool industries, these newly proposed ones lack prior theoretical justification. That is, archaeologists identified and defined them after the tools came out of the ground rather than having predicted their characteristics and the timing of their occurrence from some pre-existing model of hominin behavior and evolution. Organizing the Plio-Pleistocene stone tool evidence in terms of named stone tool industries acknowledges the behavioral variability one expects to see in this evidence, but it doesn't advance our understanding of how that variability articulates with larger processes in hominin evolution.

Box 2 *Bonobo Flintknapping*

When the bonobo "Kanzi" first learned to knap, he preferred to initiate fractures by throwing cores at the concrete floor of the laboratory in which he was being observed. Eventually, his tutors conditioned him to knap freehand, as humans do. When Kanzi knaps, he wraps his palm and fingers around the hammerstone in a power grip (fingertips in opposition to the heel of the palm), in the same way chimpanzees hold nut-cracking stones. When he strikes the core, he does so with relatively little force at short intervals (Bril et al. 2012). Kanzi knaps primarily by moving his shoulder and elbow. His wrist remains more or less immobile. He repeats this process until he obtains a sharp flake, at which point knapping ceases and cutting tool use begins. The ratio between blows struck and flakes obtained has not been precisely quantified, but videos of Kanzi knapping suggest it is probably higher than for competent human knappers. Unlike the relatively large stone percussors chimpanzees use to crack nuts, Kanzi's tools include small and thin flakes and pebble cores (Toth and Schick 2009) (Figure 4.6).

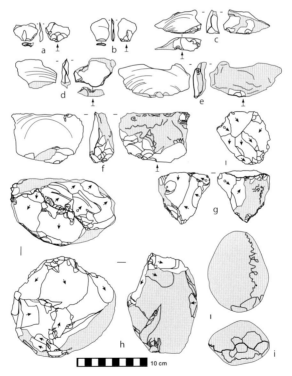

Figure 4.6 Stone tools made by a bonobo. a–f. flakes, g–i. cores. Redrawn after Toth et al. (1993).

CHAPTER 5

LOGISTICAL MOBILITY

Ladies and gentlemen, the Captain has turned on the 'Fasten Seat Belt' sign.
If you haven't already done so, please stow your carry-on luggage under-
neath the seat in front of you or in an overhead bin.

Southwest Airlines' pre-flight announcement

Every time you watch fellow airplane passengers struggle to cram their enormous carry-on luggage into the overhead bins on an airplane, you are witnes-
sing two consequences of our ancestors' logistical mobility. Humans habitually
carry things, and we often carry more than we need. When you effortlessly
stow your own small, well-packed bag in the luggage bin, you are seeing a third
consequence, tools designed for efficient carrying. This chapter considers how
distinctively human logistical mobility influenced stone tools. Logistical mobility became a detectable part of hominin land-use strategies around 1.7 Ma. The
stone tool evidence from this period onwards preserves design changes that
made stone tools more effective components of portable toolkits.

RESIDENTIAL VS. LOGISTICAL MOBILITY

Non-human primates position themselves as near as possible to food sources
and then consume them. Humans do this as well, but we also gather food, fuel,
and tool materials in bulk and move them to residential sites and other
localities. Most non-human primates practice land-use strategies with high
residential mobility. They do not move very far each day, typically less than
several kilometers, but they move every day or very nearly so. They feed as they
go and sleep in a different place each night. They do not move tools or food in
bulk to or between their residential sites. Indeed, primatologists' provisioning
chimpanzees at fixed points on the landscape is thought to lower the threshold
for interpersonal conflict and coalitionary killing among them (Goodall 1986,
Wrangham 1999). Among living primates, only humans practice logistical
mobility. We forage from fixed points on the landscape and provision those

sites with resources procured elsewhere. Logistical mobility's frequency and extent vary among ethnographic humans; nevertheless, logistical mobility features universally in human economic adaptations (Kelly 1995). Kalahari hunter-gatherers, Turkana pastoralists, Maya farmers, and American college students all supply their residential sites with resources procured in bulk elsewhere. These movements routinely involve distances of 5–10 km, but can extend to hundreds of kilometers or more. Even the most residentially mobile humans are still less mobile than any non-captive ape.

How, What, and Why We Carry

Non-human primates can carry things, but they do not do so willingly, well, for prolonged periods, or over distances equivalent to humans. Humans are nearly always carrying something, either in our hands, on our heads, or attached to us in one way or another. To not be carrying anything is so "unhuman" that nearly all of the world's cultures consider true nakedness a liminal condition, one marking important life transitions such as birth and death, as well as ceremonial and supernatural experiences.

How We Carry: Both humans and non-human primates carry stones and other tool materials from one place to another, but the costs of doing so differ. Non-human primates are quadrupedal. They use their arms as aids to locomotion. Carrying objects in one or both of their hands compromises their ability to move on the ground and in trees (Carvalho et al. 2012). Their lack of lumbar lordosis (a forward curve of their lumbar vertebrae) means that when apes and monkeys carry an object in their hands they typically do so in front of themselves. When they attempt to walk bipedally and carry things, their center of gravity shifts forward. To avoid falling over, apes and monkeys "walk" by shifting their body from side-to-side, a mode of progression that expends much of their momentum with each step. Our recurved spine allows us to keep our center of gravity above our pelvis when walking and carrying things. Lumbar lordosis also allows our rib-cage and pelvis to rotate in opposite directions, stabilizing us and storing torsional force between steps (Bramble and Lieberman 2004). The energetic consequences of these differences are not trivial. Human bipedal walking is 75 percent less energetically costly than either quadrupedal or bipedal walking by chimpanzees (Sockol, Raichlen, and Pontzer 2007). Lumbar lordosis is also one among several anatomical features that make humans exceptionally powerful and accurate throwers (Rhodes and Churchill 2009).

Unlike non-human primates, ethnographic humans devise tools for carrying things. All pre-industrial societies make containers of plant fibers, leather, and wood and use them as aids to logistical mobility. On the move, humans carry these devices in their hands, on their head, or suspended from their waist or shoulders. A small number of historic groups use dogs and other animals as aids to carrying, but these practices are thought to have arisen only in post-Pleistocene times. Carved stone and ceramic vessels are less often used as carrying aids during logistical movements, probably due to their weight and the risk of breakage.

What We Carry: What humans carry in logistical movements differs from the things non-human primates transport. Non-human primates carry tools and food for short distances. They do not transport fuel or architectural materials for the simple reason that they do not control fire or build architectural structures more substantial than nightly sleeping platforms. Humans transport tools, food, fuel, and building materials, but the distances and quantities vary. The distances humans move food, fuel, and building materials increase over time because these resources can be depleted at or near residential sites. As a result, the archaeological signature of logistical mobility varies along with prolonged occupations of the same site.

When non-human primates transport tools, they typically do so after having first located a food source, to which they bring tools directly from the nearest available source. Non-human primates transport stone tools directly to food sources without modifying them. When non-human primates transport plant food, they move it very short distances, rarely more than a few meters. Prolonged use of the same site does not seem to alter the lithic signature of non-human primate stone tool use, other than by increasing the amount of stone at those sites.

Ethnographic humans carry stone tools with them to food sources, but they also carry them while searching for food sources, while moving between food sources, and during residential movements as well. Transporting stone tools entails an energetic cost, but the countervailing benefit of doing so is that one does not need to pass up a potential resource for want of a stone cutting tool (Binford 1979, Kuhn 1992). Ethnographic stone tool users either deliberately cache stone tools at strategic points on the landscape, or they practice *de facto* caching (i.e., use tools from abandoned habitation sites), as ways to further reduce the costs of carrying stone tools. They also modify stone and other tool materials to reduce transport costs. The foods humans transport over long distances are overwhelmingly nutrient-dense foods extracted from sources that require skill to find, procure, and extract. Examples of such foods include parts of large vertebrate carcasses, plant underground storage organs, and seeds/nuts that require mechanical processing (Kaplan et al. 2000). For readers living in modern-day industrial societies, equivalent nutrient-dense efficiently transportable foods include candy, honey, energy bars, and trail mix.

Why We Carry: Carrying and logistical mobility have profound evolutionary implications. When individual non-human primates carry food, they move from where they collected it to where they themselves process and consume it. There is no larger social dimension to these activities, no ape equivalent of a dining room or a restaurant. Apart from males who will trade food for copulations, non-human primates do not systematically share food with unrelated individuals of their own species. Humans transport food over both long and short distances to residential sites at which we share food with other humans. We also store food at these localities. Logistical mobility, combined with central place foraging and food sharing/storage, allows humans to breed cooperatively in ways non-human primates cannot (Kaplan et al. 2000). Each non-human primate parent cares for her own offspring. Infants may be put briefly in care of a near relative, but they are rarely out of their biological mother's sight. Among all known pre-industrial human societies, child-care is a corporate/collective responsibility. Knowing that other adults will provision them with food, fuel, and other resources, an individual human will watch over the offspring of other individuals. Knowing that someone is watching over their children, individual humans will undertake more risky logistical forays in search of food, fuel, or other resources. Cooperative breeding also creates an environment in which children learn social and technical skills consistently. Rather than learning how to crack open nuts or make stone tools by observing their own parents, whose skills may be sub-par, they can do so by observing the best nut-crackers and flintknappers in their community.

Differences in Tools Transported by Humans vs. Non-human Primates

Differences in human vs. non-human primate mobility influence stone tool use in ways that allow predictions about how the lithic record should have changed when logistical mobility like that practiced by recent humans became part of ancestral hominin adaptations (see Table 5.1).

Increases in Raw Material Transportation Distances: Non-human primates transport stone tools relatively short distances, typically less than a kilometer, though a few further movements have been observed (Boesch and Boesch 1984a, Toth and Schick 2009). Ethnographic humans routinely carry stone and other tool materials 5–10 km and further. It follows that when hominins began carrying out logistical movements comparable to those of living humans, the archaeological record ought to preserve evidence for systematic raw material transfers greater than those carried out by non-human primates and greater than those by earlier hominins. This being said, contrasts between non-human primate and ethnographic human lithic raw material movements do not provide a prediction about either the speed, magnitude, or short-term tempo of these changes. Maximum transport distances could have shifted abruptly by orders of magnitude, or they could have increased gradually and/or recursively over time.

Tool Designs that Enhance Portability and Increase Utility: Non-human primates do not modify the stones they transport. The stone tools ethnographic humans bring along on logistical movements are usually modified, and they differ from stone tools made and used at residential sites in

TABLE 5.1. *Differences in non-human primate vs. ethnographic human stone tool use related to logistical mobility*

Characteristic of stone tool use	Non-human primates	Ethnographic humans
Stone tool transport	Short distances <5 km	Longer distances >5 km
Tool designs	None, material selection only	Designs for enhanced portability, utility
Non-residential sites provisioned with tools	Extractive sites	Extractive sites, strategic caches
Residential sites provisioned with tools.	No	Yes

several ways. Transported tools are designed to perform more than one distinct function. An arrowhead, for example, would be shaped so that it could function as a knife or drill. Such tools often feature relatively high quantities of cutting edge per unit of mass or volume so that they can be reused/resharpened after use in tasks entailing high rates of edge attrition. Such tools' main disadvantage as transported personal gear is that they are both design compromises and modified reductively. Like many components of portable toolkits, they perform adequately in a range of tasks and less well in specialized tasks than other less-portable tools. Because one modifies stone tools by removing mass, however, resharpening them and reshaping them for particular tasks reduces their future potential utility more so than that of other portable gear such as cordage, which can be reshaped without loss of mass and repaired by addition.

Readers unacquainted with portable toolkits used by ethnographic hunter-gatherers will find a familiar example of tools with these design features in Swiss Army™ knives, Leatherman™ folding tools, and similar "multi-tools." These metal implements contain multiple functionally differentiated blades (e.g., knife, can-opener, screwdriver). Their cutting blades are relatively thin (high edge/mass ratio), allowing easy reuse/resharpening. Such tools function adequately for a wide range of tasks, but not so well for prolonged periods in more specialized tasks. For example, their <10 cm long saw blades are sufficient to cut a branch for use as fuel or as a walking stick, but not for architectural carpentry.

When logistical mobility became an important factor in hominin land-use strategies, the archaeological record should preserve evidence for tool designs that enhance portability and for strategies for boosting tool utility involving reuse/resharpening. Increased logistical mobility ought to have created powerful incentives for devising carrying aids, but preservation biases may preclude our detecting them. Most such tools and containers used by ethnographic humans are made of leather, wood, and plant fibers, organic materials rarely preserved in Pleistocene contexts.

Non-residential Sites Provisioned with Stone Cutting Tools: Both humans and non-human primates provision "extractive" sites with stone tools, but they differ in the kinds of sites they frequent and how they use them. Extractive sites are places where food or other resources are procured in bulk and either consumed on the spot (by apes) or accumulated for transport elsewhere (by humans). For example, both humans and chimpanzees process nuts in bulk beneath the trees from which the nuts have fallen. Though chimpanzees have been observed concealing stone tools they brought to extractive sites at those sites, only humans place stone cutting tools in strategically placed caches independent of food sources. Earlier hominin logistical mobility ought to have resulted in such strategic caching sites, though preservation biases may limit our ability to identify them as such. Unlike chimpanzees, humans also discard stone tools while on the move as they approach and encounter lithic raw material sources. Only humans make and use stone tools at large vertebrate death sites.

Residential Sites Featuring Stone Tools: Unlike non-human primates, ethnographic humans transport stone tools to their residential sites, and they make stone tools at those sites. At ethnographic residential sites and recent archaeological localities interpreted as such, stone tools are associated with hearths, architecture, storage features, and food waste. Logistical mobility should have had a similar effect on earlier hominin behavior and ought to be expressed in similar archaeological patterning. This being said, applying this prediction to the prehistoric record is far from straightforward. Residential sites created by recent hunter-gatherers vary widely in archaeological "visibility" (e.g., Yellen 1977, Binford 1978, Hayden 1979). Moreover, many social and ecological factors influence central place foraging and food sharing/storage by ethnographic humans (Testart 1982, Winterhalder 1986, Speth 1990, Hill and Kaplan 1993, Kaplan et al. 2000, Kramer and Russell 2015).

Predictions for the Archaeological Record

Differences between human and non-human primate stone tool use related to logistical mobility suggest that when logistical mobility like that practiced by living humans evolved, the lithic archaeological record should begin to exhibit the following qualities:

1. Increases in raw material transportation distances.
2. Tool designs that enhance portability and increase utility.
3. Non-residential sites provisioned with stone cutting tools.
4. Residential sites featuring stone tools.

EARLY-MIDDLE PLEISTOCENE EVIDENCE

The Early-Middle Pleistocene Period (0.3–1.7 Ma) spans the later Early Pleistocene (0.7–2.5 Ma) and the early Middle Pleistocene (0.13–0.73 Ma). Two observations, one from hominin fossils and the other from zooarchaeology, recommend the Early-Middle Pleistocene (EMP) as the "period of interest" for hominin logistical mobility. Recent humans who depend heavily on logistical mobility do so by walking and running long distances. The period 1.6–1.8 Ma marks the appearance of hominins capable of a running/striding gait like recent humans (Lieberman 2013, Fleagle and Lieberman 2015). This same period also sees increasing numbers of archaeological sites juxtaposing stone tools together with large animal bones featuring stone tool cut-marks indicating carcass division and transport (Domínguez-Rodrigo and Pickering 2003, Blumenschine and Pobiner 2007). (The end of this focal period is somewhat more arbitrarily imposed and reflects changes in the lithic evidence discussed in Chapter 6.) Evidence of EMP hominin activity comes from much of Africa, all of Europe to about 52° N latitude, and most of the lower elevations in southern and eastern Asia (Figure 5.1). Overviews of the EMP fossil and archaeological evidence can be found in Langbroek (2004), Barham and Mitchell (2008: 108–200), Dennell (2009), Gamble (1999: 98–173), Klein

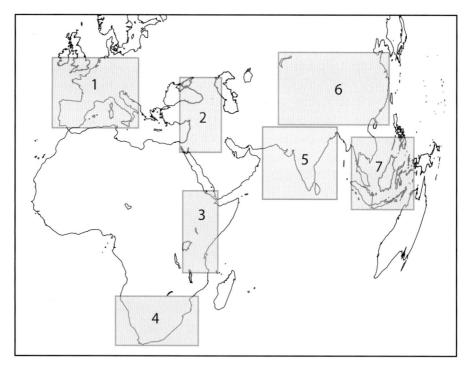

Figure 5.1 Locations of important Early-Middle Pleistocene sites. 1. Western Europe Group, 2. Southwest Asia Group, 3. Eastern Africa Group, 4. Southern Africa Group, 5. South Asia Group, 6. East Asia Group, 7. Southeast Asia Group.

(2009: 279–435), Lieberman (2011, 2013), also papers in Fleagle et al. (2010). Descriptions of EMP stone tools usually employ one or another of the typologies published by M. Leakey (1971), Kleindienst (1967), Bordes (1961) and Debénath and Dibble (1994).

Early-Middle Pleistocene Paleoenvironment

At a global scale, the EMP encompasses a transition from a warm, humid, but overall cooling world with numerous low-magnitude changes in climate to a world beset by prolonged glaciations and greater climatic variability (Zachos et al. 2001). Oceanic sediment cores show that prior to 0.9 Ma, the Earth experienced alternating cooler and warmer climates along 40,000–50,000-year-long cycles. Around 0.9 Ma, these cycles' wavelength increased to around 110,000–120,000 years. The bulk of longer cycles were cooler periods during which glaciers extended from the Arctic onto North America and Eurasia. Glaciers also formed on the peaks of mountain ranges, most notably from the Alps to the Himalayas and along the Rocky Mountains and the Andes. As ever-greater amounts of water became locked up in ice, sea levels dropped up to 150 m below their current elevation. Warm and humid "interglacial" periods roughly 10,000–15,000 years long punctuated these longer glacial cycles. Roughly eleven such glacial cycles occurred over the last million years.

The effects of glacial cycles varied geographically. In Africa, colder periods corresponded with periods of aridity and desert growth and warmer ones with extensive lakes forming and joining one another by vast networks of rivers. This being said, the correlation between tropical climates and glaciation is neither simple nor straightforward. The Mediterranean Basin appears somewhat insulated from these cycles, but their impact north of the Alps and Himalayas was profound. During interglacial periods, hippopotamus swam in the Thames River, while during glacial periods, reindeer and mammoths roamed this same region (Agusti and Antón 2003). The picture of climate change in southern and eastern Asia is less clear, although it likely involved expansions and contractions of the extensive forests that formerly covered much of these regions (Dennell 2009).

Early-Middle Pleistocene Hominins

Fossils of the Genus *Homo* dominate the hominin fossil record for the period 0.3–1.7 Ma. Most sources recognize at least two groups of EMP hominins, *Homo erectus* and *Homo heidelbergensis*. African fossils dating 1.4–1.8 Ma are commonly described as *Homo ergaster* (Table 5.2). In Africa and western Eurasia, most *Homo ergaster/erectus* fossils are older than *H. heidelbergensis* fossils. The ages and taxonomic status of many fossils from South and East Asia remain unsettled. EMP hominins differ from Plio-Pleistocene hominins in having

TABLE 5.2. *Early-Middle Pleistocene hominins*

Hominin taxon	Dates	Geographic range & representative fossils
Homo ergaster ("early African *H. erectus*")	1.4–1.8 Ma	Africa: East Turkana (KNM-ER) 3732, 3733, 3883, 47200, West Turkana (KNM-WT) 15000, Swartkrans 847 Asia: Dmanisi 2700 and 2735
Homo erectus	0.5–1.4 Ma	Africa: Olduvai H9, Olorgesailie 1, Daka 1, Buia 1 Asia: Trinil, Sangiran 17, Ngandong 9, Sambungmacan, Ngawi, Zhoukoudian Europe: Atapuerca SE, Ceprano, Dmanisi 2282 and 2280
Homo heidelbergensis	>0.2–0.5 Ma	Africa: Bodo, Ndutu, Kabwe (Broken Hill). Europe: Atapuerca Sima de los Huesos 4–6, Swanscombe, Steinheim, Arago, Petralona (Asia: Narmada, Dali, Maba?)

Source: Klein (2009)

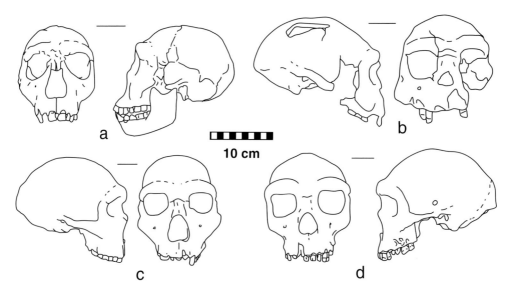

Figure 5.2 Crania of Early-Middle Pleistocene *Homo*. a. *Homo ergaster* (Nariokotome/KNM WT-15000), b. *H. erectus* (Sangiran 17), c. Eurasian *H. heidelbergensis* (Petralona 1), d. African *H. heidelbergensis* (Broken Hill 1). Scale is approximate.

smaller teeth and larger brains (>800–1000 cm³ vs. <600 cm³), more vertical faces and exterior noses, among other things (Lieberman 2011). Their skulls contrast with *H. sapiens* in having larger and more projecting faces, prominent bar-like brow ridges, receding foreheads, and a braincase that is widest at its temporal rather than parietal bones (Figure 5.2). EMP hominins' stature and other aspects of their cranial and post-cranial skeletal remains vary widely, but larger adults were about as tall and heavy as *H. sapiens* adults. This said, discoveries of very small *H. erectus* individuals in Africa and Asia reveal wide variation in stature, and possibly wide variation in sex-related size differences (sexual dimorphism). EMP fossils also contrast with Plio-Pleistocene ones in sharing morphological features that enable recent humans to walk and run for prolonged periods over long distances (Bramble and Lieberman 2004, Lieberman et al. 2008). These features include narrow feet, long legs, and a spinal column with a lumbar curve. EMP hominins probably did not walk or run in exactly the same ways as living humans do, but they share with us the capacity for "endurance" running and walking that undergirds ethnographic land-use strategies entailing high levels of logistical mobility.

Early-Middle Pleistocene Stone Tools

The lithic record for the Early-Middle Pleistocene Period extends over three continents and for more than a million years. Table 5.3 presents data on the occurrences of Modes A–I among a sample of EMP assemblages. Hammerstones, bipolar cores, pebble cores, platform cores, and simple retouched pieces occur in most of these EMP assemblages. Retouch on flake fragments is more clearly the result of hominin activity than in Plio-Pleistocene assemblages. Most EMP assemblages feature scrapers/notches/denticulates, but burins, and points (mainly "awls"), occur in many assemblages as well. More novel elements of the EMP stone tool evidence include long core-tools, bifacial hierarchical cores (BHCs), and blade cores.

Long Core-tools: Long core-tools (LCTs) are the most iconic EMP lithic artifacts (see Box 3). LCTs vary widely in size, shape, and the extent to which they have had flakes detached from them. Most are elongated in two dimensions with their mass distributed asymmetrically along the longer of these two axes. Most LCTs are between 10 and 20 cm in length (about the same size as a human hand with fingers and thumb aligned parallel to one another) (Figure 5.3). Some LCTs were made by detaching flakes from cobbles and tabular pieces of rock, others by retouching large flakes struck from boulders or from BHCs. LCTs have complex surface topography, and, as a result, flakes detached from them vary widely in size and shape. Some part of LCT variation may reflect greater or lesser amounts of reduction and/or resharpening or the effects of raw material variation. Others may reflect shapes imposed for particular functions (Jones 1979, Villa 1983, McPherron 1999). Traditional typologies recognize numerous morphological types of LCTs, including "handaxes," "picks," and "cleavers," but these all grade into one another, and no evidence indicates they differ from one another functionally.

TABLE 5.3. *Representation of Modes A–I among Early-Middle Pleistocene lithic assemblages*

Site and assemblage	A	B	C	D1	D2	D4	D5	E1	F1	F2	F3	G1	G2	Reference
Western Europe														
Atapuerca, Gran Dolina TD6 (Sp)	+		+	+										1
Atapuerca, Sima del Elefante (Sp)	?		?											2
Bilzingsleben (G)	+	?	+	+	+		+					+		3
Ceprano (It)	+		+	+			+	+						1
Hoxne (UK)	+	r	+	+	?			+						4
Isernia La Pineta (It)	+	+	+											5
Orce Basin Sites (Sp)	+	+	+											1
Piro Nord (It)	+	+	+											6
Terra Amata (Fr)	+	+	+	r			r	+				+		7
Torre in Pietra (It)	+	+	+	+	+	+		+		+	+	+		8
Vallonet Cave, Ensemble III (Fr)	+		+											1
Southwest Asia														
Gesher Benot Yaacov (Is)	+		+	+	+		+	+	r					9
Latamne (Sy)	+		+	+		r	+	+			+	+		10
Nor Geghi Units 1–4 & Slope (Ar)	+		+	+			r	+	+	+	+	r		11
Tabun Cave Level Eb–Ed (Is)		+	+	+	+	+		+	+			+		12
Tabun Cave Level F (Is)		+	+	+	+	+		+	+	?				12
Tabun Cave Level G (Is)		+	+	+	+	+						+	?	12

(*continued*)

Site											Ref
Ubeidiya (Is)	+	+	+	+	+	+	+	+	+	+	13
Eastern Africa											
East Turkana/Koobi Fora (K)	+	+	+	+	+	+	+	r	+	+	14
Konso KGA other sites (Et)				r	+	r	+				15
Konso KGA6–A1 Locus C (Et)	+			+	+		+		+	+	15
Lake Baringo Komilot Locus 1 & 2 (K)	+	+	+		+			+	+		16
Lake Baringo lower K3 GnJh 42, 50 (K)		+	+	+			+	+	+	r	17
Lake Baringo upper K3–LHA, GnJh17 (K)	+	+	+	+	+	+	+		+	r	18
Melka Kunture, Garba IV (Et)		r	r	r	+	r	+	+	+		19
Melka Kunture, Gombore I (Et)		r	+	+			+		+		19
Melka Kunture, Gombore II (Et)		+	+	+	r	+	+		+		19
Olduvai Beds III–IV (Tz)	+	+	+	?	+	+	+	+	+	+	20
Olduvai Mid–Upper Bed II (Tz)	+	+	+	?	+	+	+	+	+	+	21
Olorgesailie (K)	+	?	+	+	+	+	+	+	+		22
Peninj, EN & ES sites (Tz)							+		+		23
Peninj, ST Site Complex (Tz)	+	+	r	+	+	+	+	+	+		24
Southern Africa											
Kathu Pan 1 (SA)	+	+	+	+	+	+	+	+	+	+	25
South Asia											
Attirampakkam (In)	+	+	+	+	+	+	+		r		26
Southeast Asia											
Mata Menge (Ia)	+	+	+	+	+	+	+	+	+		27

(continued)

TABLE 5.3. (*continued*)

Site and assemblage	A	B	C	D1	D2	D4	D5	E1	F1	F2	F3	G1	G2	Reference
Eastern Asia														
Dongutuo (Ch)			+	+								+		28
Lantian Chenjiawo (Ch)			+	+										28
Lantian Gongwangling (Ch)	+		+	+										28
Xiaochangliang (Ch)			+	+								+		28
Zhoukoudian Locality 1 (Ch)	+	+	+	+	+		+					+		28

KEY: Column Headings: A. Anvil percussion, B. Bipolar core reduction, C. Pebble core reduction, D1. Orthogonal retouch, D2. Macrolithic backing/truncation, D4. Burination, D5. Convergent distal retouch, E1. Long core-tool production, F1. Preferential bifacial hierarchical core (BHC) reduction, F2/3. Recurrent BHC reduction, G1. Platform core reduction, G2. Blade core reduction. Symbols: + = present, r = reported as "rare," ? = report ambiguous.

Country Codes: Armenia (Ar), China (Ch), Ethiopia (Et), France (Fr), Germany (G), India (In), Indonesia (Ia), Israel (Is), Italy (It), Kenya (K), South Africa (SA), Spain (Sp), Syria (Sy), Tanzania (Tz), United Kingdom (UK)

References: 1. de Lumley et al. (2009), 2. Carbonell et al. (2008), 3. Mania (1995), 4. Singer, Gladfelter, and Wymer (1993), 5. Peretto (1994), 6. Arzarello et al. (2007), 7. Villa (1983), 8. Grimaldi (1998), 9. Goren-Inbar et al. (1992), 10. Clark (1967), 11. Adler et al. (2014), 12. Garrod (1937), 13. Bar-Yosef and Goren-Inbar (1993), 14. Isaac and Isaac (1997), 15. Beyene et al. (2013), 16. Tryon, McBrearty, and Texier (2005), 17. Johnson and McBrearty (2010), 18. Tryon et al. (2005), 19. Chavaillon et al. (1979), 20. Leakey and Roe (1994), 21. Leakey (1971), 22. Isaac (1977), 23. Domínguez-Rodrigo et al. (2009), 24. de la Torre and Mora (2009), 25. Wilkins and Chazan (2012), 26. Pappu et al. (2003), 27. Brumm et al. (2010), 28. Keates (2000).

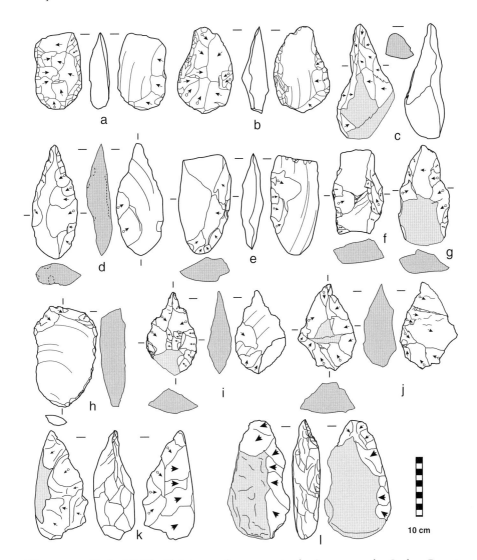

Figure 5.3 Early-Middle Pleistocene long core-tools. Sources: a–b. Gesher Benot Yaacov, Israel, c. Ubeidiya, Israel, d–e. Olorgesailie, Kenya, f–g. Olduvai Gorge, Tanzania, h–j. East Turkana, Kenya, West Turkana, Kenya, k–l. Kokiseli 4. Redrawn after Leakey (1971), Isaac (1977), Goren-Inbar and Saragusti (1996), Isaac et al. (1997), Shea and Bar-Yosef (1999), Lepre et al. (2011).

Bifacial Hierarchical Cores: Bifacial hierarchical cores (BHCs) appear in Africa and Asia around 1.5 Ma (Figures 5.4 and 5.5). Recurrent radial/centripetal BHCs occur in some of the earliest EMP assemblages. That many archaeological descriptions fail to distinguish recurrent radial/centripetal BHCs from "discoid" pebble cores makes it difficult to gauge their abundance and variability. The earliest preferential BHCs and the flakes

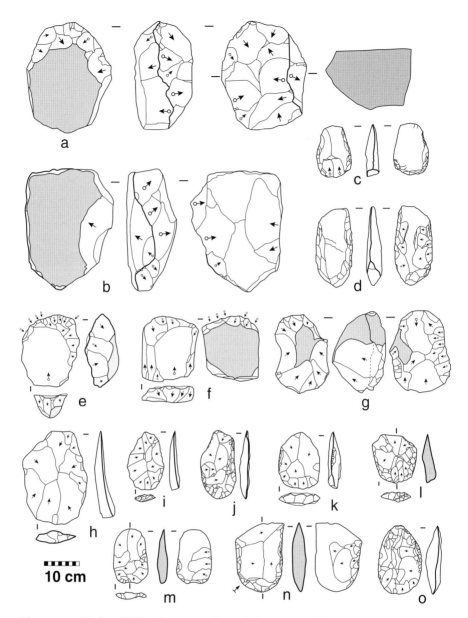

Figure 5.4 Early-Middle Pleistocene large flake cores and long core-tools made on flakes. a–b. large non-hierarchical cores, c–d. long core-tools made on large flakes struck from large non-hierarchical cores, e–f. large bifacial hierarchical cores with preferential removals, g. large bifacial hierarchical core with overshot flake refitted to it, h–i. large flakes struck from bifacial hierarchical cores, j–l. large flakes with retouch on portions of their edge, m. large flake with ventral thinning flake removals, n–o. long cutting tools made on large flakes (n = flake cleaver, o = unifacially flaked handaxe). Sources: Gesher Benot Yaacov, Israel (a–d), Lake Baringo, Kenya, Kapthurin Formation (e–o). Redrawn after Leakey et al. (1969), Madsen and Goren-Inbar (2004), Tryon et al. (2005).

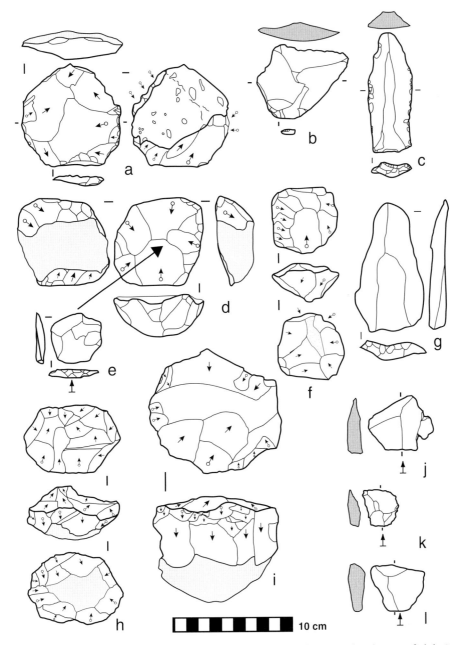

Figure 5.5 Early-Middle Pleistocene bifacial hierarchical core technology. a, f, d, h, i. recurrent bifacial hierarchical cores, b, c, e, g, j–l. flakes struck from recurrent bifacial hierarchical cores. Sources: Nor Geghi 1, Armenia (a–c), Komilot Locus 1 & 2, Kapthurin Beds, Lake Baringo, Kenya (d–g), ST Site Complex, Peninj, Lake Natron, Tanzania (h–l). Redrawn after Tryon et al. (2005), de la Torre and Mora (2009), Adler et al. (2014).

struck from them are relatively large (>10 cm long). Most such cores feature at least one relatively large flake scar that extends up to or past the midpoint of the core's flake propagation surface. Larger flakes detached from these cores vary widely in size and shape. They are often the longest and widest flakes in an assemblage but neither exceptionally thin nor narrow. Their medio-lateral cross-section is usually either lenticular (biconvex) if they were detached from the center of the core's flake propagation surface or wedge-shaped if they were detached from near the lateral edge of the core. These large flakes grade by varying degrees of retouch into LCTs and large retouched pieces. Recurrent laminar BHCs become more common after 0.3–0.5 Ma. Around this time as well, flakes struck from preferential BHCs become shorter, usually less than 10 cm, and relatively thinner (Adler et al. 2014). Among these younger assemblages, a series of shorter flake removals from the distal and lateral margins of the flake detachment surface often predetermines the shape of their large preferential flakes (Chazan 1997).

Blade Cores: A few EMP archaeological assemblages preserve evidence for blade core reduction (Figure 5.6). The best-documented such occurrences date to around 0.3–0.5 Ma in the Baringo Basin in Kenya and in the East Mediterranean Levant at Tabun, Yabrud, and Qesem Caves (Johnson and McBrearty 2010, Shimelmitz, Barkai, and Gopher 2011). At these sites, hominins detached blades systematically and retouched them in distinctive ways. In contrast with occasional finds of blades from Plio-Pleistocene contexts, orthogonal retouch on these blades is often located at the distal end of the blade, perpendicular to the tool's long axis. Retouched lateral edges are often steeply backed. In contrast with blade core reduction in more-recent contexts, EMP blade core reduction seems to have involved little prior shaping of an elongated cylindrical core out of some non-cylindrical piece of stone prior to blade removal. Instead, and for the most part, EMP hominins selected elongated pieces of lithic raw material and then detached flakes parallel to this object's long axis. In other words, they adapted knapping skills to the rock in the form they found it, rather than shaping the rock to fit some pre-existing metric or morphological template.

Geographic and Chronological Variation: These three novel features of EMP stone tool production are not evenly distributed in time and space. LCTs are found mainly in Africa and western and southern Eurasia, usually in contexts significantly younger than the first appearance dates for stone tools in any given region (Shea 2010). LCTs rarely appear at sites in East, Southeast or northern Asia. BHCs are rare but widespread throughout much of Africa and Eurasia in EMP times. Evidence for systemic blade core reduction occurs mainly in African and Southwest Asian contexts dating to less than 0.5 Ma.

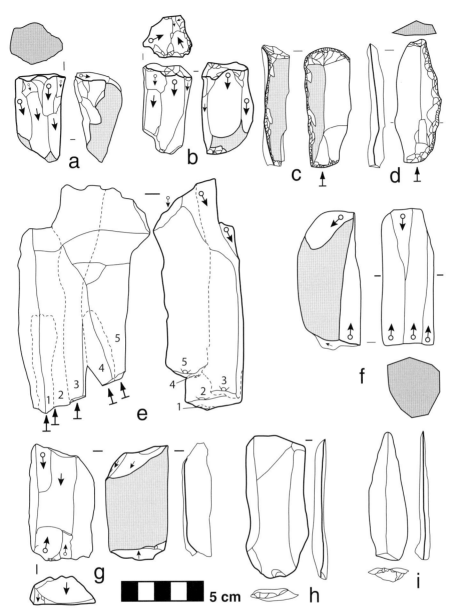

Figure 5.6 Early-Middle Pleistocene blade cores, blades, and retouched blades. a–b, f–g. blade cores, c–d. retouched blades, e. refitting set of five blades, h, i. blades. Sources: Qesem Cave, Israel (a–d), Site GnJh 17, Kapthurin Formation, Lake Baringo, Kenya (e–f), Kathu Pan 1, South Africa (g–i). Redrawn after Cornelissen (1992), Gopher et al. (2005), Wilkins et al. (2012).

TABLE 5.4. *Summary comparison of Modes A–I among Plio-Pleistocene and Early-Middle Pleistocene lithic assemblages*

Modes	Plio-Pleistocene (n = 14)	Early-Middle Pleistocene (n = 40)
A. Anvil percussion	9	31
B. Bipolar core reduction	6	13
C. Pebble core reduction	10	36
D1. Orthogonal retouch	8	32
D2. Macrolithic backing/truncation	4	13
D4. Burination	3	10
D5. Convergent distal retouch	2	17
E1. Long core-tool production	2	22
F1. Preferential BHC reduction	0	10
F2. Recurrent laminar BHC reduction	0	6
F3. Recurrent radial/centripetal BHC reduction	0	5
G1. Platform core reduction	5	19
G2. Blade core reduction	0	5

LOGISTICAL MOBILITY AND STONE TOOLS: PREDICTIONS EVALUATED

Table 5.4 presents a summary comparison of the EMP and Plio-Pleistocene evidence. Because some modes/submodes represented in the EMP sample are absent from the Plio-Pleistocene, statistical comparison can only be carried out in terms of stone percussors, bipolar cores, non-hierarchical pebble cores, retouched pieces, long core-tools, and unifacial hierarchical cores (Modes A–D and G, Submode E1). Thus compared, the EMP and Plio-Pleistocene samples differ from one another at a modest level of statistical significance (p =.04 at 5 degrees of freedom, chi-square = 11.40). The EMP evidence exhibits about an even number of matches and mismatches with the predicted effects of logistical mobility.

Matches

Increases in Raw Material Transportation Distances: Data on the maximum known raw material transport distances from EMP sites in East Africa (Feblot-Augustins 1997) support the predicted increase in transport distances. All but a few EMP sites perched on lithic raw material outcrops (e.g., Olduvai MNK) contain lithic raw materials from 2–13 km distant. The statistical characteristics of assemblages dating 1.2–1.6 Ma (mean = 8 km, sd = 4, n = 12) are essentially identical to those of assemblages dating to 1.6–1.9 Ma, but assemblages dating 0.3–1.2 Ma show significantly more distant raw material movements on average (t = 3.5, p<.01). These data are consistent with the predicted increase in raw material transportation, and they hint that this increase occurred after some delay, rather than as a sudden shift to longer transport distances.

Tool Designs that Enhance Portability and Increase Utility: Long core-tools' characteristic elongation, symmetry, and greater circumference are all consistent with efforts to enhance portability and tool utility among components of transported toolkits. LCTs differ from pebble cores, platform cores, and other Plio-Pleistocene cores in their elongation. Elongation provides more working edge from which flakes can be detached. It also presents a user with longer cutting edges, allowing more cutting work to be done with each arm movement. LCTs' relatively narrow edges allow knappers to detach small, thin flakes systematically and without compromising the edge's ability to cut things. LCTs' symmetry may also enhance their utility in cutting tasks (Machin, Hosfield, and Mithen 2007).

Bifacial hierarchical cores and blade cores are not especially common in EMP assemblages, but the qualities of flakes detached from them also suggest accommodations to portability, prolonged use, and elevated tool discard thresholds. Hierarchical cores allow relatively longer flakes to be detached from cores than would otherwise be possible with non-hierarchical cores. All other things being equal, longer flakes preserve more potentially useable working/cutting edge than shorter flakes.

Resharpening a use-dulled edge by retouch is one of the most common ethnographic strategies for increasing tool utility. Owing to their complex topography, retouched edges may not cut as well as unretouched ones, but they can cut adequately enough for many purposes. These qualities are precisely those one sees among many components of ethnographic humans' portable toolkits. EMP assemblages also preserve more consistent evidence for stone tool curation by retouch.

Patterned variation in which sides of flakes tool makers struck to create retouch suggests that the retouch on EMP retouched pieces was done mainly to resharpen tools rather than to impose a particular shape on them. If all one wants to do is to modify a stone tool into a particular shape, it does not matter from which side of a working edge one detaches flakes. But, retouching a flake's edge by striking its dorsal surface creates a curving edge profile that makes prolonged cutting with that edge difficult. Retouching a flake's edge by striking its ventral surface creates a cutting edge whose straight profile allows it to cut with less effort and to do so after repeated resharpening. EMP retouched pieces were overwhelmingly retouched by striking their ventral, rather than their dorsal, surface.

There is no direct evidence for EMP carrying aids, but indirect evidence hints at their existence. Most LCTs are small enough to be carried while held in the hand, but there are also LCTs >20–30 cm long. These tools are so very large that it is difficult to imagine their being carried around held directly in hand, and yet such LCTs were carried tens of kilometers or more. Such large LCTs, percussors, and other tools could have been made portable simply by wrapping cordage around them a few times to create a handle. No cordage remains have been recovered from EMP contexts, but hafted stone points from Kathu Pan 1 (South Africa) (Wilkins et al. 2012) indirectly imply its existence by at least 0.5 Ma.

Non-residential Sites Provisioned with Stone Cutting Tools: The EMP archaeological record provides abundant evidence for non-residential sites provisioned with stone cutting tools. The most obvious such localities are large vertebrate death sites, such as East Turkana FxJj 3. There, flaked stone tools surround the cut-marked bones of a largely complete hippopotamus (Isaac and Isaac 1997). At Olduvai FLK N Level 6, similar lithic evidence accompanies an elephant skeleton (Leakey 1971). Multiple other such sites grace the African EMP archaeological record (e.g., Delagnes et al. 2006). Others occur in Eurasia as well, as at Boxgrove (UK) and Torralba/Ambrona (Spain) (Howell et al. 1995, Roberts et al. 1997). These sites probably reflect a combination of hominin hunting and scavenging, but inasmuch as large animal carcasses rarely fail to attract large carnivores, one of the few certainties about them is that they were not likely to have been hominin residential sites.

Sites juxtaposing stone tools and partial remains of multiple individuals and sites lacking animal remains invite other interpretations (see Figure 5.7). Potts (1988) proposes that accumulations of stone tools and lithic raw materials at Olduvai Gorge were "strategic caches," supplies of tools and tool materials placed where hominins would have brought whole or partial prey animal carcasses for butchery. By positioning these caches at intervals around the margins of the Olduvai Gorge paleo-lake, Potts argues, hominins could have reduced the distances they needed to carry stone tools. Modern-day automated teller machines (ATMs) perform an analogous function. Positioned in transportation hubs and near retail stores, they minimize the distance their users have to transport cash, and thereby reduce their risk of robbery.

McCall (2014) proposes that large LCT accumulations found in fluvial contexts near the margins of many African and Eurasian lake basins are sites at which hominins abandoned the larger stone tools they had been carrying while foraging at lower elevations. At lower elevations, edible plant foods and large animal death sites are common, but large stones suitable for making LCTs and large flake tools are scarce. Carrying tools into these

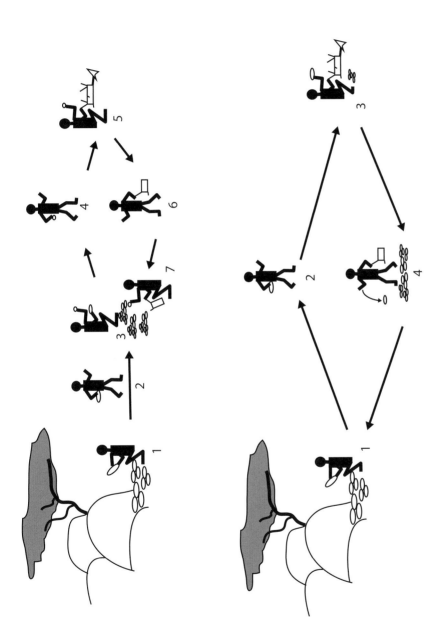

Figure 5-7 Strategic Cache (above) and Routed Foraging Models (below) for Early–Middle Pleistocene site formation. In the Strategic Cache Model (Potts 1988), lithic raw materials were procured near the margins of lake basins (1), transported to strategically advantageous locations (2), where they are deposited and/or knapped (3). Hominins forage in the area around the caches (4), and when they encounter resources (5), they transport them in whole or in part (6) back to caches for further processing with stone tools (7). In the Routed Foraging Model, tools were manufactured near raw material sources at higher elevations (1), transported to foraging areas in lower elevations (2), used to extract resources and repaired as necessary (3), carried up-slope and discarded when transport costs exceeded benefits (4).

areas would have increased hominins' opportunities for exploiting these resources. But, as hominins ascended from lower elevations and approached basin margins, where lithic raw materials are abundant, the benefits of carrying LCTs would have decreased and reached a discard threshold. Assuming these hominins followed regular paths across the landscape ("routed foraging"), McCall contends, over time large numbers of LCTs and other tools would have accumulated near one another. An analogous process can be seen today at trailheads in national parks, where visitors often abandon improvised walking sticks, food packaging, and other food waste they created while hiking.

Mismatches

The evidence does not support the prediction that EMP residential sites would be provisioned with stone tools and other materials, but this mismatch actually reflects weak evidence for EMP residential sites. During the 1960s–1970s, many EMP sites were interpreted as residential sites based on the fact that they combine stone tools with partial remains of large animal carcasses (Isaac 1978, Bunn et al. 1980). Yet, most of these sites lack hearths and evidence of architecture, universal features of pre-industrial ethnographic human residential sites (Binford 1985, McCall 2014). Combustion features interpreted as hearths occur at some EMP sites, such as Gesher Benot Yaacov (Israel) ca. 0.8 Ma (Alperson-Afil 2008), but such features are uncommon in EMP contexts (Berna et al. 2012). When combustion features occur, they are not accompanied by architecture or by evidence for food storage. This evidence allows for several alternative interpretations.

The first, as noted earlier, involves preservation bias. Archaeologists struggle to detect traces of hearths, architecture, and storage facilities left by ethnographic humans at short-term residential sites. Traces of brief fires may not survive in Pleistocene contexts. Support for this "preservation bias" hypothesis can be found in the fact that even though EMP hominins were demonstrably living north of the Alps in Europe, a habitat in which humans regularly succumb to hypothermia today during interglacial conditions, European EMP sites preserve little evidence for fire (Roebroeks and Villa 2011). The EMP may have had residential sites, but we may not be able to identify these sites as residential sites.

A second possibility is that EMP residential sites may be located in parts of the landscape under-sampled by archaeologists. Most excavations of EMP sites focus on areas around the edges of lakes and rivers and caves/rockshelters. Today, large terrestrial carnivores frequent these areas, hunting in the former, denning in the latter. Hominins living in these places for prolonged periods would have been exposing themselves to predation. It is possible that we see so little evidence for EMP residential sites because hominins systematically located those sites on or near defensible hilltops and ridgelines with a good view of the surrounding landscape. Because such elevated landforms suffer high levels of erosion, habitations on them might be poorly preserved and difficult to detect in the archaeological record.

A third possibility is that EMP hominin strategies for logistical mobility with residential sites articulated with one another in ways no longer to be seen among ethnographic humans. Gamble (1999) has explored this hypothesis, arguing that sites such as Bilzingsleben (Germany) and others that seem to preserve spatially structured evidence for hominin habitation may be "performance spaces," places where individuals gathered for social interactions independent of food-sharing and tool-production activities.

Finally, we have to entertain the possibility that the institution of central place foraging did not exist among EMP hominins. Though all humans practice this today, no other primate species does. Systematic central place foraging may have only developed as an institution among post-EMP hominins (McCall 2014).

Summary

A comparative analytical approach and strategic perspective on the EMP lithic evidence shows correlations between the evolution of a running/striding gait, increased evidence for food transport, and shifts in stone tool designs beginning around 1.7 Ma. All these changes are plausibly referable to a strategic shift involving increased logistical mobility. Previously, hominins appear to have been moving themselves and limited quantities of tool materials short distances across the landscape to places at or near where resources requiring stone tool use occurred. After 1.7 Ma they also carried stone tools with them and did so often enough to create selective pressure for stone tool designs that enhanced portability and improved utility. That residential sites with hearths and architecture comparable to those of ethnographic humans are missing from this picture of EMP stone tool use suggests (unsurprisingly) that there are differences in the social context of how EMP hominins and pre-industrial humans made, used, and discarded stone tools.

Contrast with Traditional Approaches

Archaeological studies of EMP lithic assemblages increasingly try to relate technological variability to hominin land-use strategies (e.g., Potts 1988, Isaac et al. 1997, Domínguez-Rodrigo et al. 2007). Many of these studies are quite good, but they are relatively narrow in scope. They focus on artifacts from one site or from a series of sites located near one another in the same sedimentary basin. "Big" questions for traditional archaeological approaches to the EMP lithic record focus on the meaning of large-scale geographic patterns in inter-assemblage variability (e.g., Sharon 2007). Archaeological debate about the "Movius Line" is a good example of such a big question, and the contrast with a strategic view of the EMP lithic evidence could not be starker.

Long core-tools and BHCs are common in Africa and western Eurasia but rare or absent in eastern Asia (Movius 1948; for a recent review, see Lycett and Bae 2010). The Movius Line is not in and of itself controversial. LCTs and BHCs are absent from lithic assemblages for long periods in various parts of Africa and western Asia. Archaeologists working in these places simply assign assemblages with and without LCTs to different named stone tool industries, and then move on to other issues. The Movius Line is controversial because Hallam L. Movius, Jr. (after whom it is named) interpreted the absence of LCTs and BHCs in eastern Asia as evidence for "cultural retardation" compared to the West, where successive changes in lithic technology fit well with "progressive" narratives of evolutionary change. In eastern Asia, as elsewhere, human origins research informs modern-day populations' view of their ancestors and national heritage. Understandably, Movius' explanation did not and does not sit well with Asian paleoanthropologists (Bar-Yosef and Wang 2012, Bar-Yosef 2015). Although Movius wrote more than half a century ago, many paleoanthropology textbooks in use today treat the Movius Line as if it were a real thing, a major bio-cultural division among EMP hominins. Few offer an explanation for it that is any more explicitly testable than Movius' original one.

Viewed in strategic terms, the Movius Line need reflect nothing more than sustained selective pressure against more-than-minimal investment of time and energy in stone tool production (Shea 2010). The most obvious source of such selective pressure is the ecological richness of Southeast Asian environments. More so than anywhere else in Eurasia, these warm, humid habitats resemble the African ones in which hominins first evolved. Southeast Asian habitats may have been so resource-rich that EMP hominins living there did not need to make the same kinds of long-distance logistical movements or to invest as much time and energy making efficiently transportable lithic implements as their counterparts living elsewhere in colder and drier parts of Eurasia. Unlike much of what has been written about the Movius Line, this hypothesis actually has testable predictions. If it is correct, then archaeological and fossil evidence for variation in EMP hominin mobility patterns in Southeast Asia ought to differ systematically from similar evidence from other regions in which LCTs and BHCs are common. The paleoanthropological record is not yet sufficient to test this hypothesis, but, in the future, it almost certainly will be.

Box 3 *Arguments About Handaxes*

Many archaeologists use the term "handaxe" to refer to all LCTs collectively, but handaxes are just one major morphological group of LCTs (Figure 5.8). Eye-catching artifacts, handaxes were among the first stone artifacts presented in the late eighteenth century as evidence for human geological antiquity (White 2001, Gamble and Kruszynski 2009). Handaxes are core-tools, that is, cores that feature a functional cutting edge. Beyond this, nearly everything else about them is disputed and debated.

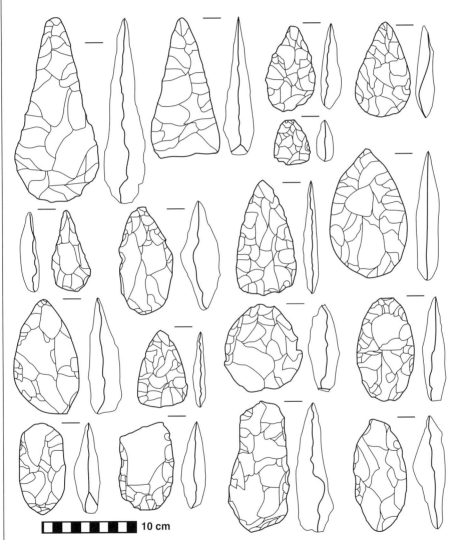

10 cm

Figure 5.8 A variety of handaxes from Pleistocene contexts. Sources: Various European, Asian, and African sites. Redrawn after Bordes (1961).

Box 3 (*Cont.*)

Handaxes are thought to have been used while held in the hand; yet, some Later Pleistocene handaxes are neither thicker nor wider than hafted stone celts from Holocene lithic assemblages. Indeed, some nineteenth-century depictions of prehistoric life showed handaxes hafted like celts, with their long axis aligned perpendicular to a wooden handle.

Kohn and Mithen (1999) view the extensive modification and attention to symmetry in handaxe design as "costly signaling," a strategy by which male hominins advertised their potential fitness as mates and social allies. Costly signaling has strategic value (for both males and females) in any activity where there is potential variation in performance (Zahavi and Zahavi 1997). Invoking it as a factor in handaxe design is not in and of itself controversial (cf. Nowell 2009). This hypothesis remains controversial in part because there is no way to test it directly.

The recurrence of morphologically distinctive handaxe types across wide areas and over prolonged periods suggests hominins made them working from pre-existing mental templates and socially transmitted production techniques (Crompton and Gowlett 1993, Wynn 1995, Gamble, Gowlett, and Dunbar 2014). Recently, however, Corbey and colleagues (2016) contend that LCTs' widespread and long-lasting consistency may have an epigenetic component, much as do bird songs. This hypothesis, too, is controversial because it does not specify a particular genetic cause or a plausibly homologous aspect of human or non-human primate tool use.

Machin and colleagues (2007) view handaxe symmetry as reflecting, in part, a design for efficiency in butchery tasks. Yet, experimenters' views diverge over whether handaxes work better than unmodified flakes for butchery (Jones 1980, Schick and Toth 1993, Shea 2015a).

Some handaxes were made on the spot, used, and discarded without significant transport or curation (Austin 1994). Yet, isolated handaxe tip- and edge-resharpening flakes made of exotic lithic raw materials show that other handaxes were also components of portable toolkits (Geneste 1988, Soressi and Hays 2003). Some typological differences among handaxes are consistent with the effects of curation by resharpening, while others seem to reflect the imposition of particular edge shapes (McPherron 1999). Still others seem to reflect variation in lithic raw materials (Jones 1979, Villa 1983).

Many archaeologists see increasing handaxe "refinement" (width to thickness ratios of their tip) as tracking a gradual improvement in hominin cognitive evolution (Leakey 1954, Bordes 1968, Wynn 2002, Stout 2011, Shipton 2013). But, Later Pleistocene handaxes exhibit wide variation in handaxe refinement, and not all of them are symmetrical (Roe 2003). Nor is it clear why handaxe refinement ought to be the target of selective pressures in hominin cognitive evolution.

In considering various arguments about handaxes, it helps to remember that as an artifact-type, "handaxe" lumps together diverse artifacts from a wide range of

Box 3 (*Cont.*)

contexts. The earliest handaxes occur in African contexts dating to around 1.7 Ma, the most recent date around 45 Ka in western Eurasia. (Stone tools essentially identical to handaxes even occur in ethnographic contexts, but they are usually called by some other name.) Examples range from enormous specimens >30 cm long to diminutive pieces a few centimeters in length. Some handaxes have extensive and invasive flake scars all over their surface; others feature only minor retouch on a portion of their circumference. In many assemblages, handaxes grade into scrapers and other retouched pieces. "Handaxe" almost certainly combines artifacts involved in a wide and heterogeneous range of hominin behavior. Using the term to describe stone tools is more or less equivalent to using the term "car" for all automotive vehicles with more than two tires.

Unsurprisingly, archaeologists also disagree over what to call handaxes and other LCTs. Some use the term "large cutting tools." This work uses "long core-tools" because it is more accurate, or at least minimally interpretive. Most LCTs are not particularly large, but rather roughly the size of a cell phone. Only small numbers of them preserve wear traces or other evidence of having been used to cut things. On the other hand, all LCTs are elongated in at least one axis, thus "long," and most feature flake scars large enough (>2 cm long) to justify calling them cores. Most also feature symmetrical retouched edges, thus justifying calling them "core-tools." Whatever one's views on "large cutting tools" vs. "long core-tools," one can use the same acronym, LCTs.

CHAPTER 6

LANGUAGE AND SYMBOLIC ARTIFACTS

No, you're doing it wrong.
> Everyone, to someone else at some point

In 1866, the Linguistic Society of Paris decided that no light could be shed on the origins of spoken language and it banned debate about the subject. That ban was still in place while archaeologists working in France and adjacent countries developed many of the traditional ways of describing stone tool variation we still use today. With this bit of history in mind, one can appreciate the skepticism that greets archaeologists' claims that we can infer the form of language or inherent cognitive ability from stone tools. This chapter evaluates how language impacted the Middle-Late Pleistocene lithic record. Between 50 and 300 Ka that record shows increasingly complex and patterned variation. This variation suggests the influence of language and symbol use arising from our species' unique neural plasticity.

LANGUAGE VS. NON-HUMAN PRIMATE COMMUNICATION

Primates communicate using facial expressions, body positions, gestures, and vocalizations. Much non-human primate communication varies minimally within species, suggesting it has a strong neurogenetic basis. Nevertheless, many primates use vocalizations as aids to deception, such as giving an alarm call when no threat is present. For the most part, however, non-human primate communication reflects immediate emotional states.

Humans use facial expressions, body positions, gestures, and vocalizations to communicate, but we also use spoken language and symbolic artifacts. Language is a system by which symbols are assigned meanings and then combined generatively to create new meanings. Human language can be vocal (speech), gestural (sign language), and even "exosomatic." That is, it can involve artifacts, such as writing, personal adornment, and artifact design variation invested with symbolic meanings. The potentially infinite range of meanings language allows us to create can include factual or deceptive information, abstract concepts, and conjectural states. These new meanings are achieved through both internalized rules about the structure of how information is presented (syntax) and learned principles that vary situationally to achieve differences in meaning (grammar) (Chomsky 2002). Because language is learned, it has both cumulative and emergent properties (Tomasello 2005). We retain vocabulary and use it in novel combinations. For example, the "mouse" we use to navigate computers' graphical user interface was named after a rodent to which this artifact bears a superficial resemblance. These properties even seem present among chimpanzees, bonobos, and gorillas taught to use sign language (Hillix and Rumbaugh 2004). For example, "Koko," a gorilla, uses the sign for "dirty" (as in a soiled diaper) as a general-purpose epithet. Other than in such captive/experimental settings, however, apes do not routinely recombine gestures to generate messages that are more than the sum of their parts. Like knapping stone tools, linguistic communication is something apes can be taught to do in a rudimentary fashion, but it is not something they do independently of human intervention.

Language Origins

Language probably did not arise, fully formed, like Athena from Zeus' forehead. Fossils, neuroanatomy, and genetics show that the capacity for spoken language evolved (Lieberman 2006, Lieberman and McCarthy 2014). This chapter focuses less on *how* language evolved than on what morphological, neurological, and genetic evidence tell us about *when* it originated and its consequences for the stone tool evidence.

The morphological basis for contrasts between non-human primate vocalization and human speech involves our long supralaryngeal vocal tract and differences in brain size and synaptic malleability. Non-human primate vocalizations can travel over enormous distances even through dense vegetation. (No one who has ever been close to agitated, vocalizing chimpanzees or bonobos soon forgets the sound.) Skeletal landmarks on hominin fossil crania and hyoid bones suggest australopithecines that lived around 3.5 Ma possessed laryngeal air sacs but that *H. heidelbergensis* who lived around 600 Ka did not. In their place, humans have a relatively enlarged oral cavity that performs a similar function in generating loud vocalizations. Human voices carry in dense vegetation, too, but to achieve similar effects to those of non-human primates, we have to use whistles, horns, drums, electronic amplifiers, or other artifacts. Only a small number of hominin fossils allow plausible reconstructions of their supralaryngeal vocal tract. Most of these reconstructions suggest that *H. heidelbergensis* and species descended from it possessed a capacity for speech, albeit speech whose qualities differed from speech by living *H. sapiens* (Lieberman, Crelin, and Klatt 1974, Mithen 2005).

Humans speak well because of our oddly shaped heads. Non-human primates retain an evolutionarily primitive mammalian condition of facial prognathism. Their faces are positioned anterior to (in front of) their brain. Their relatively unflexed upper respiratory tract allows them to ingest food quickly and safely and to breathe while eating/drinking. Living humans' faces are positioned beneath the front of our brain. Such orthognathism creates a flexed upper respiratory tract similar to that of juvenile apes. As apes' faces grow, the tongue moves upwards into the oral cavity. Humans retain this juvenile primate pattern, except that as we mature, our larynx, tongue, and connected tissues descend partway below the lower border of the mandible (Lieberman 2011). This condition allows us to produce "quantal" speech, sequences of sounds that are less susceptible to confusion and resistant to small errors in tongue placement. It also makes it difficult for us to breathe while eating/drinking and easy for us to choke when doing so. This fact alone conveys some measure of spoken language's importance in human evolution. It was, literally, a capacity to die for.

Human brain volume is about 1500–2000 cm^3, between three and four times panin brain volumes. Some of this difference is allometric (size-scaled). Humans are larger than most apes, and our brains are correspondingly bigger, but our brains also have three times more neurons (nerve cells) than chimpanzees (Moore 2014). That part of our brain involved in long-term information storage, the posterior temporal cortex, is relatively larger than that among apes. The prefrontal cortex, the part of the brain engaged in complex tasks, such as the regulation of emotions, is enlarged as well. Neural pathways linking regions of the prefrontal cortex with the basal ganglia, posterior cortical regions, and subcortical structures, such as the hippocampus and cerebellum, are implicated in linguistic and cognitive capabilities. Ongoing genetic studies suggest that synaptic connectivity and malleability in these circuits increased since 500 Ka, with human-specific enhancement possibly occurring after 250 Ka. Genes that are up-regulated in the human brain also appear to have come into place around this time, along with epigenetic events that enhanced the effects of transcription factors such as FOXP2, which is implicated in the formation of neural circuits that confer motor control and cognition – including language and emotional regulation. Though there is probably a minimum brain size necessary to support the neural architecture for spoken language, there is no consensus about what exactly this "linguistic Rubicon" is.

Functional magnetic resonance imaging, positron emission tomography, and similar studies of brain function show spoken language involves a distributed network linking various parts of the neocortex to one another by the basal ganglia. In humans, these networks are more complex and more strongly linked to those parts of the cortex that are involved in vocalization among other mammals. That non-human primates all vocalize, and that those primates phylogenetically closest to us can be taught to communicate with humans using hand gestures and keyboards with symbols on them, suggest that the neurological underpinnings of human spoken language likely reflect subtle shifts in the functions of pre-existing structures rather than the appearance of a novel structure or function (Lieberman 2015).

Recent research on the genetic basis for spoken language focuses on the role of a particular polymorphism, FOXP2 (Fisher and Ridley 2013). In mice, FOXP2 is involved in the development of nerves and muscles of vocalization (among other things). Replacing mouse FOXP2 with human FOXP2 (FOXP2$_{human}$) enhances information transfer in the basal ganglia and associative learning. Non-defective FOXP2$_{human}$ increases the length and synaptic plasticity of the basal ganglia and other structures related to associative motor learning and performance of complex and contingent tasks such as grammar. Living humans with defective copies of FOXP2$_{human}$ have severe speech-related pathologies and other cognitive difficulties. FOXP2 in Neandertal and other archaic Eurasian hominin DNA differs from chimpanzee FOXP2 by two amino acid substitutions. FOXP2$_{human}$ differs from fossil hominin FOXP2 by an additional amino acid substitution (Wood 2006). Enard and colleagues (2002) conclude that a reduction in genetic variation (a "selective sweep") in favor of FOXP2$_{human}$ occurred around 240–270 Ka among populations ancestral to living humans.

Two crucially important factors in the differences between human spoken language and non-human primate vocalization include delayed maturation (prolonged juvenility) and post-reproductive longevity. Compared to non-human primates, humans mature slowly, and we live very long lives (Burkart et al. 2009). Maturing slowly increases the proportion of our lifespan during which we retain "cognitive plasticity," an ability to learn new things, such as a new language, relatively easily. Longevity increases the storehouse of individual experience. Experience communicated among age-peers and across generations constitutes an "institutional memory" with almost immeasurable adaptive power. Ancestral solutions to a breech birth or a once-in-a-century drought can be recalled, evaluated, and deployed as needed.

Language has costs that are not shared by non-human primate modes of communication. Non-human primates easily learn vocalizations and gestures by imitation and trial and error. They do not need to be taught. On the other hand, when an individual non-human primate dies, all they have learned dies with them. To retain value, information expressed in spoken language needs to be transmitted socially and maintained trans-generationally. Great-grandmother's solutions to a breech birth or a drought have little value if her descendants no longer remember them or understand the metaphors by which she expressed them.

Language and Human Tool Use

Language and tool use both involve complex and situationally variable combinations of actions. Both engage many of the same parts of the brain, namely neural circuits involving the basal ganglia supporting motor control and cognitive acts, including working memory, syntax, and learning the referents and accessing

TABLE 6.1. *Differences in non-human primate and human tool use related to language and symbolic artifacts*

Variable	Non-human primates	Humans	Linguistic homology
Solutions to problems	Individually and collectively stereotyped	Polymodal/variable at all scales	Synonyms
Operational chains	Simple, complete	Simple-complex, complete-fragmentary	Simple vs. complex sentences
Combinatory technology	Absent	Present	Syntax and grammar
Tool functional variability	Monofunctional	Monofunctional & multifunctional	Homonyms, metaphors
Spatial and temporal variation	Long-term temporal and spatial stability	Patterned temporal and spatial variation	Dialects, historical changes in vocabulary, grammar
Symbolic artifact design variation	Absent	Ubiquitous	Accents, strategic vocabulary choices

words (Stout 2011). Many of the ways in which human stone tool use differs from non-human primate stone tool use are strikingly similar to the differences between human and non-human primate communication (Table 6.1).

Non-human vocalizations vary within a relatively limited range in any community, but they lack synonyms and metaphors. In contrast, language and human tool use both have uniquely variable qualities. Just as there is more than one way to say, "I love you," there is also more than one way to detach a flake from a core. Non-human primate tool use varies in relatively simple ways and a stereotyped manner. For example, chimpanzees split open nuts by bipolar percussion. For this, they use unmodified stone or wood hammers/anvils, an arrangement with one moving part and a stationary part. These nut-cracking strategies vary minimally within co-resident groups. Humans co-residing with one another open nuts by percussion, but also by more complex devices such as lever-clamps ("nutcrackers"), millstones, and by parching and by boiling.

Non-human primates' tools are homogeneous and generally non-combinatory. They consist either of one object (such as a stone) or an aggregate of objects made of the same material, such as a sponge made of leaves or a sleeping platform made of vegetation. Tools made by humans routinely combine different materials with contrasting mechanical properties. Our technologies have a fundamentally linguistic structure. Tools have to be assembled and used in procedurally structured ways (analogous to syntax), but these procedures retain a nearly infinite capacity for variation (analogous to grammar). Though one might think there are only a limited number of ways to make arrows by combining metal points, fibers, mastic, a wooden shaft, and fletching, arrows vary widely both within major regions and globally (Leakey 1926, Oswalt 1976).

Like their vocalizations and gestures, non-human primates' stone tools are monofunctional. They are made for one combination of motion and contact material. Human tools differ from non-human primate tools in their multifunctionality. Many readers have probably used a screwdriver to open a can of paint, a very different task from that for which screwdrivers were originally designed. In this respect, our tools are like our metaphors. Much to the trademark owners' chagrin, "Swiss Army™ knife" is often invoked as a term for multipurpose tools in general, including stone tools (Bower 2015).

Just as our languages have historical changes in grammar and vocabulary as well as regional accents and dialects, human artifact designs vary in temporally and spatially patterned ways. We know little about long-term variability of non-human primate vocalization, but nut-cracking stones from a 5000-year-old chimpanzee nut-cracking site are essentially identical to chimpanzee nut-cracking stones in use today (Mercader et al. 2002). No language, and few tools used by humans 5000 years ago, are identical to any in use today. Patterned differences in non-human primate vocalization, grooming behaviors, and technological choices correspond with rivers, mountains, and other geographic barriers that separate groups from one another (Whiten and Boesch 2001). Geography shapes the distributions of human languages and technology, too, but neither rivers nor mountain ranges have ever been longstanding barriers to the spread of any language or technology. Nearly all dimensions of ethnographic material culture exhibit such complexly variable "quasi-linguistic" patterning, broad distributions with considerable internal chronological and geographic variability. Quasi-linguistic patterning in material culture emerges not so much from language itself but from the underlying neural plasticity and behavioral variability of which language is the least ambiguous expression.

Other than objects incorporated into agonistic displays, wild-living non-human primates do not use tools or purposefully shaped variation in tool designs to communicate with one another. All human societies do. Much like regional accents and vocabulary choices, symbolic aspects of artifact design can be subtle or overt. College students, for example, signify their changing social affiliations (athlete, fraternity/sorority member, engineer, art major, etc.) through choices of clothing and other personal adornments whose meanings are negotiable and situationally variable. College faculty and staff do this, too, of course; but, as reflecting their relatively stable and formal roles, they use media with overt symbolism, such as uniforms, business attire, and academic regalia. That such symbolic "stylistic" variation so permeates human material culture today suggests that prehistoric humans almost certainly used stone tools as media for symbolically encoded social messages.

Predictions for the Archaeological Lithic Evidence

Differences between human and non-human primate tool use related to language suggest that when spoken language and symbolic artifacts became widespread, the stone tool evidence should exhibit the following qualities:

1. Different solutions to the same kinds of technological problems will co-occur with one another.
2. There will be evidence for stone tools being combined with other materials into multi-component implements, such as hafted tools.
3. Morphologically homogeneous sets of stone tools will exhibit wear and residues from different modes of use.
4. Spatial and temporal variation in artifact production techniques and designs will exhibit "quasi-linguistic" patterning.
5. There will be evidence for symbolic dimensions to lithic artifact variability.

THE MIDDLE-LATE PLEISTOCENE EVIDENCE

Anatomical, neurological, and genetic evidence suggest a wide range of dates as the period of interest for language origins. No one disputes that humans who lived after 40 Ka possessed linguistic capabilities equivalent to living humans. In later Pleistocene "cave art," we see the same abstraction and visual metaphors one finds in contemporary language (Soffer and Conkey 1997). Hypotheses that hominins possessed quantal speech before 300 Ka currently enjoy relatively little support. Therefore, in seeking lithic correlates for language origins, this chapter focuses on the period 50–300 Ka. This Middle-Late Pleistocene (MLP) Period encloses the later Middle Pleistocene (128–728 Ka) and most of the Late Pleistocene (12.5–128 Ka).

The MLP archaeological record preserves first appearance dates for non-lithic evidence of complex behavior that almost certainly required spoken language. These activities include manufacturing glue and hafted stone tools (Wadley 2010, Barham 2013), mortuary rituals (Pettitt 2010), personal adornment (d'Errico et al. 2005, Bouzouggar et al. 2007), complex pyrotechnology – including heat treatment of stone tools (Brown et al. 2009), thermally induced color alteration of mineral pigments (Hovers et al. 2003), as well as astronomically scheduled exploitation of marine resources (Marean et al. 2007). Living non-human primates do not do any of these things spontaneously, nor do they appear capable of learning to do them.

Middle-Late Pleistocene Paleoenvironment

Archaeological sites and hominin fossils dating to 50–300 Ka occur throughout Africa and in all but the northernmost latitudes of Eurasia (Figure 6.1). Middle-Late Pleistocene archaeological contexts are usually dated by radiopotassium, uranium-series, or various trapped-electron methods (thermoluminescence, electron-spin resonance, or optically stimulated luminescence). All but the youngest MLP sites lie beyond radiocarbon dating's effective range.

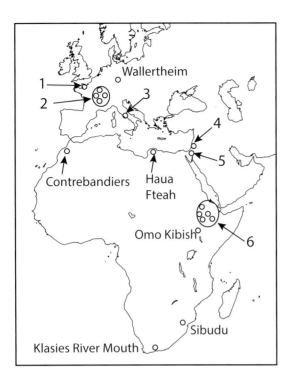

Figure 6.1 Locations of Middle-Late Pleistocene sites. 1. La Cotte de St. Brelade, 2. Abri Vaufrey, Combe Capelle Bas, Champ Grand, and Pech de L'Azé I, 3. Grotta Moscherini, Guattari, Sant' Agostino, and Breuil, 4. Qesem, Tabun, El Wad, Skhul, Qafzeh, Berekhat Ram, Biqat Quneitra, 5. Rosh Ein Mor, Boker Tachtit, Boker, Tor Faraj, 6. Gademotta/Kulkuletti, Herto, Aduma, Porc Epic, Mochena Borago.

The period 50–300 Ka encompasses much of the five most-recent Pleistocene glacial–interglacial cycles, namely marine oxygen-isotope stages (MIS) 3–13. (Even-numbered marine oxygen-isotope stages are colder "glacial" periods while odd-numbered ones are warmer "interglacial" ones.) During the coldest parts of these glacial periods, polar ice sheets extended from the Arctic Ocean onto North America as far south as New York City and onto Europe as far as northern Germany. During interglacial periods, glaciers retreated to the Arctic Circle and sea levels rose to near their current elevation.

The MLP archaeological record is much richer than earlier periods. For recent overviews of the African MLP evidence, see McBrearty and Brooks (2000), Willoughby (2007), Barham and Mitchell (2008: 200–308), Basell (2008), Henshilwood and Lombard (2014), Tryon and Faith (2013), Wadley (2015), and papers in Garcea (2010). Dennell (2009), Petraglia (2007), Shea (2003, 2007), and Norton and Jin (2009) furnish regional syntheses of Asian MLP evidence. For Europe, see Gamble (1999: 174–267), Klein (2009: 435–614), Scott (2011), and Jöris (2014).

Middle-Late Pleistocene Hominins

The best-documented MLP hominin fossil taxa include *Homo heidelbergensis,* *H. neanderthalensis* (Neandertals), and our species, *H. sapiens* (Figure 6.2 and Table 6.2).

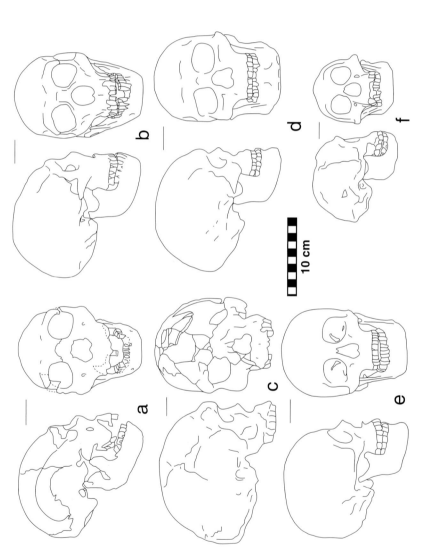

Figure 6.2 Middle–Late Pleistocene hominin crania. a. *Homo heidelbergensis* (Atapuerca SH-5). b. *H. neanderthalensis* (Shanidar 1), c. later Middle Pleistocene *H. sapiens* (Herto), d. Later Pleistocene *H. sapiens* (Zhokoudian Upper Cave 1), e. twentieth-century *H. sapiens* (redrawn after Lieberman [2011: 555]). f. *H. floresiensis* (Liang Bua 1). Scale is approximate.

TABLE 6.2. *Middle-Late Pleistocene hominins*

Hominin taxon	Locations and dates	Sites with representative fossils
Homo heidelbergensis	Eurasia, Africa >200–500 Ka	Atapuerca SH, Spain Steinheim, Germany Petralona, Greece Bodo, Ethiopia Kabwe, Zambia
Homo neanderthalensis	Western Eurasia >45–250 Ka	Feldhöfer, Germany Le Moustier, France La Chapelle Aux Saints, France Shanidar, Iraq Kebara, Israel Amud, Israel
Homo sapiens	Africa, Asia, Australia 200 Ka to present	Omo Kibish, Ethiopia Herto, Ethiopia Skhul, Israel Qafzeh, Israel
Homo sp. indet.	Asia >40 Ka	Denisova Cave, Russia Dali, China Jinniushan, China Maba, China Xuijiayao, China Chaoxian, China
Homo floresiensis	Island Southeast Asia >40–93 Ka	Liang Bua, Indonesia

Homo heidelbergensis fossils occur in Europe, Africa, and western Asia between 200 and 500 Ka (Stringer 2012). *Homo heidelbergensis* had somewhat smaller brains (1100–1400 cm^3) than either Neandertals (1245–1740 cm^3) or *H. sapiens* (>1350 cm^3). Post-cranially, *H. heidelbergensis* had a robust, yet essentially "modern," appearance. *Homo heidelbergensis* is thought to include the last common ancestors of *H. sapiens* and Neandertals.

Neandertal fossils occur throughout Europe and western Asia between 45 and 250 Ka (Trinkaus and Shipman 1993). Neandertal skeletons retain many of the rugged "archaic" features of their *H. heidelbergensis* ancestors, but they differ in having somewhat shorter distal limbs (forearms, lower leg) and thick trunks (i.e., barrel chests and wide hips) (Trinkaus and Howells 1979). These characteristics minimize surface area, conserving heat. Living humans with bodies shaped like this either live in cold habitats or are descended from people who did so until recently (Churchill 2006).

Thus far, *H. sapiens* fossils dating to 50–195 Ka are known from Africa and that part of Southwest Asia immediately contiguous to Africa (Trinkaus 2005). These early human fossils have relatively narrow trunks and long limbs, more or less like those of contemporary Africans, tropical Asians, and Aboriginal

Australians. Long limbs and a narrow trunk increase surface area, allowing people shaped like this to shed heat efficiently and to stay cool in hot climates. Though anthropology textbooks and other works often refer to all *H. sapiens* fossils as "modern" humans, there are significant morphological differences between all Pleistocene *H. sapiens* fossils and post-Pleistocene humans (Howells 1989, Lieberman 2011, Caspari and Wolpoff 2013, Cieri et al. 2014).

Middle-Late Pleistocene Stone Tools

Table 6.3 summarizes the stone tool evidence from a sample of archaeological sites dating to 50–300 Ka. MLP and EMP samples preserve almost identical evidence for major differences in tool production (i.e., the same number of Modes A–I), but the MLP sample exhibits greater typological variation (i.e., more variation among submodes). The most striking contrasts between EMP and MLP evidence are (1) increased size variation, both among flakes struck from bifacial hierarchical cores and among retouched tools, and (2) increasingly patterned variation in elongated bifaces. There are also complex and contingent patterns of variation in hierarchical core technology.

Flakes and Retouched Pieces

MLP assemblages contain both large (>10 cm long) and small (<2–3 cm long) flakes struck from BHCs, unifacial hierarchical cores, and from pebble cores. The largest and the smallest of these flakes are broader and thinner than EMP flakes. All other things being equal, thinner and broader flakes recover more potential cutting edge per unit mass of stone. MLP flakes from hierarchical cores exhibit complexly patterned size and shape variability. In some assemblages, very large and very small flakes are endpoints of a continuum. In others, size variation skews toward larger or smaller values. In some assemblages, this variation is correlated with raw material size and availability, other times not, or less clearly so.

Retouched pieces also vary widely in size and shape (see Figure 6.3). Extensively retouched flakes are usually smaller than superficially retouched ones in the same assemblages. This is consistent with the hypothesis that much variation among scrapers/notches/denticulates and other retouched pieces reflects curation-related retouch (Dibble 1995). However, this relationship does not appear to be simple and linear (Hiscock and Clarkson 2009). Many MLP assemblages contain large and extensively retouched flakes as well as smaller, less-extensively retouched ones. Retouch patterns are sometimes correlated with flake shape. Elongated flakes and blades, for example, often feature sharp retouched edges and burin removals at their distal end and backing retouch on their lateral edges. Some retouch on thinned bifaces and on flakes from hierarchical cores seems to have been applied in order to impose

TABLE 6.3. *Representation of Modes A–I among Middle-Late Pleistocene lithic assemblages*

Samples	A	B	C	D1	D2	D3	D4	D5	D6	D7	E1	E2	E3	E4	F1	F2	F3	G1	G2	G3	Reference
Europe																					
La Cotte de St. Brelade Levels D–H (UK)	+		+	+	+		+	+							+		+				1
La Cotte de St. Brelade Levels 6–C (UK)	+		+	+	+		+	+			+				+		+				1
Abri Vaufrey Levels IX–XI (Fr)	+		+		+		+				+						+	+			2
Abri Vaufrey Levels IV–VIII (Fr)	+			+	+		+	+								+	+	+			2
Combe Capelle Bas (Fr)	+		+	+	+		+	+							+		+				3
Champ Grand Levels B, D (Fr)	+	+	+	+	+		+	+				+				+	+	+	+		4
Pech de L'Azé I Layer 4 (Fr)	+	+	+	+	+						+	+					+	+			5
Wallertheim D (Gr)				+	+		+	+								+	+		+		6
Grotta Moscherini Levels 1–6 (It)		+	+	+	+		+	+								+	+	+	+		7
Grotta Guattari Levels 1–5 (It)			+	+	+		+	+								+	+	+	+		7
Grotta Sant' Agostino Levels 1–4 (It)		+	+	+	+			+							+	+	+	+	+		7
Grotta Breuil Levels 3–4 (It)		+	+	+	+			+								+	+	+	+		7
Southwest Asia																					
Qesem Cave (Is)	+		+	+	+		+				+						+	+	+		8
Tabun Cave Level Ea (Is)			+	+	+		+				+				+	+	+	+			9, 10
Tabun Cave Level D/Unit IX (Is)			+	+	+		+				+				+	+	+	+			10
Berekhat Ram (Is)	+			+	+		+				+				+	+	+	+			11
Rosh Ein Mor (Is)			+	+	+			+								+	+	+	+		9
Tabun Cave Level C (Is)			+	+	+		+	+			+				+	+	+	+			9
Skhul Cave Level B (Is)	+		+	+	+		+	+			+				+	+	+	+			12
Tabun Cave Level B (Is)			+	+	+		+	+			+				+	+	+	+			9
Qafzeh Cave Units I–XXIV (Is)	+		+	+	+		+	+							+	+	+	+			13
Biqat Quneitra (Is)	+		+	+	+		+	+			+				+	+	+	+			14
El Wad Cave Level G (Is)				+	+		+	+							+	+	+		+		9
Boker Tachtit 1–4 (Is)				+	+		+	+							+	+	+		+		15

(continued)

TABLE 6.3. (*continued*)

Samples	A	B	C	D1	D2	D3	D4	D5	D6	D7	E1	E2	E3	E4	F1	F2	F3	G1	G2	G3	Reference
Boker (Is)	+			+	+	+	+	+										+	+		16
Tor Faraj Level C (Jr)		+	+	+	+	+	+	+	+						+	+	+	+	+		17
Northern Africa																					
Haua Fteah (Middle Paleolithic) (Ly)			+	+	+	+	+	+	+	+	+				+		+	+	+		18
Contrebandiers Cave Levels 4–6 (Mr)	+		+	+	+		+	+	+	+		+	+			+	+	+			19
Eastern Africa																					
Gademotta/Kulkuletti (Et)	+	+	+	+	+		+	+		+	+	+	+		+	+	+	+			20
Omo Kibish Members 1–3 (Et)	+	+	+	+	+			+		+	+	+		+		+	+	+	+		21
Herto (Upper) (Et)	+				+		+	+			+	+		+	+	+	+	+	+		22
Aduma Ardu Beds (Et)	+		+	+	+		+			+	+	+				+	+	+	+		23
Porc Epic Cave (Et)	+	+	+	+	+	+	+	+		+		+	+			+	+	+	+		24
Mochena Borago Lower T-Group (Et)	+	+	+	+	+	+	+	+				+			+	+	+	+	+	+	25
Southern Africa																					
Klasies River Mouth (SA)	+	+	+	+	+	+	+	+	+	+		+	+		+	+	+	+	+		26
Sibudu (SA)		+	+	+	+		+	+	+	+		+			+	+	+	+	+		27

KEY: Column Headings: A. Anvil percussion, B. Bipolar core reduction, C. Pebble core reduction, D1. Scraper retouch, D2. Macrolithic backing/truncation, D3. Microlithic backing/truncation, D4. Burination, D5. Convergent distal retouch, D6. Concave proximal retouch, D7. Flake core reduction, E1. Long core-tool production, E2. Thinned biface reduction, E3. Tanged biface production, E4. Celt production, F1. Preferential BHC reduction, F2. Recurrent laminar BHC reduction, F3. Recurrent radial/centripetal BHC reduction, G1. Platform core reduction, G2. Blade core reduction. Symbols: + = present.

Country Codes: Ethiopia (Et), France (Fr), Germany (Gr), Israel (Is), Italy (It), Jordan (Jr), Libya (Ly), Morocco (Mr), South Africa (SA), United Kingdom (UK).

References: 1. Callow and Cornford (1986), 2. Rigaud (1989), 3. Dibble and Lenoir (1995), 4. Slimak (2007), 5. Bordes (1972), 6. Conard and Adler (1997), 7. Kuhn (1995), 8. Barkai, Gopher, and Shimelmitz (2006), 9. Garrod (1937), 10. Shimelmitz and Kuhn (2013), 11. Goren-Inbar (1985), 12. McCown (1937), 13. Hovers (2009b), 14. Goren-Inbar (1990), 15. Marks and Kaufman (1983), 16. Jones, Marks, and Kaufman (1983), 17. Henry (2003), 18. McBurney (1967), 19. Dibble, Hajraoui, and Olszewski (2012), 20. Wendorf and Schild (1974), 21. Shea (2008), 22. Clark et al. (2003), 23. Yellen et al. (2003), 24. Pleurdeau (2005), 25. Brandt et al. (2012), 26. Singer and Wymer (1982), 27. Villa, Delagnes, and Wadley (2005).

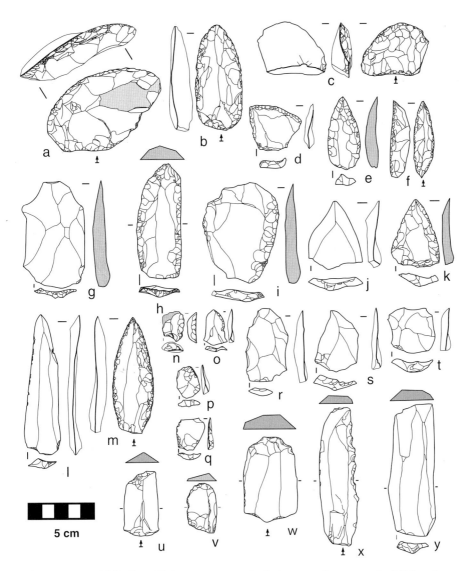

Figure 6.3 Middle-Late Pleistocene retouched pieces and unretouched flakes from hierarchical cores. a–f, h–i, k, m, and u–x. retouched pieces, g, j, l, n–t, and y. unretouched flakes from hierarchical cores. Sources: Abri Vaufrey, France (a, c), La Quina, France (b), Kunji Cave, Iran (d–e), Shanidar Cave, Iraq (f), Rosh Ein Mor, Israel (g), Qafzeh Cave, Israel (h–i), Kebara Cave, Israel (j, k), Tabun Cave, Israel (l, m), Omo Kibish KHS, Ethiopia (n–q) Omo Kibish BNS, Ethiopia (r–t), Klasies River Mouth Cave, South Africa (u–y). Redrawn after Singer and Wymer (1982), Rigaud (1989), Baumler and Speth (1993), Solecki and Solecki (1993), Bar-Yosef (2000), Shea (2008, 2013b), Hovers (2009b), Jelinek (2013), Shimelmitz and Kuhn (2013).

shape and symmetry. European and northern Asian lithic assemblages tend to contain more retouched tools and more extensively retouched tools than African and southern Asian assemblages. This might reflect the fact that in Europe and northern Asia, snow would have covered raw material sources for prolonged periods. Colder conditions in both regions may also have resulted in larger site catchments (the areas around residential sites from which foragers procure resources). One or both of these factors could have increased hominins' incentives for curating stone tools by resharpening them and by elevating tool discard thresholds.

Elongated Bifacial Cores

Long core-tools (LCTs) occur in African, European, and southern Asian MLP lithic assemblages (Figure 6.4). LCTs become less common in assemblages from Africa and southern Asia after 200–300 Ka, but they continue to appear in European and montane western Asian sites to around 40–45 Ka. LCTs from European MLP assemblages are often more elongated, bilaterally symmetrical and morphologically stereotyped than EMP ones (McPherron 2006) (compare the LCTs in Figure 6.4 with those in Figure 5.3).

Thinned bifaces appear for the first time in MLP samples. These artifacts range widely in size, and, to varying degrees, grade into LCTs. European examples are relatively broad, while African ones are narrower and more elongated. Thinned bifaces occur sporadically among Asian MLP assemblages as well.

Tanged bifaces, including tanged points, and celts appear in African MLP assemblages.

Hierarchical Core Technology

Bifacial hierarchical core technology varies widely throughout the MLP (Figure 6.5). Most assemblages of any size preserve evidence for recurrent radial/centripetal BHCs and preferential BHCs. Recurrent laminar BHCs are more variable in their occurrence. BHCs become less common in archaeological lithic assemblages throughout much of Africa and western Eurasia after 50 Ka.

MLP blade core reduction differs from its EMP counterpart by occurring at numerous sites across the same region for tens of thousands of years. Northern Europe, the East Mediterranean Levant, and southern Africa all preserve evidence for such episodic "irruptions" of blade production. As with the EMP evidence, however, MLP blade core reduction often occurs recursively. It appears among assemblages near to one another in space and time, then it either disappears or becomes uncommon for prolonged periods (i.e., tens of thousands of years).

MLP assemblages feature cores-on-flakes and hierarchical cores less than 2–3 cm long, or "mini-cores." The most common mini-cores and cores-on-flakes have a flake scar less than 3 cm long initiated on a truncated edge that

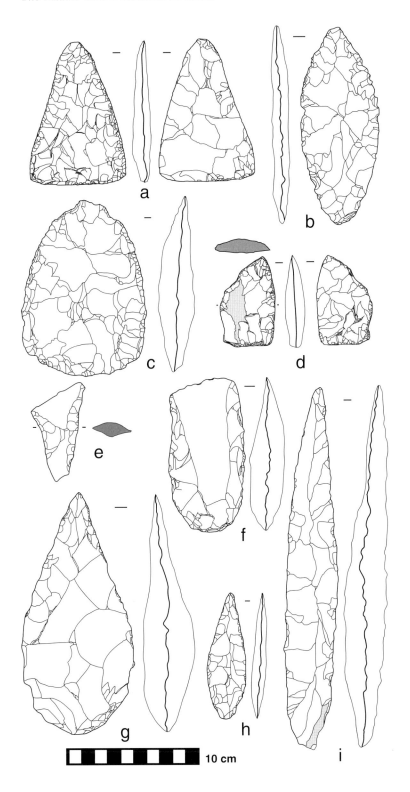

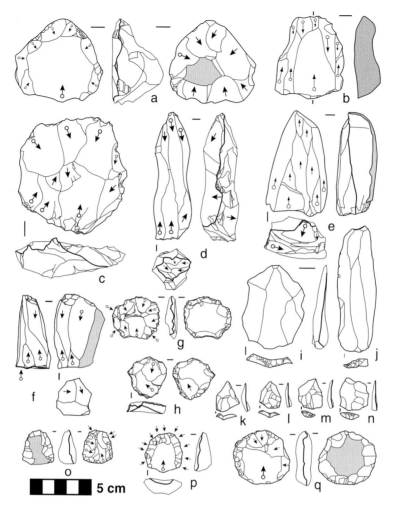

Figure 6.5 Middle-Late Pleistocene hierarchical cores and flakes. a–e. bifacial hierarchical cores, f. blade core, g, h. cores-on-flakes, i–n. flakes struck from bifacial hierarchical cores, o–q. bifacial and hierarchical mini-cores. Sources: Ar Rasfa, Jordan (a, i), Har Oded, Israel (b), Reincourt-Les-Baupame, France (c, d, j), Hayonim Cave, Israel (e, f), Biqat Quneitra, Israel (g, h), Omo Kibish, Ethiopia (k–p), Pech de L'Azé, France (q). Redrawn after Boutié and Rosen (1989), Goren-Inbar (1990), Tuffreau (1992), Dibble and McPherron (2006), Shea (2008), Ahmad and Shea (2009), Meignen (2011).

Caption for Figure 6.4 *(cont.)*

Figure 6.4 Elongated bifaces from Middle-Late Pleistocene contexts in Eurasia (a–d) and Africa (e–i). a, c–g, and i. long core-tools, b, h. thinned bifaces. Sources: Abilly (Indre-et-Loire), France (a), Mauern, Germany (b), Little Cressingham (Norfolk) UK (c), Koenigsaue, Germany (d), Mbalambala (Dundo), Angola (e, h), Kalambo Falls, Zambia (f–g), Kalina Point (Gombe), Democratic Republic of the Congo (i). Redrawn after Bohmers (1951), Bordes (1961: plate 56), Clark (1984: 263, 287, 2001: 330, 382), Debénath and Dibble (1994: 158), Mellars (1996: 129).

propagates either under a prominent dorsal scar ridge or under the flake's bulb of percussion. MLP hierarchical mini-cores include BHCs, platform cores, and blade cores. Cores-on-flakes and mini-cores both indicate lowered thresholds for core procurement and higher thresholds for artifact discard. That is, MLP hominins used smaller objects as cores and retained cores longer than EMP hominins did.

LANGUAGE AND SYMBOLIC ARTIFACTS: PREDICTIONS EVALUATED
Overview of the Predictions

Table 6.4 compares occurrences of Modes A–I among MLP assemblages to the EMP evidence discussed in Chapter 5. Evaluating these data statistically is neither simple nor straightforward. Burins, tanged pieces, cores-on-flakes, thinned bifaces, tanged bifaces, and celts are not represented in the EMP sample. Yet, even with data on these distinctive MLP artifacts omitted from comparison, EMP and MLP lithic samples still differ

TABLE 6.4. *Occurrences of Modes A–I among Early-Middle Pleistocene and Middle-Late Pleistocene lithic assemblages*

Modes	Early-Middle Pleistocene (n = 40)	Middle-Late Pleistocene (n = 35)
A. Anvil percussion	31	20
B. Bipolar core reduction	13	11
C. Pebble core reduction	36	27
D1. Orthogonal retouch	32	34
D2. Macrolithic backing/truncation	13	34
D3. Microlithic backing/truncation	10	3
D4. Burination	0	29
D5. Convergent distal retouch	17	29
D6. Concave proximal retouch	0	2
D7. Flake core reduction	0	8
E1. Long core-tool production	22	18
E2. Thinned biface production	0	9
E3. Tanged biface production	0	4
E4. Celt production	0	1
F1. Preferential BHC reduction	10	23
F2. Recurrent laminar BHC reduction	4	23
F3. Recurrent radial/centripetal BHC reduction	5	30
G1. Platform core reduction	19	25
G2. Blade core reduction	5	19

at a high level of statistical significance (chi-square = 83.98 at 12 degrees of freedom, p <.01).

Multiple Simultaneous Solutions to Problems: Collectively, MLP stone tool assemblages preserve evidence for Modes A–G, but few assemblages feature all of them. Most assemblages feature multiple submodes of any given mode. Preferential and radial/centripetal submodes of BHC preparation occur in most assemblages. Similarly, blade core reduction rarely appears without accompanying evidence of platform core reduction. We cannot know how many different ways individual hominins made stone tools, but repetitive patterns of stratigraphic associations show multiple ways of making technologically similar artifacts "at the same time," at least in the geological sense. This evidence contrasts with the EMP record, in which there is less typological/submode variation within broader technological modes.

Combinatory Technology: Wear patterns, mastic residues, and retouch patterns show that some MLP artifacts were used while attached to handles (Barham 2013) (Figures 6.6 and 6.7). Tanged pieces/points, microliths, and celts, and other MLP stone tools were retouched in ways that could facilitate hafting. Abrupt changes in retouch patterns on celts and retouched pieces show where an edge was covered by a handle. Microwear/residues also suggest that unretouched flakes were sometimes hafted. A variety of hafting arrangements have been proposed for MLP stone tools, but few actual handles have been found in contexts older than 40 Ka.

Functional Variability: Microwear and residue analyses indicate wide functional variation among broadly defined MLP stone tool categories (Béyries 1988, Anderson-Gerfaud 1990). In nearly every sample involving multiple examples of the same named artifact-type, wear patterns and residues suggest variable combinations of tool motions and contact materials. Woodworking and hide-scraping are among the most commonly inferred functions for MLP tools, but these tasks have high edge-attrition rates and distinctive wear traces. Retouched points and triangular flakes of roughly the same size were used both as hand-held and hafted cutting tools as well as for weapon tips (Shea 1997). The range of individual artifact functional variation remains poorly understood, though some mismatches between wear patterns and residues suggest multiple and sequential uses in different tasks (Hardy et al. 2001).

"Quasi-linguistic" Variation among Artifacts: Evidence for quasi-linguistic patterning in MLP lithic variation can be seen in distinctive artifact designs with regional distributions seemingly uninterrupted by geographic barriers. For example, one sees patterned differences in LCT morphology between northwestern Europe ("*bout coupé*" handaxes), western Europe

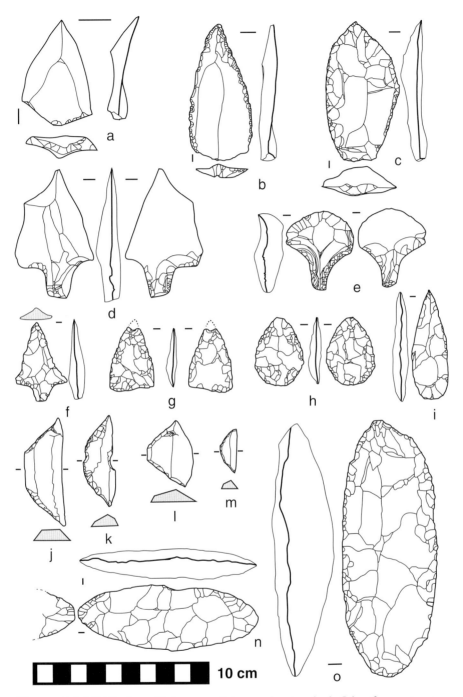

Figure 6.6 Middle-Late Pleistocene flakes and retouched flake fragments. a–c. retouched and unretouched triangular flakes, d–f. tanged points/pieces, g–i. thinned bifaces, j–m. microliths, n, o. celts. Sources: Kebara Cave, Israel (a), Rosh Ein Mor, Israel (b), Biache-St. Vaast, France (c), Oued Djebbana, Algeria (d–e), Mbalambala, Angola (f, n), Lukenya Hill Unit A, Kenya (g–h), Porc Epic Cave, Ethiopia (i), Klasies River Mouth Cave, South Africa (j–m), o. Kalina Point (Gombe), Democratic Republic of the Congo (o). Redrawn after Tixier (1960), Merrick (1975), Crew (1976), Singer and Wymer (1982), Clark (1984), Béyries (1988), Bar-Yosef (2000), Pleurdeau (2005).

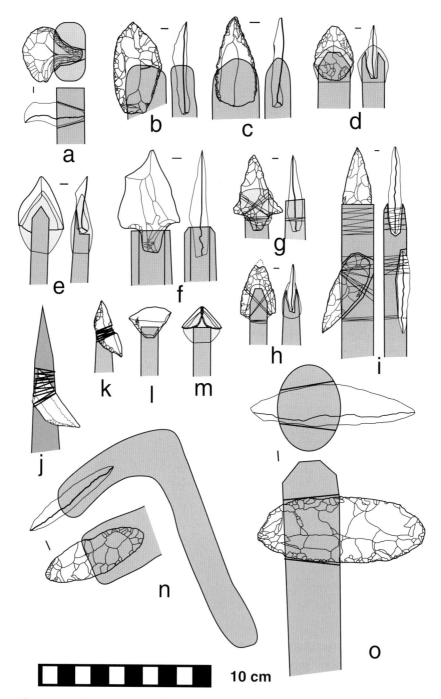

Figure 6.7 Conjectural hafting arrangements for Middle-Late Pleistocene artifacts.
a. tanged piece hafted as a scraper, b. scraper hafted as knife, c–h. retouched points and
pointed flakes hafted as knives/weapon tips, i. retouched points hafted as weapon tip
and barb, j–m. backed pieces hafted as barbs and weapon tips, n, o. celts hafted as adzes
and axes. For sources, see Figure 6.6.

(triangular handaxes), and Central Europe (*kielmessern* = "keeled knives") (Figure 6.4 a–d). Later Pleistocene sites in equatorial Africa also feature distinctive elongated LCTs, or "lanceolates" (Figure 6.4 h–i). Additional examples of such distinctive artifacts with regional distributions include tanged points from North Africa (Figure 6.6 d–f), backed pieces from southern Africa (Figure 6.6 j–m), and heavily retouched oval "Quina" scrapers from Western Europe, and sharply angled "Yabrudian" scrapers from the Southwest Asia (Figure 6.3 a–c). Unlike the EMP evidence, in which similar artifacts occur throughout that 1,400,000-year-long period, some distinctive MLP artifacts only appear for tens of thousands of years or less. This patterning does not approach the rapid turnover and local-scale variation seen in recent human material culture, but it is similar enough to millennial or sub-millennial scale lithic artifact variation after 50 Ka to suggest that it springs from a common evolutionary cause.

Why MLP lithic variation differs from the post-MLP evidence invites several possible explanations. The MLP lithic record everywhere is less well documented than its post-MLP successor. Having fewer assemblages may make it more difficult for archaeologists to detect patterns in MLP stone tool design variation. Thus far archaeologists have sought patterned variation in the MLP evidence mainly in artifact morphology, among which there is much convergence due to the reductive nature of lithic technology. Cultural differences among MLP tool makers may be more clearly expressed in operational chains than in artifact morphology. Research on MLP operational chains is increasingly a routine part of archaeological lithic analysis. Future research may yet reveal additional short-term and regionally patterned MLP lithic variation.

The relationship between population densities and innovation may also explain the "coarse grain" of MLP typological variation. Several recent cross-cultural studies suggest that larger populations living in higher densities have higher rates of technological innovation and offer more opportunities for innovations to diffuse than smaller populations living at lower densities (Shennan 2001, Powell, Shennan, and Thomas 2009, but see Collard, Buchanan, and O'Brien 2013). MLP humans are thought to have been fewer in number and to have lived at lower population densities than most post-MLP humans (Mellars and French 2011, Churchill 2014). If these two hypotheses are correct, then demographic factors rather than differences in linguistic or other cognitive capabilities may account for some of the contrasts between MLP and post-MLP stone tool variation.

Symbolic Artifact Design Variation: Some MLP artifacts were made from visually striking raw materials. Others were extensively retouched in ways similar to overtly symbolic artifacts from recent contexts. The difficulty with identifying such artifacts as having symbolic meaning is that one cannot reject alternative functional/mechanical explanations for them. For example, MLP hominins may have selected and preferentially curated visually striking raw materials because they are easier to spot on the ground than other materials. Modern-day survival gear and emergency equipment is also brightly colored for the same reason. That the MLP lithic evidence yields an equivocal finding about symbol use more plausibly reflects the inadequacy of traditional archaeological methods for analyzing stone tools than it does MLP hominins' ignoring stone tools' potential as symbolic media.

Cause vs. Consequence

Several archaeologists have noted similarities between the procedural complexities of composing a sentence and attaching stone tools to handles (Ambrose 2001, Barham 2010, Wadley 2010). Some have argued that cognitive abilities originally developed in the service of making hafted tools were later co-opted into the realm of social interactions. This is not impossible, but the only evidence we have of pre-MLP hafted tools are points from Kathu Pan 1 (South Africa) currently dated to 500 Ka (Wilkins et al. 2012). If hafting gave rise to language, one would expect evidence for hafting to be more widespread than it currently appears to be in the archaeological record.

Based on evidence at hand, it seems far more likely that linguistic abilities developed in social interactions reflecting genetic and epigenetic events that enhanced the capabilities of neural circuits and structures that regulate cognition – including language, motor control, and emotional regulation (Lieberman and McCarthy 2014). As these capacities evolved, they may have influenced technological adaptations through feedback processes too complex to be reduced to a simple cause/consequence dichotomy. Put simply, language, symbol, and technology co-evolved with one another. Even today, their relationships vary. Some aspects of human material culture exhibit more linguistically structured variability than others. "Folk art," clothing, and hand-made crafts vary more and in overtly symbolic ways than nails, screws, and other industrial products. In seeking evidence for language in the lithic archaeological record, we should expect similar variability in its effects. Potentially symbolic artifacts may not have been symbolic. As psychologist Sigmund Freud put it, "Sometimes a cigar is just a cigar."

Contrasts with Traditional Approaches

Historically, archaeological approaches to investigating the origins of language focus on evidence from the Upper Paleolithic Period in Europe, ca. 13–50 Ka

(Mellars 1991, Renfrew 1996, Mithen 1998, Lewis-Williams 2002). Many archaeologists consider this the period during which the archaeological record first exhibits evidence for "behavioral modernity" (see Box 4). In theory, focusing on Upper Paleolithic Europe allows archaeologists to compare evidence associated with *H. sapiens*, who were assumed to be fully capable of spoken language, to older evidence associated with Neandertals, who are thought to have been language impaired (Nowell 2010). Also in theory, focusing on Europe allows archaeologists to treat habitat as a "control" variable. But archaeological, fossil, and genetic evidence increasingly suggests Neandertals had some linguistic capacities. Moreover, much of the time Neandertals spent in Europe (>45–250 Ka) coincided with relatively warm (though cooling) interglacial conditions, ones that contrast starkly with the cold and hyper-variable climates 13–50 Ka.

Systematic prismatic blade production is one of the most conspicuous derived features of the European Upper Paleolithic stone tool evidence. Blades vary in number and in how they were made, but few Upper Paleolithic assemblages lack evidence for prismatic blade production. And yet, blades occur in European assemblages associated with *H. neanderthalensis*, and in African assemblages associated with early *H. sapiens* and *H. heidelbergensis*. Many lithic assemblages associated with *H. sapiens* both before and after 40 Ka lack evidence for prismatic blade production. These observations allow two mutually exclusive interpretations. Either blade production has no value for diagnosing "behavioral modernity" (Bar-Yosef and Kuhn 1999), or species other than *Homo sapiens* were "behaviorally modern" (d'Errico 2003). The latter would be an impressively postmodern inversion of the term's original meaning.

Viewed as products of technological strategies, these widespread occurrences of blade production pose no theoretical conundrums whatsoever. Blades are simply elongated flakes knapped from unifacial hierarchical cores in response to various selective pressures. These pressures might have included tabular raw materials, the need to boost cutting edge recovery rates, tool standardization, portability, accommodations to hafting, or other circumstances. That blade production varies so widely, not only prior to the Upper Paleolithic Period but also during it and afterwards as well, supports the hypothesis that prismatic blade production was merely a tool making strategy and not an expression of behavioral modernity. Sometimes, a prismatic blade is just a stone tool.

Box 4 *Behavioral Modernity and Behavioral Variability*

Archaeologists use the term "behavioral modernity" to distinguish the evidence associated with recent (<40 Ka) *Homo sapiens* from that associated with earlier humans and other hominins. Because prehistoric archaeology began in Europe, "behavioral modernity" and "modern human behavior" are defined in terms of evidence dating to less than 36–45 Ka, the period encompassing first appearance dates for *H. sapiens* across much of that continent (Nowell 2010). Putatively modern behaviors include producing symbolic artifacts (art, personal adornment, mortuary rituals), carving bone and antler tools, knapping prismatic blades, specialized big-game hunting, and occupying harsh (i.e., cold and/or arid) environments. Humans living outside of Europe are identified as behaviorally modern when their archaeological record exhibits some of these features (d'Errico 2007). All living humans are behaviorally modern (Figure 6.8), even though few living humans carve bone tools, hunt big game, or knap prismatic blades.

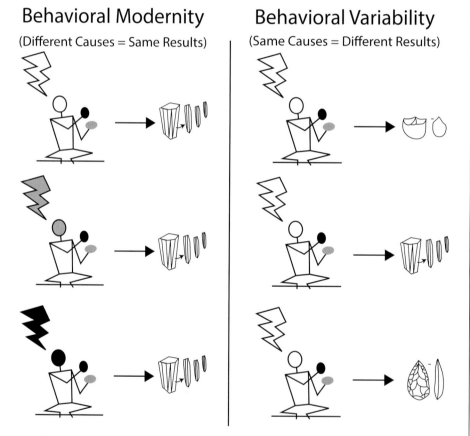

Figure 6.8 Behavioral modernity vs. behavioral variability. In behavioral modernity, different stimuli result in the same "modern" behaviors, such as blade production. In behavioral variability, the same stimulus can result in different behaviors and different stone tools.

Box 4 (*Cont.*)

Paleoanthropologists are increasingly skeptical about behavioral modernity's value in human origins research (McBrearty and Brooks 2000, Henshilwood and Marean 2003, Shea 2011a). Critics point to the obvious risk of projecting unique properties of the European evidence to other regions, to the lack of theoretical justification for viewing particular behaviors as "modern," and to the concept's underlying teleology (i.e., the idea that all humans evolved convergently).

The author and other colleagues have argued that human origins research is better served by investigating behavioral variability (Potts 1998, Shea 2011a, b, Eren, Diez-Martin, and Domínguez-Rodrigo 2013, Tryon and Faith 2013). Behavioral variability is when the same stimulus evokes different responses in the same subject. Compared to other primates, humans exhibit wide behavioral variability. Everything we do, collectively and individually, we do in more than one distinct way. We maintain both simple and complex solutions to nearly every problem we face. We excel at repurposing solutions to one set of problems to fit novel circumstances. Unlike modernity, which is a metaphor, variability is a statistically measurable property of archaeological evidence, especially the stone tool evidence. Hypotheses about behavioral variability can be empirically falsified in ways that arguments about behavioral modernity cannot.

CHAPTER 7

DISPERSAL AND DIASPORA

> Dispersal is the destiny of a successful species.
> Robert Foley and Roger Lewin (2003), *Principles of Human Evolution*

Humans today live in a global diaspora, a wide geographic distribution that makes us immune to all but biosphere-level extinction threats. Our nearest primate relatives, the great apes, live in small regions within tropical Africa and Asia. All of them are endangered species. This chapter considers how human dispersal and diaspora affected stone tool variation. Between 9–50 Ka, humans extended their geographic range to Sahul (Pleistocene Australia and New Guinea), northern Eurasia (Europe and northern Asia), and the Americas. Lithic evidence for these dispersals contrasts in a predictable, patterned way, not only with the stone tools made by humans prior to 50 Ka, but also among the regions to which humans dispersed after 50 Ka.

DIASPORA VS. ENDEMISM

Our closest non-human primate relatives are endemic species. They live in a narrow range of habitats, on a single continent or island archipelago, and in communities of closely related individuals. Deep genetic divisions among populations of chimpanzees, bonobos, gorillas, and orangutans who live near one another show they have been living this way for a very long time (Disotell 2013). Human diaspora differs from non-human primate endemism at all scales, from the landscape over which individuals range in their lifetime, to the distances between social intimates, to our species' overall geographic range. As a result, the human genome is relatively homogeneous across even vast distances (Oppenheimer 2004, Wells 2009).

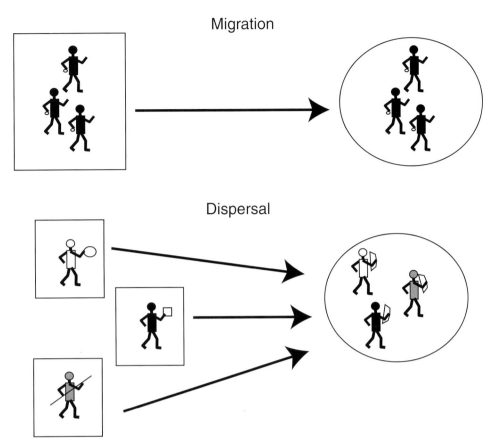

Figure 7.1 Population movements: Migration (above) and dispersal (below).

Human Population Movements

Most historic human population movements fall somewhere along a continuum between migration and dispersal (Figure 7.1). In migrations, an entire community relocates. Its pre-existing biological and social relationships remain largely intact. In dispersals, individuals or small groups of individuals relocate and form new social relationships. When the Mormons moved from Nauvoo, Illinois to Utah Territory in 1840s, they were migrating. When the author's ancestors moved to North America from Europe, renounced their former nationalities, and became Americans, they were dispersing.

Descriptions of migration by "food producers," people who subsist on domesticated plants and animals, dominate ethnographic and historical accounts of population movements. How such movements differ from those by hunter-gatherers and/or by Pleistocene humans remains unclear. On the one hand, hunter-gatherers did not have to linger in one place tending planted fields or herds, so they may have been able to disperse faster than ethnographic food-producing populations. On the other hand, high infant mortality and long inter-birth intervals could have kept hunter-gatherer population growth rates so low that there were few incentives for large-scale population movements. On the third hand, climate was more variable during Pleistocene times than it has been recently (Burroughs 2005). Such environmental variability could have both raised and lowered the thresholds for human dispersal at the same time in different contexts.

Several qualities make humans uniquely successful dispersers (Foley 2002, Gamble 2013). Jungles and forests do not limit human geographic ranges as they do those of arboreal primates. Because humans are generalist feeders, our geographic range varies independently of specific plant or small animal food sources (Ungar 2007). Being effective long-distance walkers/runners, we can travel further in daily foraging trips than non-human primates. Because we can swim, rivers and other water bodies that block non-human primate population movements are not obstacles. Spoken language and symbolic artifacts allow us to construct spatially extensive and adjustable social networks that disperse the risk of subsistence failure and ensure access to mates in new habitats (Alexander 1987).

All primates use tools to gain access to food sources that are concealed from view or enclosed in inedible tissues (van Schaik and Pradhan 2003). Humans also use tools to change the nature of those resources (e.g., plant and animal domestication) and to make new resources available. Few readers who own dogs think of them as tools, but they are, in essence, biotechnology. Fire, technically a physical reaction, is also a tool. Many foods we humans eat either require cooking or are significantly improved by cooking (Wrangham 2009). Predictably, humans use fire as an aid to subsistence and to making other tools in every habitat we occupy. Stone tools enjoy an even wider range of applications than fire. Not only are stone tools found everywhere human fossils are, they are also found in Pleistocene contexts lacking evidence for fire.

Human Dispersal and Stone Tool Use

The longest fossil records for *H. sapiens* and for our nearest primate relatives occur within a few degrees latitude of the Equator. Humans who live in these areas today do so at high population densities and by subsisting mainly on plant foods (Kelly 1995). Dispersing away from this region challenged ancestral humans in at least five major ways:

1. It required insulation from atmospheric cold.
2. It forced them to find alternative energy sources to tropical plant foods.
3. Means had to be developed for crossing water, including life-threateningly cold water.
4. Social networks had to be maintained over large areas and among groups living at low population densities.
5. Novel habitats required dispersing humans to "fine-tune" their technological strategies.

TABLE 7.1. *Differences in non-human primate and human tool use related to dispersal*

Variable	Non-human primates	Humans
Insulation from atmospheric cold	Nests	Fire, clothing, artificial shelter
Crossing water	None	Watercraft
Alternative energy sources to plant foods	Technologically assisted predation on insects, small animal prey	Technologically assisted predation on large and small animals
Maintaining extensive social networks	Physiological only (grooming)	Social networks reinforced with symbolic artifacts

The ways in which ethnographic humans use tools to meet these needs and how they contrast with non-human primate tool use provide insights into what qualities we should expect to see in the lithic evidence for human dispersal (Table 7.1).

Insulation from Atmospheric Cold: Dying from overheating (hyperthermia) is hard work. One has to expose oneself to heat sources, not drink water, and/or exert oneself to the point where physiological cooling mechanisms fail (Lundin 2003). Hypothermia kills all by itself. Immersion in cold water can cause death in minutes. Tropical primates rarely have to cope with potentially lethal cold temperatures. When resting in cold habitats, both humans and non-human primates huddle together, minimizing convection, and they interpose vegetation or other materials between themselves and the ground, reducing heat loss by conduction. Other than this, non-human primates' strategies for dealing with atmospheric cold are limited to seeking shelter from wind and to their physiological defenses (fur, body fat). Humans, in contrast, cope with atmospheric cold by kindling fires, by constructing artificial shelters, and by making clothing from leather and other materials. Of these three activities, leather production is most likely to leave a detectable signature in the lithic record. Before metal tools became available, ethnographic humans used stone scraping tools to turn animal hides into leather. Hide-scraping entails high rates of edge attrition, and it leaves readily detectable wear traces (Brink 1978). Ethnographic humans who used stone tools to scrape hides often did so with hafted elongated flakes and blades whose working edges were positioned perpendicular to their long axis. This arrangement allowed repeated resharpening without the need to unseat the tool from its handle. Traditional archaeological typologies identify retouched pieces hafted and used this way as "endscrapers."

Alternative Energy Sources to Tropical Plant Foods: Tropical habitats can be no less seasonal than temperate ones, but important differences remain. Non-human primates living in tropical and warm-temperate habitats cope with seasonal variation in plant foods by switching among food sources and by augmenting their diets with insects. Some panins hunt, but protein and fat from larger mammals does not comprise a major part of their diet. Only chimpanzees devise tools to assist them in hunting, and (as of this writing) such so-called "spear" use has only been observed at one field site (Pruetz and Bertolani 2007). Humans who live in temperate and colder latitudes cope with seasonal short-falls in plant foods by fishing and by systematically preying on large terrestrial herbivores (Marean 2007, Speth 2010). Tropical hunter-gatherers do this too, but fish and hunted game are more crucial components of hunter-gatherer diets in colder habitats (Kelly 1995). Nearly all ethnographic humans who hunt large terrestrial mammals in cold habitats do so by using complex projectile weapons, such as the spearthrower and dart, the bow and arrow, or, more recently, firearms. These versatile weapons allow their users to attack either large or small prey (Churchill 1993). When hunting large prey, pre-industrial humans often tip their complex projectile weapons' missile components with stone and bone/antler armatures and barbs (Ellis 1997). Stone weapon armatures create large wounds that increase blood loss and quicken the death of the prey animal, thereby reducing pursuit and handling costs (Wilkins et al. 2014). Ethnographic humans rarely use stone tools as tips of spears or arrows used for fishing, but they do employ them as tips for weapons used against marine mammals (Ellis 1997), crucial sources of fat for ethnographic humans living in cold habitats (Speth 2010).

Crossing Water: Deep water is a formidable obstacle to most non-human primate movements. Immersed in deep water, most apes sink and drown. Yet, those same African rivers demarcating major genetic divisions among African apes teem with swimming human children and throng with wooden dugout canoes. Boats allow nearly friction-free movements of people and goods as well as access to aquatic resources. All humans who live near water have watercraft of one kind or another (McGrail 2001). That most pre-industrial watercraft were made of wood, reeds, leather, and other perishable materials complicates the search for stone tool evidence of watercraft. But, before metal tools became available, humans shaped dugout canoes using hafted stone celts with ortho-gonal cutting edges ("adzes" and "chisels"). Many of these celts had abraded cutting edges that made straighter and more precise cuts than retouched edges. Dispersal aided by watercraft should have been accompanied by evidence for the production and use of celts, possibly abraded-edge celts.

Maintaining Extensive Social Networks: Primates obtain mates and allies through social networks. Non-human primates' social networks are organized along lines of biological relationships, and are reinforced by mutual grooming. Because grooming requires close physical proximity, these net-works are small in scale and spatially and temporally unstable. The death of one or more individuals can cause them to unravel. Such small, unstable social networks constrain non-human primates' potential for dispersal. Individual chimpanzees seeking out mates or food in new territory bear all the risk of dispersal themselves. As primatologist Irven DeVore put it, "a lone ape is a dead ape" (personal communication).

Compared to non-human primates, humans are "hyperprosocial." We actively seek out opportunities to form cooperative coalitions with one another (Bowles 2006, Marean 2015). Coalitions aid human dispersal by spreading risks to individuals among coalition members. Unlike their chimpanzee counterpart, a human seeking new mates or food sources in unfamiliar territory knows that if they fail or if they get in trouble, they can count on support from other coalition members, either the ones they left behind or people they encounter. Coalition members benefit from sharing such risks most obviously by gaining information about new potential sources of mates and resources. They also benefit by having outlets for a growing population and destinations for dissidents, outlets that reduce potential intra-coalitionary conflicts.

Human social networks work so well because they incorporate "fictive kinship," an evolved capacity to treat distantly related or unrelated individuals altruistically, as if they were close kin. One of the most memorable literary examples of such fictive kinship is from Shakespeare's play *Henry V*, in which the young king rallies his outnumbered and exhausted soldiers before the Battle of Agincourt (October 25, 1415) as follows:

> We few, we happy few, we band of brothers;
> For he today that sheds his blood with me
> Shall be my brother; be he ne'er so vile,
> This day shall gentle his condition;
> And gentlemen in England now a-bed
> Shall think themselves accurs'd they were not here,
> And hold their manhoods cheap whiles any speaks
> That fought with us upon Saint Crispin's day.

As primates, humans are visual creatures. Visual and other clues to shared social identities increase altruism, or "compliance," in social relations among living humans (Burger et al. 2004). All humans use symbolic artifacts to broadcast information about social identities and coalition memberships (Wobst 1977, Hodder 1982). Using artifacts for this purpose, rather than grooming, overcomes potential linguistic and cultural barriers to compliance. It allows human social networks to scale upwards infinitely and to remain stable over wide regions for prolonged periods. The media for these symbolic messages include nearly all dimensions of material culture, including artifact design variation. If extensive social networks incorporating fictive kinship were involved in human dispersal, then their lithic "fallout" ought to include long-lasting and widespread patterns of lithic artifact design variation (Sackett 1982, Carr 1995). Among ethnographic hunter-gatherers, hunting weapons are often on hand among encounters with strangers (Wiessner 1983). Therefore, such artifact style variation should be more clearly apparent among lithic armatures for hunting weapons than among other artifacts, such as those used for tool making and maintenance tasks at habitation sites.

Technological Fine-tuning: Non-human primate technologies vary, but because of their users' endemism, they vary in response to a relatively narrow range of ecogeographic variables. As a result, the probability of "technological convergence," of multiple panin individuals and groups independently inventing similar solutions to similar problems, is intrinsically high. Chimpanzee nut-cracking stones and other tools from Guinea, Ivory Coast, and Liberia resemble one another in ways that the clothing, baskets, religious icons, and other tools humans make in those countries do not. Humans "fine-tune" their technologies to local conditions. Because we are so geographically dispersed, such fine-tuning diverges over time and space and varies in ecogeographically patterned ways.

Humans use technology to obtain food and to insulate themselves from their environment. As one might expect, the subsistence technology ethnographic humans use in tropical habitats like those in which our species evolved is less complex than the subsistence aids humans use in colder and drier habitats to which we are physiologically less well adapted (Oswalt 1973, 1976, Collard, Kemery, and Banks 2005). The complex spears ethnohistoric Inuit used to hunt seal differ starkly from the relatively simple spears Aboriginal Australians used to hunt kangaroo. Both differ from the spears historic Comanche used to hunt bison from horseback on the plains of North America. These observations allow two predictions. First, we ought to see differences between the tools made by the first humans in any given region and those made by their successors. Second, lithic evidence for such technological fine-tuning ought to be more pronounced in colder and drier habitats than in warmer and more humid ones.

Predictions for the Archaeological Lithic Evidence

Contrasts between human and non-human primate tool use referable to our species' dispersal suggest that the stone tool record for population movements by Pleistocene humans should exhibit the following characteristics:

1. Specialized hide-working tools and weapon armatures will occur in colder habitats.
2. Heavy-duty carpentry tools/celts will be made and discarded near major rivers and coastlines.
3. Patterned artifact style variation will appear, especially among lithic weapon armatures.

4. There will be differences in artifact design variation between sources and destinations of dispersing human populations.

5. There will be ecogeographically patterned differences between earlier and later stone tools in particular regions.

This chapter tests these predictions using evidence for Late Pleistocene dispersals by *Homo sapiens* originating from Eurasia. It does so not because these predictions are irrelevant to earlier hominin dispersals or to human dispersals within Africa or between Africa and southern Asia. Rather, it does so because the archaeological record for these later dispersals is less fraught with ambiguities than earlier dispersals. The geochronology, fossil record, and archaeological evidence for dispersals by *H. ergaster, H. erectus*, and *H. heidelbergensis*, as well as for *H. sapiens* in Africa and southern Asia before 45 Ka are simply too coarse-grained to use for this purpose, at least for now.

THE LATE PLEISTOCENE AND EARLY HOLOCENE EVIDENCE

The oldest-dated *Homo sapiens* fossils come from sites near Kibish in the Lower Omo Valley (Ethiopia) dating to around 200 Ka (Figure 7.2). The first non-African human fossil evidence appears along the East Mediterranean Coast between 90 and 130 Ka. By 45 Ka, human fossils occur in Southeast and East Asia. First appearances of *H. sapiens* across southern Asia are not correlated with major changes in the stone tool evidence. After 50 Ka, *H. sapiens* fossils appear for the first time in Sahul (Pleistocene Australia and New Guinea), northern Eurasia, and the Americas. In Sahul and the Americas, our species' arrivals mark the beginning of an archaeological record. Much of northern Eurasia was already populated by other hominins, including Neandertals and "Denisovans." Nevertheless, our species' arrival there also coincides with major changes in lithic and other evidence. This chapter focuses on the period 9–50 Ka, one that encompasses most of the last Late Pleistocene glaciation and the first several millennia of the Holocene Epoch (<12.5 Ka).

Late Pleistocene Paleoenvironment

Popular images of life in Late Pleistocene times depict icy wind-swept landscapes, but there were actually rapid, wide-ranging, and short-term climate shifts throughout this period (for an overview, see Burroughs 2005). Average global temperatures are estimated to have been as much as -5–$6°$ C, significantly below those at present (0.6° C). Late Pleistocene sea levels were as much as 150 m below their current elevation. Such lowered sea levels made possible crossings between continents and islands that today require long and risky ocean voyages. The Earliest Holocene (10–12.5 Ka) began with a period of rapid warming followed by an abrupt return to glacial conditions called the

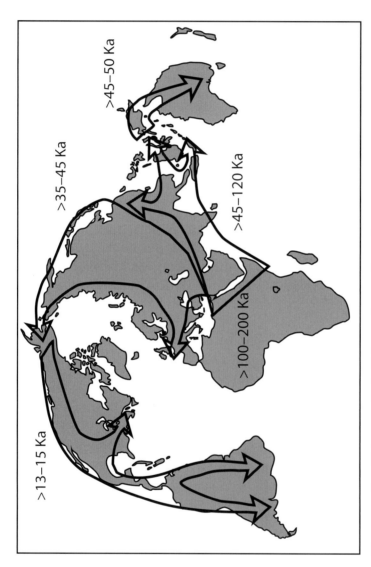

Figure 7.2 Late Pleistocene/Early Holocene human dispersals.

Younger Dryas Event (11.5–12.8 Ka) (Straus and Goebel 2011). After this millennium-long "cold snap," warmer conditions returned, persisting and increasing to the present day.

Dispersal to Sahul

Stone tools appear in Sahul and adjacent islands around 45–50 Ka (O'Connell and Allen 2004) (see Figure 7.3). This dispersal originated on the easternmost "Sundaland," the peninsula comprising much of Southeast Asia and the Indo-Malaysian archipelago. Cranial variation among early "Sahulians" hints at continuities with older *Homo* populations from Indonesia (Caspari and Wolpoff 2013). Early Holocene sea-level rise flooded Sundaland's and Sahul's Late Pleistocene coastlines. This flooding limits archaeologists' knowledge

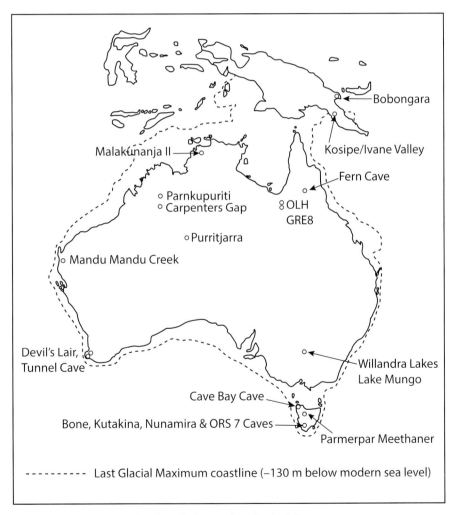

Figure 7.3 Locations of early Sahulian archaeological sites.

about coastal adaptations in this part of the world prior to the peopling of Sahul. For recent reviews of the evidence from Sahul, see Lourandos (1997), Mulvaney and Kamminga (1999), Hiscock (2008), Habgood and Franklin (2008), O'Connell and Allen (2012), and White (2014). Holdaway and Stern (2004) provide an excellent overview of the Sahulian stone tool evidence.

Stone Tools Made By Early Sahulians: Figure 7.4 shows examples of stone tools associated with human dispersal to Sahul, and Table 7.2 summarizes the stone tool evidence for selected Sahulian assemblages dating to 11–62 Ka.

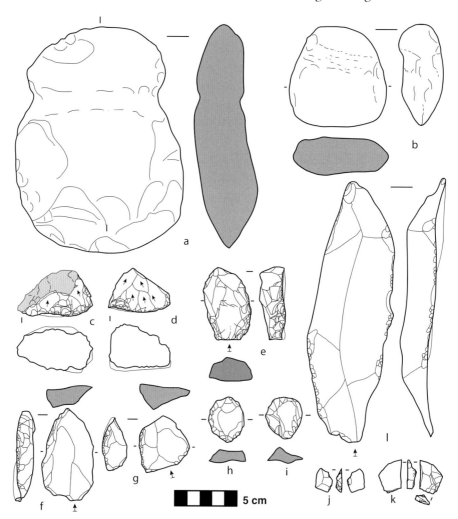

Figure 7.4 Stone tools associated with human dispersal to Sahul: a. celt ("waisted axe"), b. abraded-edge celt, c–d. platform cores, e–g. retouched flakes/scrapers, h–i. "thumbnail" scrapers, j–k. backed pieces, l. blade. Sources: Huon Peninsula, New Guinea (a), Malangangerr Cave, Australia (b), Lake Mungo/Willandra Lakes, Australia (c–g), Bone Cave, Tasmania (h–k), Lancefield Swamp, Australia (l). Redrawn after Bowdler et al. (1970), Mulvaney (1975), Gillespie et al. (1978), Groube et al. (1986), White and Lampert (1987), McNiven (2000).

Samples by region	A	B	C	D1	D2	D3	D4	D5	D7	E1	E2	E4	G1	H	Reference
New Guinea															
Bobongara, Huon			+									+			1
Kosipe/Ivane Valley			+	+								+			2
Australia															
Carpenters Gap 3 Levels 8–14				+	+			+							3
Fern Cave		+	+									+			4
GRE8 Units 5–9			+	+	+	+					+				5
Malakunanja II	+	+	+	+				+		+	+			+	6
Mandu Mandu Creek Unit 2			+	+						+			+		7
OLH midden			+	+											5
Parnkupiriti Site 3			+	+											8
Puritjarra Units 2b–2d			+	+	+								+		9
Willandra Lakes/Lake Mungo	+			+	+		+		+						10
Devil's Lair Cave		+	+	+					+						13
Tasmania															
Bone Cave Upper Levels		+	+	+									+		11
Bone Cave Lower Levels		+	+	+									+		11
Cave Bay Cave	+	+	+	+									+		12

(continued)

TABLE 7.2. (*continued*)

Samples by region	A	B	C	D1	D2	D3	D4	D5	D7	E1	E2	E4	G1	H	Reference
Tunnel Cave Levels 7B–10a		+		+											13
Kutakina Cave			+	+											14
Nunamira Cave			+	+											15
ORS 7			+												15
Parmerpar Meethaner (Units 3–4)			+	+		+									15

KEY: Column Headings: A. Anvil percussion, B. Bipolar percussion, C. Pebble core reduction, D1. Scraper retouch, D2. Macrolithic backing/truncation, D3. Microlithic backing/truncation, D4. Burination, D5. Convergent distal retouch, D7. Flake core reduction, E1. Long core-tool production, E2. Thinned biface production, E4. Celt production, G1. Platform core reduction, H. Abraded-edge tool production. Symbols: + = present.

References: 1. Groube et al. (1986), 2. Summerhayes et al. (2010), 3. O'Connor et al. (2014), 4. Lamb (1996), 5. Slack et al. (2004), 6. Clarkson et al. (2015), 7. Morse (1988), 8. Veth et al. (2009), 9. Smith (2006), 10. Hiscock and Allen (2000), 11. Holdaway (2004), 12. Bowdler and Jones (1984), 13. Dortch (2004), 14. Kiernan, Jones, and Ranson (1983), 15. Cosgrove (1995).

Low numbers of observations for the Sahulian samples in terms of submodes complicates comparing these data with the MLP sample discussed in Chapter 6. If one compares these data in terms of Modes A–G, omitting Modes H–I (edge-abraded tools and groundstone tools) because they are absent from the MLP sample, and omitting bifacial hierarchical cores because they are absent from the Sahulian sample, the remaining samples still differ from one another significantly (chi-square = 10.9, p = 0.05 at 5 degrees of freedom).

Flaked stone artifacts from Late Pleistocene and Early Holocene Sahul include pebble cores, platform cores, and flakes with various retouched, backed, and truncated edges. Except for relatively small "thumbnail" scrapers from sites in Tasmania, retouched tools and cores show little standardization. Prismatic blades and backed pieces are rare (McNiven 2000), and microlith production is largely a Holocene phenomenon (Hiscock 2002). Flaked and abraded-edge celts occur in assemblages from New Guinea and northern Australia (Habgood and Franklin 2008).

Dispersal to Northern Eurasia

First appearances of *H. sapiens* fossils in northern Eurasia coincide with novel ways of making stone tools and of making/using other artifacts. These fossils and this evidence first appear in eastern Europe/western Asia around 40–50 Ka (see Figure 7.5). Eurasian humans' cranial features and limb proportions resemble tropical humans, specifically Africans (Trinkaus 2005, Grine et al. 2007). The archaeological record suggests humans moved into northern Eurasia across a broad front stretching from western Asia to the Pacific Coast.

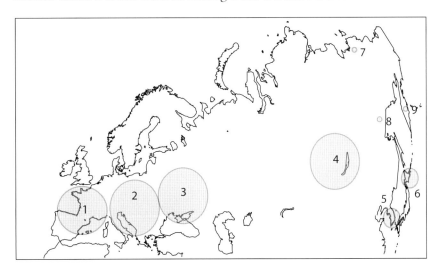

Figure 7.5 Geographic groups of northern Eurasian Late Pleistocene archaeological sites included in this study. 1. Western Europe, 2. Central Europe, 3. Eastern Europe, 4. Siberia/Mongolia, 5. South Korea, 6. Northern Japan, 7. Eastern Siberia. 8. Dyuktai Cave, and 9. Ushki 1. Specific sites assigned to these assemblage groups are listed in Table 7.3. (For Dyuktai Cave and Ushki, see Table 7.4.)

These movements' timing seems to have followed a west–east gradient of lower temperatures and increased aridity: with Europe colonized first; central and eastern Siberia colonized somewhat later. For recent overviews of this evidence, see Gamble (1999: 268–417), Straus (1995), Hoffecker (2004, 2011), Hoffecker and Elis (2003), Zilhao (2014), Klein (2009: 615–725), Graf (2013), and papers in Brantingham and Kuhn (2004), Conard (2006), Goebel et al. (2011), and Kaifu and colleagues (2015).

Stone Tools Made By Early Northern Eurasians: Figure 7.6 shows stone tools associated with *H. sapiens* in northern Eurasia after 40–45 Ka. Table 7.3 summarizes the lithic evidence for selected assemblages from this region. Several factors complicate comparing these data to the MLP sample. Microblade cores (Submode G3) and abraded-edge tools and groundstone tools (Modes H and I) are absent from the MLP sample. Compared in terms of Modes A–C and Submodes D1–D7, E1–E4, F1–F3, and G1–G2, the northern Eurasian lithic sample differs from the MLP sample at a high level of statistical significance (p<.01, chi-square = 109.5 at 18 degrees of freedom).

Northern Eurasian Late Pleistocene lithic assemblages differ from older ones in southern Asia and from their local northern Asian precursors older than 50 Ka mainly in showing more consistent evidence for blade and microblade core reduction, tanged pieces/points, and thinned bifaces. Individual artifacts often combine design features, such as scraper edges, backing/truncation, burin removals, and bifacial retouch in ways rarely seen among older stone tools. Microblade cores, bladelets, microliths, and small tanged pieces and tanged points are common. Non-lithic artifacts, carved stone, and microwear traces show that stone tools were used to shape bone, antler, ivory, and other durable materials to a greater extent than during earlier times. LCTs and bifacial hierarchical cores are less common, even absent, in these assemblages, but this may reflect differences in the typologies archaeologists working in this region use to describe stone tools older and younger than 40–50 Ka. (A bit of circular reasoning may be at work as well, for in many regions, LCTs found on the surface are routinely attributed to pre-50 Ka contexts even though their actual ages are unknown.)

Dispersal to the Americas

Humans moved into the Americas from eastern Eurasia via "Beringia," that part of easternmost Siberia and Alaska conjoined by lower Late Pleistocene sea levels. This movement began with a recolonization of easternmost Siberia and Beringia after around 18 Ka. At this point in time, continental glaciers blocked land routes from eastern Beringia to the rest of North America. Though there are tantalizing hints of a possible earlier human presence south of the glaciers, the overwhelming majority of genetic, fossil, and archaeological evidence point to dispersal commencing after 13–15 Ka (Waguespack 2007) (Figure 7.7). These data suggest an earlier watercraft-assisted dispersal along the Pacific Coast (Dixon 2013)

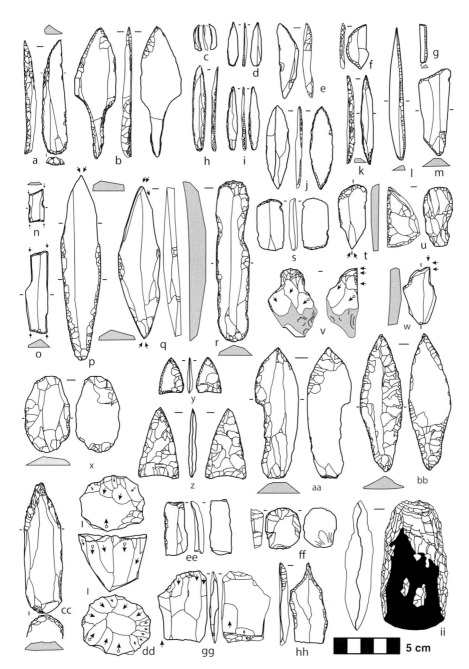

Figure 7.6 Stone tools associated with human dispersal to northern Eurasia: a, c, e–m, and ee. backed and/or truncated blades, b, d, j, cc, hh. points, n–q. burins, r–s, ff. scrapers, t. scraper/burin, u–w. core-scrapers, x. scraper/truncated piece, y–z. thinned bifaces with proximal concavities, aa–bb. tanged points, dd. blade core, gg. bipolar core/core-on-flake, ii. abraded-edge celt. Regional provenience: Western Europe (a–w), Eastern Europe (x–bb), northern Asia (cc–hh), Japan (ii). Site provenience: Les Cottés (a), Font Robert (b), Roc de Combe (c), Vignaud (d), Klissoura Cave 1 (e–f), Font Yves (h), Abri Dufour (i), Puyjarrige (j), La Gravette (k), Le Flageolet (s), Avdievo (x), Kostienki Ic (y–aa), Kostienki 8 (bb), Kara-Bom (cc, gg), Mal'ta (dd–ff, hh), Hintabayashi B (ii), unspecified French sites in de Sonneville-Bordes (1963) (g, l–r, t–w). Redrawn after de Sonneville-Bordes (1963), Demars and Laurent (1992), Derev'anko (1998), and Takashi (2012).

TABLE 7.3. *Representation of Modes A–I among Late Pleistocene and Early Holocene stone tool assemblages from northern Eurasia sorted by geographic groups (1–7)*

Site and level by geographic group	D1	D2	D3	D4	D5	D6	D7	E1	E2	E3	E4	F1	F2	F3	G1	G2	G3	H	I	Reference
Western Europe																				
Abri Castanet, Levels A–C	+	+		+	+											+	+			1
Abri Facteur Tursac, Levels 10–21	+	+	+	+	+											+	+			2
Abri Pataud, Levels 6–14	+	+	+	+	+		+								+	+	+			3
Cueva Morín, Levels 3–9	+	+	+	+	+	+	+								+	+	+			4
La Ferrassie, Levels F–H	+	+	+	+	+	+									+	+	+			5
La Ferrassie, Levels J–L	+	+	+	+	+	+									+	+	+			5
La Riera Cave, Levels 1–20	+	+	+	+	+	+			+	+					+	+	+			6
Laugerie Haute, Levels H–G	+	+	+	+	+	+										+	+			1
Le Solutré	+	+	+	+	+	+			+	+						+	+			7
Central Europe																				
Dolní Věstonice II	+	+	+	+	+	+	+									+	+		?	8
Geißenklösterle	+	+	+	+	+	+	+									+	+			9
Klithi	+	+	+	+	+										+	+	+			10
Pavlov I	+	+	+	+	+	+									+	+	+			11

(continued)

(continued)

Site																	No.
Stranska Skala IIIC	+	+	+		+	+	+	+	+	+	+	+		+	+	+	12
Vedrovice V, AH 2	+	+	+	+	+	+	+	+	+	+	+	+		+	+	+	13
Vogelherd IV, V	+	+	+	+	+	+	+	+	+	+	+	+	+	+	+	+	14
Willendorf II, AH	+	+	+	+	+	+	+	+	+	+	+	+	+	+	+	+	14
2–4																	
Eastern Europe																	
Eliseevichi	+	+	+	+	+	+		+	+	+			+			+	15
Kabazai II Units I–III	+	+	r	+		+	+	+	+	+	+	r	+	+	+	+	16
Kabazai V	+	+	+	r		+	+		+	+			+	+	+		16
Kostienki 14 Level Ivb	+	+	+	+	+	+	+	+	+	+	+	+	+	+	+	+	17
Mezerich	+	+	+	+	+	+	+	+	+	+	+	+		+	+	+	15
Mezin	+	+	+	+	+	+	+	+	+	+	+	+	+	+	+	+	15
Pushkari I	+	+	+	+	+	+	+	+	+	+	+	+	+	+	+	+	15
Radomyshl'	+	+	+	+	+	+	+	+	+	+	+	+	+	+	+	+	15
Starosele Levels 1–4	+	r	r	?.	+	+	+	+	+	+	+	+	+	+		+	16
Timonovka I	+	+	+	+	+	+	+	+	+	+			+		+	+	15
Timonovka II	+	+	+	+	+	+	+	+	+	+			+		+	+	15
Mongolia/Siberia																	
Afontova Gora II	+	r	+	+	+	+	+	r					+	+	+	+	17
Kara–Bom Levels 1–6	+	+	+	+	+	+	+	+					+	+	+	+	17
Kokorevo II	+	+	+	+	+	+	+				+	+	+	+	+	+	17
Mal'ta	+	+	+	+	+	+	+	+	+	+	+	+	+	+	+	+	17
Tolbaga Levels 1–4	+	+	+	+	+	+	+	+					+	+	+	+	17
Tolbor 15 Levels 4–5	+	+		+									+	+	+	+	18

TABLE 7.3. (*continued*)

Site and level by geographic group	D1	D2	D3	D4	D5	D6	D7	E1	E2	E3	E4	F1	F2	F3	G1	G2	G3	H	I	Reference
Tolbor 15 Levels 6–7	+	+			+		+						+		+	+				18
Tolbor 4 Levels 4–6	+	+		+	+		+						+	+	+	+	+			18
South Korea																				
Hwaedae-ri	+	+		+	+	+										+				19
Sinbock	+	+	+	+	+	+		+	+							+	+	+	+	19
Soyangggeae	+	+	+	+	+	+					+				+	+	+	+		19
Wolseong-don	+	+	+	+	+	+					+				+	+	+			19
Yongho-dong Levels 1 & 3	+	+		+	+	+									+	+				19
North Japan																				
Kashiwadai 1	+	+	+	+											+	+	+			20
Kawanishi-C	+	+	+	+	+										+	+				20
Marukoyama	+	+	+	+											+	+				20
Minamimachi 2	+	+	+																	20
Shimaki LC 1	+	+		+			+									+	+			20
Eastern Siberia																				
Yana RHS	+	+		+	+										+	+				21

KEY: Column Headings: D1. Scraper retouch, D2. Macrolithic backing/truncation, D3. Microlithic backing/truncation, D4. Burination, D5. Convergent distal retouch, D6. Concave proximal retouch, D7. Flake core reduction, E1. Long core-tool production, E2. Thinned biface production, E3. Tanged biface production, E4. Celt production, F1. Preferential bifacial hierarchical core (BHC) reduction, F2. Recurrent laminar BHC reduction, F3. Recurrent radial/centripetal BHC reduction, G1. Platform core reduction, G2. Blade core reduction, G3. Microblade core reduction, H. Abraded-edge tool production, I. Groundstone tool production. Symbols: + = present, r = reported as "rare," ? = report ambiguous.

References: 1. de Sonneville-Bordes (1960), 2. Delporte (1968a), 3. Chiotti (2005), 4. González Echegaray and Freeman (1978), 5. Delporte (1968b), 6. Straus and Clark (1987), 7. Combier and Montet-White (2002), 8. Klíma (1995), 9. Hahn (1988), 10. Bailey (1998), 11. Svoboda (1994), 12. Svoboda and Bar-Yosef (2003), 13. Valoch (1993), 14. Hahn (1977), 15. Soffer (1985: 125), 16. Marks and Chabai (1998), 17. Anikovich et al. (2007), 18. Gladyshev et al. (2012), 19. Lee (2013), 20. Izuho (2013), 21. Pitulko et al. (2013).

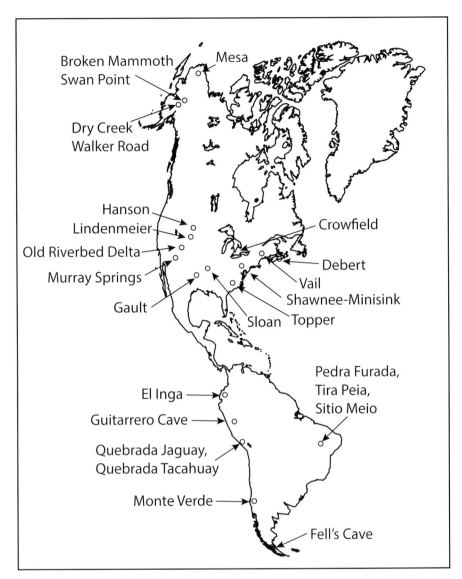

Figure 7.7 Locations of Beringian and American Later Pleistocene and Early Holocene archaeological sites.

augmented by later land movements as the continental glaciers receded (Meltzer 2009). For syntheses of the early American evidence, see Haynes (2002), Hoffecker and Elias (2007), Waguespack (2007), Goebel et al. (2008), Meltzer (2009), Moore (2014: 63–91), and papers in West (1996), Goebel and Buvit (2011), Graf, Ketron, and Waters (2013). For detailed discussion of early American stone tools, see Collins (1999) and Callahan (1979).

Stone Tools Made By Early Americans: Figure 7.8 shows stone tools associated with Late Pleistocene and Early Holocene dispersal to the Americas. Table 7.4 summarizes the stone tool evidence for a sample of early American

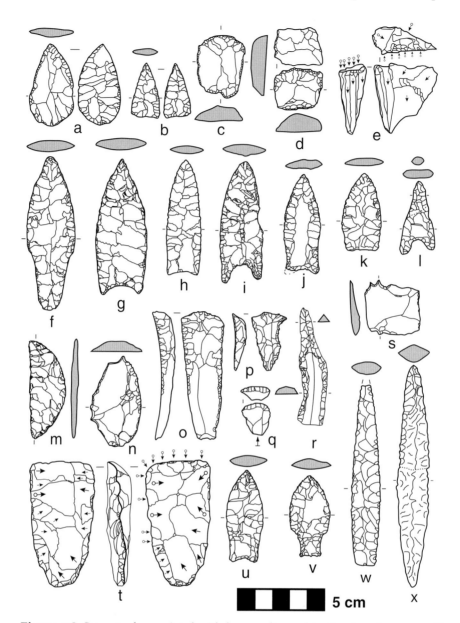

Figure 7.8 Stone tools associated with human dispersal to the Americas 10–15 Ka. a–b, f–m, and u–x. thinned and/or tanged bifaces, c, n–q. scrapers, notches, and denticulates, d. bipolar core, e. wedge-shaped core, r and s. points/perforator, t. celt. Regional provenience: a–e. Eastern Beringia, f–t. North America, u–x. Central and South America. Site provenience: Walker Road, Alaska (a), Dry Creek, Alaska (b–d), Onion Portage, Alaska (e), Kayenta, Arizona (f), Site 26 Hu 17, Humbolt County, Nevada (g), Domebo, Oklahoma (h), Debert, Nova Scotia (i), GBL 281/270 Jefferson County, Indiana (j), Meadowcroft Rockshelter, Pennsylvania (k), Vail, Maine (l), Point Sal, Santa Barbara, California (m), Unspecified "Clovis" site in Stanford and Bradley (2012) (n–s), Gault, Texas (t), Turrialba, Costa Rica (u), Fell's Cave, Chile (v), Monte Verde II, Chile (w), Taima Taima, Venezuela (x). Redrawn after Gramley (1982), Lynch (1983), Justice (1987, 2002b, a), Dixon (1999), Lavallée (2000), Stanford and Bradley (2012), Dillehay (2013), Collins (2014).

TABLE 7.4. *Representation of Modes A–I among Late Pleistocene and Early Holocene stone tool assemblages from Beringia and the Americas*

Site/Sample	A	B	C	D1	D2	D3	D4	D5	D6	D7	E1	E2	E3	E4	G1	G2	G3	H	I	Reference
Beringia																				
Broken Mammoth, Alaska			+	+	+		+	+				+	+			+	+			1
Dry Creek Levels I–II, Alaska			+	+	+							+	+		+	+	+			2
Dyuktai Cave, Siberia			+	+	+		+				+	+	+		+	+				1
Mesa, Alaska	+		+	+	+		+	+				+	+							3
Swan Point, Alaska	+		+	+	+		+	+					+		+	+	+			4
Ushki 1, Levels V–VII, Siberia				+	+		+					+	+		+	+	+			1
Walker Road, Alaska				+				+					+		+	+				2
North America																				
Crowfield, Ontario				+							+	+	+							5
Debert, Nova Scotia	+	+	+	+			+	+			+	+	+		+					6
Topper, South Carolina	+		+	+				+			+	+	+		+	+				7
Gault, Level 3, Texas	+			+	+							+	+	+		+				8
Hanson, Wyoming	+		+	+			+	+				+	+							9
Lindenmeier, Colorado	+	+	+	+	+		+				+	+	+						+	10
Murray Springs, New Mexico	+		+	+				+		+	+	+				+				11
Old Riverbed Delta, Nevada	+	+	+	+	+			+			+	+	+	+			+			12

(continued)

TABLE 7.4. (*continued*)

Site/Sample	A	B	C	D1	D2	D3	D4	D5	D6	D7	E1	E2	E3	E4	G1	G2	G3	H	I	Reference
Shawnee-Minisink Units 1–4	+	+	+	+				+				+	+	+	+					13
Sloan	+	+	+	+	+		+	+			+	+	+	+				+	+	14
Turrialba	+		+	+	+		+	+			+	+	+		+	+		+		15
Vail, Maine	+	+	+	+	+			+		+		+	+							16
South America																				
El Inga Lower Occupation			+	+			+	+	+			+	+	+	+					17
Fell's Cave Layer V	+		+	+				+					+	+						18
Guitarrero Cave Levels I–II	+	+	+	+			+	+			+	+	+	+		+			+	19
Monte Verde Level I	+		+	+								+								20
Monte Verde Level II	+	+	+	+							+								+	20
Quebrada Jaguay		+	+	+																21
Quebrada Tacahuay		+	+	+				+												22
Vale de Pedra Furada	+	+	+		+															23

KEY: Column Headings: A. Anvil percussion, B. Bipolar percussion, C. Pebble core reduction, D1. Scraper retouch, D2. Macrolithic backing/truncation, D3. Microlithic backing/truncation, D4. Burination, D5. Convergent distal retouch, D6. Concave proximal retouch, E1. Long core-tool production, E2. Thinned biface production, E3. Tanged biface production, E4. Celt production, F1. Preferential bifacial hierarchical core (BHC) reduction, F2. Recurrent laminar BHC reduction, F3. Recurrent radial/centripetal BHC reduction, G1. Platform core reduction, G2. Blade core reduction, G3. Microblade core reduction, H. Abraded-edge tool production, I. Groundstone tool production. Symbols: + = present.

References: 1. West (1996), 2. Hoffecker (2001), 3. Kunz and Reanier (1995), 4. Holmes (2001), 5. Deller and Ellis (2011), 6. MacDonald (1985), 7. Smallwood, Miller, and Sain (2013), 8. Bell (2000), 9. Frison and Bradley (1980), 10. Wilmsen and Roberts (1978), 11. Haynes and Huckell (2007), 12. Madsen, Schmitt, and Page (2015), 13. McNett (1985), 14. Morse (1997), 15. Snarskis (1979), 16. Gramley (1982), 17. Waters and Pevney (2011), 18. Bird (1988), 19. Lynch (1985), 20. Collins (1997), 21. Sandweiss et al. (1998), 22. deFrance et al. (2001), 23. Boëda et al. (2013).

assemblages. Due to low numbers of observations, microliths and cores-on-flakes (Submodes D3 and D6), microblade cores (G3), abraded-edge tools (Mode H), and groundstone tools (Mode I) have to be excluded from statistical comparison of the early American lithic sample to the MLP sample. Bifacial hierarchical cores (Mode F) are absent from the early American sample, and for that reason excluded as well. The remaining data for the early American sample differ from the MLP evidence at a high level of statistical significance (p<.01, chi-square = 44.9 at 13 degrees of freedom).

Comparing the early American sample to that from northern Asia, a comparison that includes microblades (Submode G3), also reveals statistically significant differences (p<.01, chi-square = 92.9 at 15 degrees of freedom). Early American stone tools differ from those found in northern Eurasia by lacking bifacial hierarchical cores, in rare occurrences of microliths, and in more elaborate forms of tanged bifacial points. Prismatic blades and microliths occur in some assemblages from Beringia and North America (Collins 1999), but they are rare further south and in younger contexts. Celts are also relatively uncommon. The earliest American tanged bifaces (stemmed points, fluted points, and lanceolate points) have wide regional distributions and broadly patterned geographic variation in tool designs (Morrow and Toby 1999).

DIASPORA AND STONE TOOLS: PREDICTIONS EVALUATED

Table 7.5 compares occurrences of Modes A–I among the Later Pleistocene/Early Holocene lithic evidence for human dispersal to data for MLP assemblages. Most of the differences between early Sahulian and MLP lithic samples involve the absence of long core-tools and bifacial hierarchical cores, and relatively sparse inventories of retouched pieces. The northern Eurasian sample also lacks evidence of long core-tools and bifacial hierarchical cores, but it features abundant retouched pieces, as well as widespread evidence for blade and microblade core reduction. These same qualities also distinguish the early American lithic evidence from the MLP sample, except that blade cores and celts are uncommon in the New World.

Overview of the Predictions

The Sahulian, northern Eurasian, and early American lithic evidence supports most of the predictions about how dispersal should affect stone tool variation.

Specialized Hide-working Tools and Projectile Weapon Armatures in Colder Habitats: "Endscrapers" on blades are common in lithic assemblages from colder regions, such as northern Eurasia and North America. Not all endscrapers were necessarily used for hide-scraping, of course, but

TABLE 7.5. *Occurrence of Modes A–I among Middle-Late Pleistocene and Early Holocene lithic assemblages and lithic assemblages associated with human dispersal to Sahul, northern Eurasia, and the Americas*

Modes	MLP (n = 37)	Sahul (n = 21)	Northern Eurasia (n = 47)	Americas (n = 28)
A. Anvil percussion	20	3	24	17
B. Bipolar core reduction	11	7	19	8
C. Pebble core reduction	27	17	32	18
D1. Orthogonal retouch	34	17	47	26
D2. Macrolithic backing/truncation	34	3	47	14
D3. Microlithic backing/truncation	3	2	27	0
D4. Burination	29	1	41	12
D5. Convergent distal retouch	29	2	41	18
D6. Concave proximal retouch	2	0	14	1
D7. Flake core reduction	8	2	21	2
E1. Long core-tool (LCT) production	18	1	3	9
E2. Thinned biface production	9	1	7	20
E3. Tanged biface production	4	0	3	21
E4. Celt production	1	3	8	6
F1. Preferential BHC reduction	23	0	4	0
F2. Recurrent laminar BHC reduction	23	0	5	0
F3. Recurrent radial/centripetal BHC reduction	30	0	6	0
G1. Platform core reduction	25	5	17	10
G2. Blade core reduction	19	0	43	10
G3. Microblade core reduction	0	0	36	6
H. Abraded-edge tool production	0	1	2	1
I. Groundstone tool production	0	0	2	4

hide-scraping is among the most consistent function inferred for these artifacts from microwear evidence (Audouin-Rouzeau and Beyries 2002). Endscrapers and blades are relatively uncommon in lithic assemblages from the tropical targets of Late Pleistocene human dispersal, Sahul and South America.

Late Pleistocene Sahul boasts few clear examples of lithic or bone armatures for complex projectile weapons, but stone artifacts similar in size and shape to those used by recent humans as tips and barbs for complex projectile weapons (spearthrower darts, arrows) are widespread in the Late Pleistocene lithic record for northern Eurasia and the Americas (Larsen-Peterkin 1993, Shea 2006b, Meltzer 2009). These artifacts include pointed flakes and blades with basal modification for hafting, thinned and/ or tanged bifaces, backed and truncated pieces, and microliths. Many such artifacts exhibit breakage patterns similar to ethnographic and experimentally utilized projectile points.

Heavy-duty Carpentry Tools: The Sahulian evidence supports the prediction that we should find evidence of heavy-duty woodworking tools and/or celts in Late Pleistocene contexts. "Waisted axes," celts with a concavity running about the midpoint of their length, are known from tectonically uplifted beaches in eastern New Guinea ca. 40 Ka (Groube et al. 1986). Abraded-edge celts and flakes appear throughout northern Australia after 20–30 Ka. Celts, abraded-edge and otherwise, also occur at Japanese archaeological sites dating to 35–40 Ka (Takashi 2012), and at Eastern European and Siberian sites after 20 Ka. Oddly, celts are rarely reported in western European stone tool assemblages until postglacial times (<12.5 Ka). Abraded-edge celts appear to be genuinely absent from early American assemblages, but some of these assemblages contain relatively large, thick, and elongated bifacial cores and retouched flakes ("heavy-duty scrapers" or "preforms") that would be classified as celts in Old World contexts. Clearer examples of celts are common in American assemblages from mid-Holocene times onwards.

Admittedly, it could be a mistake to equate the manufacturing of heavy-duty stone carpentry tools with watercraft production. On the other hand, the hypothesis that effective watercraft were in widespread use during Late Pleistocene/Early Holocene times can be inferred from two other observations. First, the fact that humans reached Sahul at all shows that they had ocean-capable watercraft by at least 45 Ka. Second, the fact that major rivers in Sahul, northern Eurasia, and the Americas do not mark disjunctions in the distribution of any lithic artifact-type or core reduction strategy suggests Late Pleistocene humans had the means to regularly cross these rivers.

Patterned Artifact Style Variation: The Late Pleistocene marks the first time when hypotheses about lithic artifact style variation become non-controversial. Often archaeologists can correctly identify retouched Late Pleistocene/Early Holocene lithic artifacts to a particular region and to within a few thousand years of their actual age by simple visual inspection. This is rarely possible with stone tools dating to more than 50 Ka. As in earlier periods, some artifact-types remain minimally variable for thousands of years and over vast areas, but in those parts of the world where archaeological scrutiny has been greatest (Europe, the Mediterranean Basin, southern Africa), archaeologists have arranged lithic artifact-types into chronological series that hold up well when tested with geochronological evidence. These artifacts' shorter temporal ranges are comparable to ethnographic material culture variation. Rather than the tens of thousands of years that separate typologically distinct MLP samples, patterned differences can be detected in post-50 Ka lithic assemblages dating thousands of years apart.

Late Pleistocene/Early Holocene lithic projectile armatures from northern Eurasia and the Americas exhibit the predicted patterns of short-term and inter- and intra-regional morphological variability. Late Pleistocene lithic artifact style variation frequently correlates with artifact design variation in other media, such as bone tools and personal adornments (Larsen-Peterkin 1993, Bar-Yosef Mayer 2005, Vanhaeren and d'Errico 2006). Such stylistic variation also occurs, albeit somewhat less clearly, among scrapers/notches/denticulates, burins, and other retouched pieces (e.g., "carinated" pieces, "Noailles," and "parrot beak" burins, "strangled" endscrapers). As noted earlier, this relative lack of clarity in stylistic patterning may reflect prolonged use and retouch leading to resharpening-related morphological convergence among artifacts that were used at residential sites and less often transported to the outer limits of foraging areas.

Differences in Artifact Designs Between Donor and Recipient Regions: The less extensively modified stone tools in Sahul, northern Eurasia, and the Americas are similar to their immediate precursors in Southeast Asia, western Asia, and Beringia, but the most extensively modified lithic artifacts found with early human fossils in Sahul (waisted axes), northern Eurasia (microblades), or the Americas (fluted points) do not occur among African or South Asian lithic assemblages prior to 50 Ka.

Prismatic blade production (especially "bladelets" and "microblades") and the knapping of thinned and tanged bifaces are two of the more obvious ways in which the Late Pleistocene lithic record for dispersal into northern Eurasia differs from the evidence in the presumed source areas for human populations in southern Asia prior to 50 Ka. While both of these ways of making stone tools occur in some African contexts older than 50 Ka, neither is common in southern Asian contexts before 50 Ka.

Late Pleistocene lithic assemblages from North America lack the microliths found in Beringian assemblages. Though "stemmed" forms of tanged bifacial points occur along the Pacific Coasts of Northeast Asia and North America, "fluted" bifacial points have no exact parallels in Asia or in Beringia. Prismatic blade and microblade core technology, which is widespread throughout northern Eurasia and Beringia, does not seem to have spread into the Americas much further south than modern-day Mexico.

Lithic evidence from Sundaland prior to 50 Ka consists mainly of hierarchical and non-hierarchical pebble cores and various simple kinds of retouched pieces with seemingly little formal patterning (Higham 2002). Flaked stone celts and abraded edge tools such as those found in early Sahulian contexts are not documented at earlier sites in Southeast Asia. Again, it must be kept in mind that Sundaland's coastlines, lower-elevation river valleys, and floodplains, its likely centers of gravity for Late Pleistocene human settlement, are now underwater and inaccessible to archaeologists.

Ecogeographically Patterned Differences Between Earlier and Later Stone Tools: Around 5–6 Ka sea levels stabilized near their modern stand and desert conditions became more widespread in interior Australia (Hiscock 2008). These changes put Sahulians between an ocean that had recently drowned their most productive habitats and an increasingly inhospitable "outback" (continental interior). Faced with these circumstances, one would expect Sahulians to have intensified their subsistence and technological strategies, attempting to eke out more energy from those habitats in which they were living. Many of the distinctive features of stone tools made around this time in Australia, including bifacial points and microlithic backed/truncated pieces, result from pressure flaking and lithic miniaturization, two forms of intensification in stone tool production (see Box 5).

For northern Eurasians, the corresponding ecological crisis would have occurred during the Last Glacial Maximum (LGM), ca. 18–22 Ka (Clark et al. 2009). Gaps in the Late Pleistocene record suggest humans abandoned much of northern Europe and drier eastern parts of Siberia around this time (Hoffecker 2004). LGM archaeological assemblages from southern Europe also feature microlithic tools and increased evidence for pressure flaking (Gamble 1999). In LGM western Europe, knappers used pressure flaking to shape tanged pieces, points, and thinned bifaces. Microlithization seems to have taken root somewhat later. Microblades were manufactured before the LGM in eastern Europe and northern Asia, but their occurrence in archaeological assemblages increased markedly during the LGM and in postglacial times.

Early Americans' first major ecological crisis appears to have been during the Younger Dryas period, ca. 11.5–12.8 Ka. This brief return to near-glacial conditions did not evoke microlith production. Instead, it coincides with the spread of distinctive styles of basally thinned ("fluted") points and stemmed bifacial points shaped by pressure flaking (Meltzer 2009). These points are often interpreted as specialized tools for killing large mammals, but they do not appear among stone tools made by big-game hunters in the Old World, something one would expect to see if function alone determined their morphology. They are more plausibly interpreted as symbolic signifiers of social networks established rapidly to minimize risks of subsistence failure among groups distributed widely across the landscape. Consistent with this hypothesis, lithic assemblages from the more arid parts of North America preserve evidence for long-distance transfers of lithic raw materials multiple orders of magnitude greater than seen among stone tool assemblages at the same time elsewhere. After the Younger Dryas, fluted points all but vanish. Relatively simple tanged and notched points become more common, and more variable within and between regions. Lithic raw material transfers also become less extensive. These changes are consistent with the fragmentation of formerly extensive social networks, something one would expect to see as warmer climates boosted local environmental productivity and risks of subsistence failure declined.

These changes in the lithic evidence from Sahul, northern Eurasia, and the Americas contrast starkly with the lack of change among stone tools made by *Homo floresiensis*, a Later Pleistocene "archaic" hominin that was apparently endemic to the island of Flores in Indonesia up to at least ca. 60 Ka (see Box 6). Some measure of *H. sapiens'* ability to fine-tune technologies may reflect capacities for behavioral variability that evolved after *H. floresiensis'* ancestors became isolated from hominin populations living on mainland Eurasia.

Contrasts with Traditional Approaches

Traditional archaeological approaches to explaining the lithic evidence for Late Pleistocene/Early Holocene human dispersals are deeply concerned with routes. This concern is the source of many problems. Archaeologists' methods for identifying specific dispersal routes accept what one might call the "Hansel and Gretel Fallacy," the assumption that for thousands of years human groups left consistent and distinctive lithic "signatures" along their dispersal routes in much the same way the two children in the German folktale left white pebbles along their path through the woods so that they could find their way home.

No recent human social networks have archaeological signatures as consistent through time and space as the Late Pleistocene stone tool industries archaeologists treat as proxies for human social groups. Indeed, the many efforts contemporary emigrants/immigrants make to maintain their ethnic heritage in a diaspora show that maintaining a particular social identity under such circumstances is very hard work. That ethnographic and historic efforts to do this invariably fail suggests that it is a mistake to project stable ethnic-cultural entities with unique archaeological signatures onto evolutionary/geological timescales. The lithic record for Late Pleistocene human dispersal almost certainly includes substantial quantities of tools made by individuals who changed their social identities as they dispersed into new lands, altering their stone-toolmaking habits and lithic "signature" in the process.

Hypotheses about human dispersal routes are often shown using a map of the modern world traversed by straight or slightly curving arrows. (My students in New York call them "subway map models.") Recent dispersals by non-human species rarely follow such simple trajectories. Rather, they follow paths of least resistance along watercourses and topographic features (Crosby 1986). They ebb and flow along with climate change and demographic shifts. Except at the broadest geographic scales and least levels of temporal resolution, none are as simple as archaeologists' maps for human dispersals. Viewed at evolutionary/geological timescales, prehistoric human dispersals from any one region to another probably involved all the routes that were physically available and logistically possible. Testing hypotheses about which routes were more important than others in the long run requires data unequivocally referable to historical relationships among prehistoric humans, such as genetic data from fossils and living humans (Oppenheimer 2004, Hawks 2013). Archaeology may be able to suggest hypotheses about failed dispersals, but paleoanthropologists seeking conclusive evidence for successful ones should seek them in the human genome. On this issue, the stone tools are not so much mute as they are unreliable informants.

Box 5 *Pressure Flaking and Lithic Miniaturization*

Many Later Pleistocene contexts preserve evidence for pressure flaking and lithic miniaturization. Both ways of making stone tools increase the amount of effective cutting edge that can be recovered from a stone tool, but at the cost of increased allocation of time and energy in tool production. Pressure flaking and lithic miniaturization are both evolutionarily significant developments in lithic technology. Each is a kind of "lithic intensification," a strategy in which one works harder for the same or greater return. Intensification can be an important source of behavioral variability and social evolutionary change. That pressure flaking and lithic miniaturization appear in Later Pleistocene times is consistent with the hypothesis that over the last 3.5 million years, hominin stone tool use acquired an increasingly obligatory character. Unfortunately, uncertainties about the antiquity of pressure flaking and lithic miniaturization make it difficult to cite this evidence to support that hypothesis or to refute it.

In pressure flaking, one initiates fractures by slowly increasing pressure on an edge with a percussor made of stone, metal, bone/antler, or wood until a fracture occurs. The fractures caused in this way are often bending fractures rather than Hertzian cone fractures (Cotterell and Kamminga 1987). These fractures can either be relatively short (in which case the damage resembles retouch by percussion) or shallow and deeply invasive. Pressure flaking can be discriminated from percussion fractures by measuring microscopic features on fracture surfaces (Tsirk 2014). In practice, however, most archaeologists identify pressure flaking from macroscopic patterns of fracture variation. The artifacts most commonly identified as having been shaped by pressure flaking include backed/truncated pieces, microliths, thinned bifaces, tanged pieces, tanged bifaces, and some small blade/microblade cores. As with any visual assessment based on morphological analogy, archaeologists differ from one another in how they make these identifications. Inevitably, this creates an archaeological record for pressure flaking that reflects behavioral differences among

Box 5 (*Cont.*)

archaeologists rather than behavioral differences among prehistoric humans. Figure 7.9 shows Late Pleistocene and Early Holocene artifacts thought to have been pressure flaked together with ones pressure flaked by recent flintknappers.

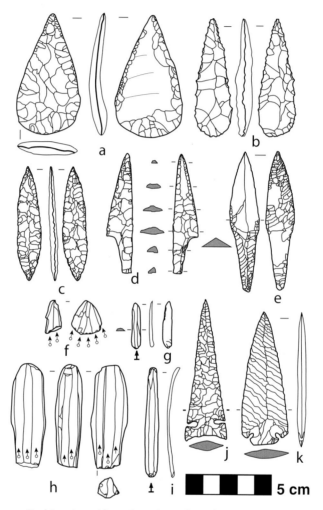

Figure 7.9 Prehistoric artifacts thought to have been shaped by pressure flaking (a–i) and twentieth-century artifacts known to have been shaped by pressure flaking (j–k): a. Omo Kibish BNS, Ethiopia (ca. 104 Ka), b. Umhlatuzana Rock Shelter, South Africa (ca. 70 Ka), c–d. Fourneau du Diable, France (ca. 20 Ka), e. Early Holocene "knife" from Byblos, Lebanon (ca. 10 Ka), f–g. microblade core and microblade from Rose Cottage Cave, South Africa (12–13 Ka), h–i, prismatic blade core and blade from Tell Seker Al-Aheimar, Syria, j. bifacial "Ishi point" made by Ishi (Yahi) Californian Native American (USA, ca. AD 1916), k. bifacial point made by Errett Callahan (USA, ca. AD 1988). Redrawn after Cauvin (1968), Demars and Laurent (1992), Whittaker (1994), Shea (2008), Nishiaki and Nagai (2011), McKay (2014), and an unpublished figure provided by Anders Hogburg and Marlize Lombard.

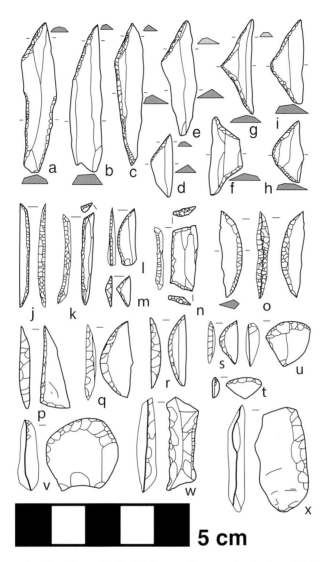

Figure 7.10 Artifacts from Early Holocene Europe (a–i), Late Pleistocene/ Early Holocene Southwest Asia (j–o), and Holocene South Africa (p-x) generally accepted as microliths. a–s, x. backed and/or truncated pieces, t–w. scrapers. Sources: Star Carr, England (a–i), various Late Pleistocene/early Holocene sites in Israel and Jordan (j–o), various Holocene sites in South Africa (p–x). Redrawn after Clark (1954), Mitchell (2002), Shea (2013b).

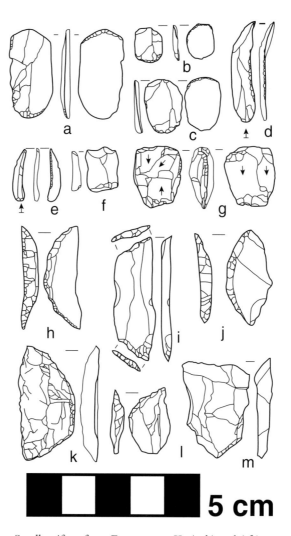

Figure 7.11 Small artifacts from Europe >17 Ka (a–h) and Africa >40 Ka (i–m) not generally accepted as microliths. a–f, h–m. backed and/or truncated pieces, g. bipolar core. Sources: Abri Dufour, France (a), Le Flageolet, France (b–c), Kostienki 1, Russia (d), La Chaise, France (e), Klissoura Cave 1, Greece (f), Champ, France (g), Salento, Italy (h), Nelsons Bay Cave, South Africa (i–j), Twin Rivers Cave, Zambia (k–m). Redrawn after Volman (1984), Demars and Laurent (1992), Barham (2000), Kozlowski (2000).

Box 5 (*Cont.*)

Lithic miniaturization is a strategy (or, more precisely, a group of strategies) in which flakes less than 3 cm long are systematically detached from cores (Kuhn and Elston 2002). This can entail either selecting small rocks for use as cores, prolonged curation and reduction of larger cores, or both. Common techniques for detaching small flakes include bipolar or freehand percussion, indirect percussion, and/or pressure flaking. Unfortunately, variable and inconsistently applied definitions of "microliths" among different archaeological research traditions hamper research on lithic miniaturization. Few traditional definitions of microliths have specific size criteria. Most include artifacts shorter than 20–30 mm long and less than 4–5 mm wide, but longer backed/truncated pieces are often described as microliths. All traditional definitions recognize small backed and truncated tools as microliths, but many also recognize small unretouched blades ("bladelets" or "microblades") as microliths, too. Artifacts that fit the morphometric criteria for microliths are often not identified as such because they occur in older contexts than those in which traditional archaeological frameworks recognize microliths (<15–20 Ka). Small bipolar cores and cores-on-flakes are not generally recognized as microliths even though they are indisputably microlithic. More seriously, traditional archaeological frameworks do not recognize unretouched flakes as microliths. They fail to do this even though ethnographic stone-tool-using humans routinely used unretouched flakes shorter than 2–3 cm for cutting tasks, even though non-human primates do so as well (suggesting the practice is evolutionarily primitive), and in spite of the fact that hierarchical cores shorter than 2–3 cm grace the archaeological record from the Plio-Pleistocene times onwards. As a result, archaeological identifications of microlith production actually only register the production of certain kinds of retouched microliths and/or small blades, rather than the overall systemic reductions in stone tool size. Figures 7.10 and 7.11 show examples of artifacts generally accepted as microliths and artifacts of the same size that are not considered microliths by traditional archaeological typologies.

Box 6 *What Does* Homo floresiensis *Tell Us about Brain Size and Stone Tools?*

Since the earliest days of human origins research, many paleoanthropologists have accepted the hypothesis of a causal link between hominin brain enlargement ("encephalization") and stone tool production (Bowdler 1986). In 2003 the scientific world was stunned by the discovery of fossils of *Homo floresiensis*, diminutive hominins barely a meter tall whose brains were no larger than those of chimpanzees and bonobos (Morwood and Jungers 2009). Excavations at Liang Bua Cave on the island of Flores, Indonesia, recovered remains of *H. floresiensis* together with flaked stone tools in contexts dating from 60–>130 Ka. The stone tools associated with *H. floresiensis* include large flakes that were struck from boulders outside the cave and then transported into Liang Bua, where they were flaked about their circumference (Moore et al. 2009). There are few differences among the stone tools from Liang Bua and the lithic evidence from Mata Menge, a site on Flores dating to 800 Ka (Brumm et al. 2006) (Figure 7.12). Liang Bua and Mata Menge both provide evidence for pebble cores and bifacial hierarchical cores. Neither site

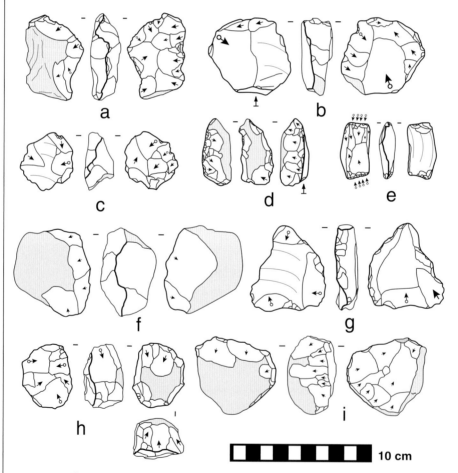

Figure 7.12 Stone tools from Liang Bua (a–e) and Mata Menge (f–i), Indonesia. a, h, i bifacial hierarchical cores, f. non-hierarchical cores, b, c, g. cores-on-flakes, d. scraper, e. bipolar core-on-flake. Redrawn after Moore et al. (2007).

Box 6 (*Cont.*)

preserves evidence for long core-tools or for the use of fire, both of which are associated with *H. erectus* in older Asian contexts (Goren-Inbar et al. 2000).

Assuming the stone tool evidence associated with *H. floresiensis* fossils is correctly attributed to that hominin, this association suggests the following:

Stone cutting tool production and transport by hominins did not require large brains. Further support for this hypothesis can be found in observations that bonobos can knap and use stone tools. MLP humans do not have big brains because they made stone tools.

Hierarchical core reduction does not require brains as large as those among MLP hominins. This hypothesis is supported by occurrences of bifacial and unifacial hierarchical cores among EMP contexts in Africa.

The Flores evidence further supports the link between logistical mobility and long core-tool production (see Chapter 5). *Homo floresiensis* had relatively long forearms, short lower legs, and elongated feet. These features suggest a form of terrestrial locomotion with a stronger arboreal component than among other Middle and Late Pleistocene hominins. Both the Mata Menge and Liang Bua assemblages lack the long core-tools that Chapter 5 attributes to prolonged walking/running and logistical mobility.

CHAPTER 8

RESIDENTIAL SEDENTISM

A house is just a place to keep your stuff while you go out and get more stuff.

    George Carlin (1937–2008)

Compared to other primates, humans are extremely sedentary. Because we reside in the same places for prolonged periods, we accumulate a lot of stuff. Our accumulations, in turn, influence our behavior. The more stuff we have, the higher the cost of moving it, and the more it takes to make us move. This chapter examines how residential sedentism affected lithic evidence in the East Mediterranean Levant. This region has a detailed record for how residentially mobile hunter-gatherers became sedentary food producers between 6.5 and 24 Ka. In the Levant, sedentism increased the amount of time and energy people devoted to lithic seed-pulverizing equipment, projectile weapon armatures, and carpentry tools.

SEDENTISM VS. MOBILITY

The most mobile hunter-gatherers are more sedentary than the least mobile non-human primates. Most non-human primates feed as they go during the day and rest at different sleeping sites each night. They may return to favorable locations, such as a particular tree or a rock ledge, but they do not stay in the same place continuously for days on end. Individual human sedentism varies widely, but, collectively, humans have continuously occupied some favorable sites for millennia (e.g., Cairo, Jerusalem, Rome). Our residential sedentism has countervailing costs, including increased risk of exposure to infectious diseases and the need to supply residential sites in bulk with food, fuel, and other resources. For most humans, however, residential sedentism's benefits, such as decreased infant mortality and stable social networks, outweigh its costs. Countless ethnographic accounts report formerly mobile hunter-gatherers and pastoralists becoming sedentary. Sedentary humans rarely increase their residential mobility voluntarily, other than in times of war or other social upheavals.

Residential Sedentism: Human vs. Non-human Primate Differences

What allows human residential sedentism to be so different from other primates' land-use strategies? The most obvious factors include logistical mobility (see Chapter 5), a broad and variable ecological niche, central place foraging, institutionalized division of labor, stable large-scale social coalitions, and food production.

Broad and Variable Ecological Niches: Our nearest non-human primate relatives' ecological niches are comparatively narrow and minimally variable. They subsist mainly on fruits, nuts, and roots, supplementing their diets with insects and small vertebrates. Tool use enlarges their range of food sources, but it does not substantially increase their residential sedentism. Humans' tools are distinctive in their functional variability. Bows and arrows that can kill large dangerous animals are also used on fish, birds, and smaller terrestrial prey. Traps and nets used to catch one species are repurposed for catching others. Pulverizing tools used to split open nuts are also used to grind seeds or to crush roots and tubers. Our tools' multiple potential applications allow humans to construct broad ecological niches dynamically. Consequently, we can remain in one place for prolonged periods simply by switching from higher-ranked to lower-ranked food sources and back again as necessary.

Central Place Foraging and Food Sharing: Non-human primates do not forage from fixed places, and they do not systematically share food among non-kin. They share food with their young, and with potential mates and social allies (there is also much "tolerated theft"). They do not store food for later use. In contrast, central place foraging and systematic food sharing among non-kin based on principles of delayed reciprocity are universal human behaviors. They make sedentism possible by encouraging large numbers of individuals to focus their efforts on fixed points on the landscape for prolonged periods (Winterhalder 2001, Marlowe 2005). Ethnographic humans also improve conditions at these central places by constructing hearths, durable artificial shelters, and food storage facilities.

Institutionalized Division of Labor: Differences in subsistence activities and tool use by male vs. female non-human primates are either minimal, or when patterned, so consistent among separate populations that they almost certainly arise from sex-based biological differences (Boesch and Boesch 1984b). All human societies have a division of labor of one kind or another. Among many ethnographic foragers, males pursue distant food sources with highly variable energetic return rates, such as large terrestrial or aquatic mammals. Females tend to focus their subsistence efforts closer to residential sites and on prey that have more predictable energetic returns, such as plant foods and smaller animals. Though these differences seem at first glance sex-based, they are socially constructed. Given a container and proper incentives, men can forage for plant foods and small animals just as well as women can. Armed with bows or firearms, women can hunt larger game just as well as men. Division of labor supports residential sedentism, because it enables human food-sharing coalitions foraging from the same central place to practice different subsistence strategies simultaneously (Jochim 1988).

Large, Stable, and Symbolically Reinforced Coalitions: Non-human primates form coalitions for brief periods, for grooming, hunting, and territorial aggression, but such "cooperation" among non-kin is fleeting and task-specific, more or less like cooperation among members of professional sports teams. Chimpanzees, for example, will work together to hunt monkeys, but the instant their prey has been killed, cooperation ceases and a free-for-all for possession of the carcass begins. No humans hunt like this. A human hunter who did so could reasonably expect to be scolded, cursed, shamed, ostracized, even killed.

Human sedentism supports, and is supported by, large, stable social coalitions of distantly related individuals (Hill et al. 2011). These coalitions regulate food acquisition, preparation, and redistribution, cooperative child-care, collective governance, and territorial defense. Human coalitions incorporating large numbers of non-kin are organized around fictive kinship, co-residence patterns, common language, and shared cultural beliefs. Exosomatic symbols, such as clothing, personal adornment, and artifact design variation, play crucial roles in these coalitions because they broadcast information about individuals that allows strangers to predict the likely outcome of future interactions (Wobst 1977). In most societies and under the best circumstances, one can predict interactions with an armed stranger wearing a police officer's uniform in ways one cannot predict interactions with armed strangers wearing civilian clothes.

Food Production Using Domesticated Plants and Animals: Non-human primates have co-evolutionary relationships with plants and other animals, but they have not domesticated them. Most hunter-gatherers use domesticated dogs to boost foraging returns. Doing this allows them to persist at favored residential sites (Reitz and Wing 2008). For most pre-industrial humans, however, prolonged sedentism requires food production using domesticated plants and animals (Rindos 1984). Controlling the reproductive activities of domesticated animals and planting, tending, and harvesting crops can be more energetically costly and time-consuming than hunting and gathering, but these activities can also yield windfall energetic returns of foods that can be stored and transported in bulk to level out subsistence shortfalls. Stored or not, surplus food can be used as strategic assets in social relations (Bender 1978, Hayden 1994).

TABLE 8.1. *Differences among stone tools used by residentially mobile and sedentary humans*

Variable	Mobile humans	Sedentary humans
Complex projectile technology	Spearthrower and dart, bow and arrow	Bow and arrow
Stone weapon armature design emphasis	Hunting	Hunting and anti-personnel
Carpentry tools	Flaked stone and edge-ground celts	Edge-ground celts
Functional specialization	Rare, most tools multifunctional	Some specialized tools
Artifact design variability	Stable and widely distributed	Unstable and spatially contingent
Overdesign	Rare	Common

Differences in Stone Tool Use By Mobile and Sedentary Humans

The differences between non-human primates and sedentary food-producing humans are so vast that predictions about sedentism's effect on the lithic record have to be refined by comparisons with residentially mobile humans (Table 8.1). Residentially sedentary humans differ from their more-mobile counterparts in their use of non-hierarchical core technology, seed-pulverizing technology, complex projectile technology, lithic anti-personnel weapons, abraded-edge woodworking tools/celts, and functionally specialized tools, as well as in complex and contingent patterns of artifact design variation, namely "lithic overdesign."

Non-hierarchical Core Technology: Because residentially mobile humans often reduce the mass of rock they transport by attaching stone tools to handles, their core technology emphasizes hierarchical core reduction (Binford 1979). Maintaining a stable hierarchy of fracture initiation and detachment surfaces allows knappers to obtain more morphologically consistent flakes than when the two surfaces are interchangeable (as among non-hierarchical cores). This strategy reduces the extent to which tools have to be retouched in order to fit them into pre-existing handles, and it conserves potentially useful tool mass. Conversely, sedentary knappers often emphasize expedient/non-hierarchical core reduction, producing large quantities of morphologically variable flakes near their residential sites (Parry and Kelly 1987). Doing this increases the likelihood that someone seeking a sharp unretouched flake of specific size and shape will be able to locate one by searching among pre-existing knapping products rather than have to knap a fresh tool. Residential sedentism ought to have increased incentives for non-hierarchical core reduction.

Seed-pulverizing Technology: Both residentially mobile and sedentary societies use groundstone tools to pulverize seeds and nuts in order to make them easier to cook and to digest, but such groundstone tools are more ubiquitous and more substantially modified from their natural forms among sedentary societies, especially those that practice cereal cultivation. Among residentially mobile groups, groundstone seed-pulverizing tools are usually small mortars and pestles, versatile implements that pulverize by percussion (Kraybill 1977). Residentially sedentary groups more often employ querns, handstones, and other large seed-grinding tools that pulverize by abrasion. They also make greater use of stone and ceramic cooking vessels. Residential sedentism should be correlated with increases in the occurrences of larger groundstone seed-pulverizing tools, with a shift from simple mortars/pestles to querns/handstones, and carved stone and ceramic vessels.

Complex Projectile Technology: All human societies use complex projectile weapons for niche widening and stabilization (Shea 2006b). Such weapons are also used as aids to "coalition enforcement," that is, to punish "cheaters" and "free-riders" in alliance networks (Bingham 2000). In Eurasia and the Americas, where bow/arrow and spearthrower/dart were both used in historical times, these weapon systems' use is correlated with high population densities and residential sedentism (Churchill 1993, Yu 2006, Bingham and Souza 2009).

Bows/arrows are particularly helpful in solving problems residential sedentism creates. Prolonged residence at the same site quickly depletes local prey animal populations. This requires hunters to be more opportunistic in choosing targets and to systematically target smaller and fast-moving prey. Arrows are lighter than spearthrower darts, and thus a single forager can carry more of them. Arrows are more versatile than spears. They can be launched effectively from concealment, in three dimensions (up, down, and horizontally), and against a wider range of prey than spears can. Relatively easy to operate to the point where even children can use them, bows and arrows increase the pool of potential hunters. These observations suggest residential sedentism ought to have increased the use of the bow and arrow.

Lithic Anti-personnel Weapons: Humans rank second only after large game as the principal targets for ethnographic stone-tipped projectile weapons (Ellis 1997). Prolonged residence at habitation sites near stable resources encourages territorial aggression and defense (Keeley 1996). Because arrows move so much faster than spears, ethnographic humans routinely use them as anti-personnel weapons in coalitionary conflicts. Because chasing a wounded and fleeing animal subtracts from the calories gained by killing it, stone weapon tips used by mobile foragers are designed to kill prey quickly by massive hemorrhage. Barbed tips and microlithic inserts create large wounds that do not close quickly, leaving a blood trail hunters can easily follow. In contrast, arrow tips used by humans in warfare and other forms of coalitionary killing often have long narrow blades and tangs, deep lateral notches, and barbed/denticulated edges. These features enhance functionality as anti-personnel weapons by making the points liable to break while deeply embedded in their targets, thereby making them difficult to extract. The resulting wounds disable without causing immediate death. Such wounds are advantageous in warfare, because they burden rival coalitions with wounded former combatants. They are also advantageous in coalition enforcement because they magnify the physical threat to the targets of such enforcement. If sedentism led to increased coalitionary conflicts involving stone-tipped weapons, the tips of those weapons ought to show designs optimized for use as anti-personnel weapons.

Abraded-edge Woodworking Tools/Celts: Central places from which residentially mobile and sedentary humans forage contrast with one another in the scale of their architecture (Oliver 1987). Remaining in one place for prolonged periods creates incentives to build residential structures, storage facilities, and other complex construction projects. In most parts of the world, these structures incorporate large quantities of wood that have to be precisely shaped and joined. Prior to the availability of metal tools, much of this carpentry was done with abraded-edge stone celts. Edge abrasion minimizes friction between the non-cutting tool surfaces and worked materials, transmitting more energy into cutting than with flaked-stone edges (Hayden 1989). Increases in the scale and necessary precision of architectural construction associated with residential sedentism should have increased incentives for making abraded-edge woodworking tools.

Functionally Specialized Tools: Among mobile hunter-gatherers, much division of labor involves subsistence and child-care. Among sedentary societies, the division of labor extends further, to resource extraction (e.g., mining, gathering fuel), food preparation, artifact production, and other craft specialist activities. Craft specialization involves the same person performing repetitive tasks at high frequencies. As such, it increases incentives for devising functionally specialized implements, tools engineered to be maximally efficient in a narrow range of tasks. Such energetic and kinematic efficiency is especially important among agrarian societies in which children and older adults with limited physical strength can be recruited as laborers (e.g., Kramer 2005). Specialized tools for high-repetitive tasks boost these relatively "underpowered" individuals' potential productivity. It follows that residential sedentism should have increased incentives for devising functionally specialized tools, particularly ones used for repetitive tasks with high edge-attrition rates.

Complex and Contingent Patterns of Artifact Design Variation: All humans use artifact design variation to broadcast symbolic messages about their social identities and memberships in various kinds of social coalitions. Residentially mobile humans live in relatively small communities. In communities of a few hundred individuals most people know one another well. For such people, messages about social identity encoded in symbolic artifacts are redundant with personal experience. (The village blacksmith dressed up in a suit is still the village blacksmith.) The benefits of devising artifacts to transmit symbolic messages accrue mainly in encounters with strangers who are members of the same larger culture (Wobst 1977). For example, one can safely predict that someone wearing an expensive sweater with the name of an Ivy League college on it is affiliated with that institution.

Communities of residentially sedentary humans can number in the thousands or more. Arithmetic increases in community size result in exponential increases in the number of potential interactions among the people living together. Ethnographic studies suggest humans have difficulty maintaining social relationships with more than about 150 people at any one point in time (Dunbar 1992). It follows that even in small sedentary communities, the number of these potential interactions will overwhelm individuals' cognitive capacities for keeping track of social relationships. Historically, people have tried to solve this problem by using complex and contingent artifactual symbols as clues to social identities (Coward 2010). Firemen, for example, wear different uniforms than police officers, and, while working, both move around in different kinds of automobiles than bankers and politicians. Because these artifactual signals about identities and affinities are networked with one another and with society at large, change in one is often correlated with changes in other media. Again, comparing the clothing, professional equipment, and transportation aids of firemen, police, bankers, and politicians from the 1920s with those in use today reveals not only differences between these time periods, but also differences between regions at the same time (say, in New York vs. London, or Cairo vs. Tokyo). As prehistoric humans became more sedentary we should expect to see increasingly complex, spatially and temporally contingent patterns of lithic variability that are correlated with design shifts in non-lithic evidence.

Lithic Overdesign: When strangers in residentially sedentary communities habitually use artifactual symbols to transmit socially significant information, a high "noise to signal ratio" can become a problem. So many messages are transmitted simultaneously that individual messages become degraded. The distinctive shirt, dress, or jewelry that stands out in a small gathering has less visual impact in a crowd of hundreds. To counteract high noise to signal ratios, individuals often undertake displays that are expensive, risky, or difficult to imitate in order to overcome competing messages. Sociologists describe such strategies as "conspicuous consumption" (Veblen 1899). Behavioral ecologists use the term "costly signaling" (Zahavi and Zahavi 1997).

"Lithic overdesign" is a distinctively human manifestation of conspicuous consumption/costly signaling in which labor is devoted to stone production overtly for purposes of display and in ways that do not increase tool mechanical functionality. Lithic overdesign can involve selectively using exotic or otherwise costly-to-procure lithic raw materials, exaggerated artifact size, and/or functionally superfluous patterns of surface modification by retouch or abrasion. Residential sedentism ought to have systemically increased incentives for lithic overdesign, including "extreme" flintknapping (see Box 7).

Predictions for the Archaeological Lithic Evidence

Behavioral differences among non-human primates, residentially mobile humans, and residentially sedentary humans suggest that when prehistoric humans became residentially sedentary, the stone tool evidence should exhibit the following qualities:

1. Increased emphasis on non-hierarchical core reduction.
2. Larger, more varied, and more substantially modified groundstone seed-pulverizing tools.
3. Increased evidence for the bow and arrow.
4. Stone weapon tips designed as anti-personnel weapons.
5. Abraded-edge woodworking tools/celts.
6. Functionally specialized tools.
7. Complex and contingent patterns of artifact design variation.
8. Increased artifact overdesign.

Residential sedentism undoubtedly varied throughout the Pleistocene, but it seems to have increased in many parts of the world more or less simultaneously during Late Pleistocene and Early Holocene times as a warming world experienced reduced climatic variability (Richerson, Boyd, and Bettinger 2001, Mithen 2004). Surveying the lithic record for sedentism worldwide is beyond the scope of this book. Instead, this chapter tests its predictions using evidence from the southern part of the East Mediterranean Levant during the period 6.5–24 Ka. Owing to a long history of research, the southern Levant has a uniquely well-documented archaeological record for the origins of residential sedentism.

THE SOUTHERN LEVANT IN THE LATE PLEISTOCENE AND EARLY HOLOCENE: A CASE STUDY

This chapter discusses the lithic evidence from the East Mediterranean Levant in terms of two major blocks of time, the Terminal Pleistocene, ca. 11.5–24.0 Ka, and the Early Holocene, ca. 6.5–11.5 Ka (see Figures 8.1 and 8.2). The division between Terminal Pleistocene and Early Holocene periods corresponds to a major shift across several dimensions of archaeological evidence indicating increased sedentism and food production by agriculture and pastoralism. For overviews of this evidence, see Bar-Yosef and Belfer-Cohen (1989), Henry (1989), Cauvin (2000), Kozlowski and Aurenche (2005), Simmons (2007), Goring-Morris, Hovers, and Belfer-Cohen (2009), Belfer-Cohen and Goring-Morris (2011), and papers in Kuijt (2002).

Levantine Geography and Paleoenvironment

A borderland between the Mediterranean Sea and the Arabian Desert, the southern Levant is bounded to the north by the Taurus-Zagros Mountains and

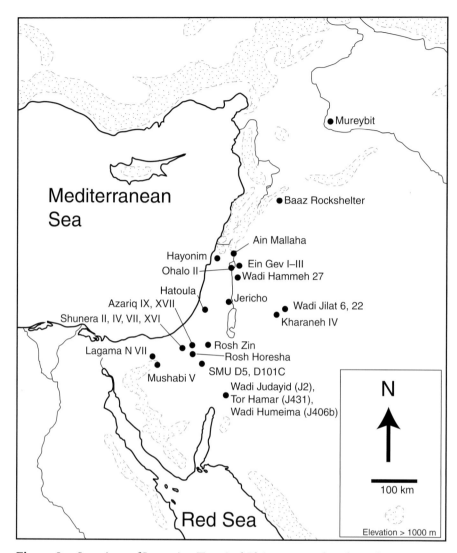

Figure 8.1 Locations of Levantine Terminal Pleistocene archaeological sites.

to the south by the Sinai Peninsula and the Red Sea. The northernmost extension of the East African Rift, the Jordan Valley, divides the Levant into coastal lowlands formerly covered with Mediterranean (oak-terebinth) woodland vegetation and eastern highlands supporting steppe–desert vegetation (Zohary 1973, Horowitz 1979). High topographic relief around the Jordan Valley and the southern flanks of the Taurus-Zagros Mountains creates numerous "ecotones," places where woodland, steppe, and desert habitats are in close conjunction with one another (Zohary 1973). Ecotones offer a wide range of potential food sources with lower search costs than the more ecologically homogeneous regions nearby. These ecotones were perennial focal points for Pleistocene and pre-agricultural Holocene human settlement.

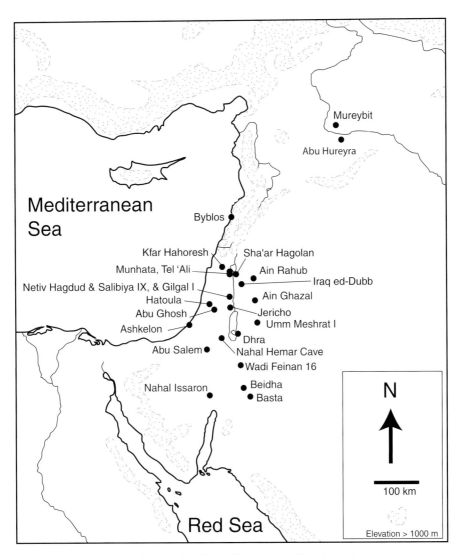

Figure 8.2 Locations of Levantine Early Holocene archaeological sites.

The Last Glacial Maximum in Southwest Asia (18–22 Ka) was cold with alternating periods of humidity and drought. According to the most recent syntheses of this evidence, precipitation increased slowly after about 15 Ka (Simmons 2007, Bar-Yosef 2011, Belfer-Cohen and Goring-Morris 2011, Zeder 2011). Thus, the Terminal Pleistocene began cold and dry with warming conditions and increasing rainfall punctuated by a cold, dry interval near its end. Those woodland-steppe ecotone habitats most favorable for human hunter-gatherer settlement expanded during the earliest part of this period. Increased numbers of archaeological sites and increased site sizes suggest human population grew as well. A brief return to glacial conditions around 11.5–12.8 Ka (the Younger Dryas Event) reversed these trends, causing a reduction in woodland

vegetation cover and retractions of human settlement into more humid habitats
and lower elevations. The earliest evidence for plant domestication appears
shortly after the end of the Younger Dryas. After 11.5 Ka, rainfall and tem-
perature both increased, with fluctuations, to about 6.5 Ka. The Early
Holocene began warm and wet, wetter indeed than the present day, but it
ended in warmer and drier conditions.

Levantine Terminal Pleistocene/Early Holocene Human Biology and Behavior

Only *H. sapiens* fossils are known from Levantine Terminal Pleistocene and
Early Holocene contexts. These fossils differ markedly from earlier Pleistocene
humans in reduced overall skeletal robusticity and in the degree to which their
faces are "feminized" (i.e., lacking prominent chins and brow ridges). These
differences may reflect dietary and/or hormonal changes among Later
Pleistocene humans (Lieberman 2011, Cieri et al. 2014).

Skeletons from both the Terminal Pleistocene and Early Holocene show
evidence for repetitive-stress-related damage to the vertebrae and forearms and
legs unlike anything seen in Pleistocene contexts (Molleson and Jones 1991,
1993, Molleson 1994). Younger individuals from Abu Hureyra (Syria) have
damage to cervical vertebrae showing they habitually carried heavy loads on
their heads, presumably in baskets, sacks, or other containers. Female skeletons
often show pathologies of the lumbar vertebrae, toes, and leg indicating they
spent long hours working while kneeling, possibly grinding seeds on stone
querns. Terminal Pleistocene and Early Holocene human teeth show a marked
increase in dental abrasion and dental caries (severe cavities). The first probably
reflects increased inclusion of grit from stone seed-grinding tools into food.
The second may result from increased carbohydrate consumption.

Terminal Pleistocene and Early Holocene settlement patterns differ in ways
that point to increased residential sedentism and larger populations. The largest
Terminal Pleistocene sites amount to little more than a few acres. Some Early
Holocene ones cover dozens of acres or more (Simmons 2007: 178). This size
difference suggests a shift from maximum on-site populations from dozens of
individuals to hundreds, or even thousands. Larger sites from both periods are
near stable water sources, such as lakes, rivers, and springs. The largest Early
Holocene sites occur on alluvial fans and other soils suitable for cereal
cultivation.

Terminal Pleistocene houses and other architecture are mostly freestanding
round or oval structures some of whose walls have stone footings. Such dwellings resemble those of many residentially mobile ethnographic hunter-
gatherers and pastoralists (Oliver 1987). Hunter-gatherers often solve social
conflicts by "voting with their feet," that is to say, by relocating their residences
within a site or by moving from one habitation site to another. Building light

freestanding structures allows them to do this at relatively low cost. At the very least, doing so minimizes the energetic loss of abandoning an existing dwelling.

Early Holocene architectural evidence points to increased residential sedentism, albeit with considerable geographic and chronological variability. Early Holocene houses are larger, rectangular, and feature stone foundations and plaster floors. Having rectangular walls makes it relatively easy to expand a household by using a standing wall as part of a new, contiguous room. Shared walls and courtyards link many rectangular Early Holocene structures to one another. Moving such a connected house is, for all intents and purposes, impossible. By making relocation costly, this architectural shift further suggests changes in the ways Early Holocene humans dealt with social conflict (i.e., "voting with your fists," or, perhaps, actually voting).

Terminal Pleistocene and Early Holocene periods also preserve contrasting evidence for plant and animal domestication and for correlated changes in human diet breadth (Simmons 2007, Twiss 2007, Belfer-Cohen and Goring-Morris 2011, Zeder 2011). Levantine humans had domesticated wolves (dogs), which they probably kept as hunting aids in the same way as many recent hunter-gatherers do (Shipman 2015). Little other evidence for food-animal domestication appears in Terminal Pleistocene contexts. Carbonized plant remains suggest occasional intensified collection of wild plants, especially fruits/nuts, cereal grasses, and legumes (peas, lentils, vetch). Early Holocene sites, in contrast, preserve evidence for domesticated sheep, goats, cattle, and (arguably) pigs, and for extensive planting of domesticated cereal grasses and legumes, as well as for cultivation of grapes and dates (Twiss 2007). Early Holocene faunal remains include "commensal" animals that thrive in proximity to human settlement, such as cats, mice, rats, pigeons/doves, and sparrows (Tchernov 1997).

Levantine Terminal Pleistocene/Early Holocene Stone Tools

For such a small region, the East Mediterranean Levant boasts a rich and varied Terminal Pleistocene/Early Holocene lithic record (Shea 2013b) (Figures 8.3 and 8.4). Table 8.2 summarizes the lithic evidence for a representative sample of Levantine Terminal Pleistocene and Early Holocene assemblages.

Most of the differences between Terminal Pleistocene and Early Holocene lithic assemblages involve variation in retouched pieces, elongated bifacial cores, blade cores, abraded-edge tools, and groundstone tools.

Scrapers/notches/denticulates, backed/truncated pieces, and burins occur in all lithic assemblages, but microliths are less common in Early Holocene contexts. Awls are the most common kind of points in Terminal Pleistocene assemblages, and these appear in a wide range of single, multiple, and elongated forms. Tanged pieces vary widely in size. Invasive retouch makes some tanged

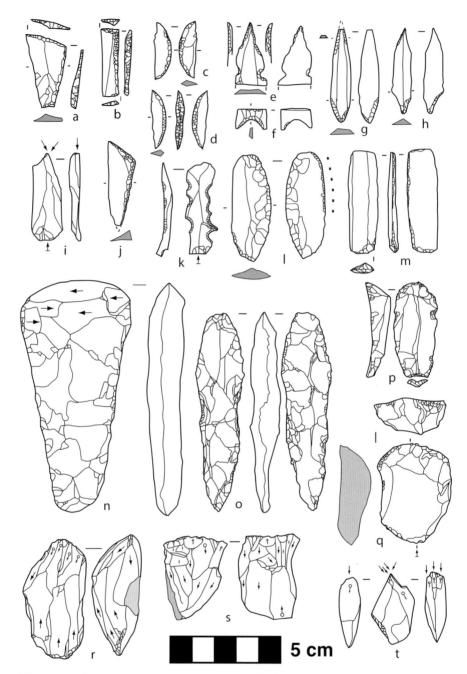

Figure 8.3 Representative Levantine Terminal Pleistocene stone tools. a–d. micro-liths, e, g–h. points, f. truncated piece, i. burin, j. backed piece, k. multiple notch, l. bifacially backed piece with sickle polish, m. backed and truncated piece, n–o. celts, p–q. scrapers, r–t. platform cores. Sources: Various sites in Negev and Sinai (a–d, h), Abu Maadi I (g), Beidha (k, m), Lagama North VIII (j), Netiv Hagdud (e–f, l, n–o), Poleg 18M (r), Poleg 18MII (t), Rosh Horesha (i), Saaïda II (q), SMU D5 (p), Tabaqat Fahl (s). Figures adapted from Shea (2013b).

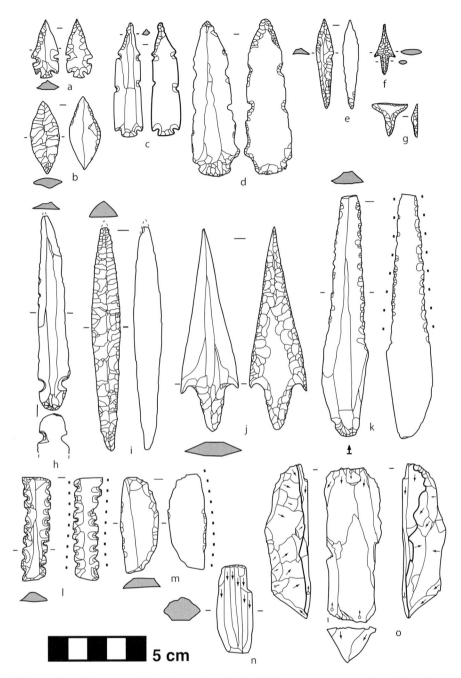

Figure 8.4 Representative Levantine Early Holocene stone tools. a–f. points, g. microlith or "transverse arrowhead," h–j. points/retouched blades, k. blade with sickle polish, l–m. sickle inserts, n–o. platform/blade cores. Sources: Abu Salem (a), Aswad I (c, k), Bouqras (n), Byblos (i, m), Givat Haparsa (f), Herzliya (g), Munhata (j), Nahal Hemar Cave (h), Nahal Issaron (e), Nahal Oren (d), Nizzanim (b), Sheikh Hassan (o), Tel 'Ali (l). Figures adapted from Shea (2013b).

TABLE 8.2. *Representation of Modes A–I in Levantine Terminal Pleistocene and Early Holocene assemblages*

Sample	A	B	C	D1	D2	D3	D4	D5	D6	D7	E1	E2	E3	E4	G1	G2	G3	H	I	Reference
Terminal Pleistocene																				
Ein Gev I–III	+	+	+	+	+	+	+	+		+					+	+	+		+	1
Kharaneh IV A–B			+	+	+	+	+									+	+			2
Ohalo II			+	+	+	+	r													3
Shunera XVI			+	+	+	+	+								+	+	+			4
Tor Hamar (J431) Level E			+	+	+	+	r	+								+	+			5
Wadi Jilat 6			+	+	+	+	+	+								+	+		+	6
Wadi Humeima (J406b)			+	+	+	+	r	+								+	+			5
Azariq IX			+	+	+	+	r									+	+		+	4
Azariq XVI			+	+	+	+	r									+	+			4
Kharaneh IV C–D			+	+	+	+	+									+	+			2
Lagama N VII			+	+	+	+										+	+		+	5
Mushabi V			+	+	+	+	r									+	+	+	+	5
Shunera II			+	+	+	+	r									+	+			4
Shunera IV			+	+	+	+	r	+								+	+			4
Shunera VII			+	+	+	+	r									+	+		+	4
SMU-D101C			+	+	+	+	+	+								+	+			7
SMU-D5		+	+	+	+	+	+	+		+					+	+	+			8
Wadi Jilat 22 B–E	+		+	+	+	+	+	+		+					+	+	+		+	6
Ain Mallaha	+	+	+	+	+	+	+	+			+			+	+	+	+		+	9
Baaz Rockshelter AH II–III	+		+	+	+	+	+	+	+						+	+	+		+	10
Hatoula L.3	+		+	+	+	+	+	+								+	+			11

(continued)

Site	Ref.
Hayonim Cave Level B	12
Jericho Natufian	13
Mureybit, Phases I–II	14
Rosh Horesha	15
Rosh Zin	16
Wadi Hammeh 27	17
Wadi Judayid (J2)	5
Abu Hureyra 1	18
Early Holocene	
Abu Salem (SMU-G12)	19
Salibiya I	20
Dhra	21
Gilgal I	22
Hatoula L.2 PPN	11
Iraq ed-Dubb	23
Jericho early / PPNA	13
Jericho PPNA	13
Netiv Hagdud	24
Salibiya IX	24
Wadi Feinan 16	25
Byblos	26
Mureybit, Phases III–IV	27
Abu Ghosh	28
Ain Ghazal	29
Basta Area B	30
Beidha I–VI	31

(continued)

TABLE 8.2. *(continued)*

Sample	A	B	C	D1	D2	D3	D4	D5	D6	D7	E1	E2	E3	E4	G1	G2	G3	H	I	Reference
Jericho PPNB	+		+	+	+		+	+			+		+	+	+			+	+	13
Kfar Hahoresh	+	+	+	+	+	+	+	+	+		+	+		+	+	+		+	+	32
Nahal Hemar					+			+	+						+	+			+	33
Nahal Issaron			+	+			+	+	+			+		+	+	+			+	34
Tel 'Ali	+		+	+	+		+	+	+			+	+	+	+	+			+	35
Ain Rahub	+	+	+	+	+		+	+	+	+	+		+	+	+	+	+			36
Ashkelon	+	+	+	+	+	+	+	+	+	+				+	+	+		+	+	37
Jericho PN	+		+	+	+		+	+	+			+	+	+	+			+	+	13
Munhata Levels 2–6	+	+	+	+	+		+	+	+	+	+	+		+	+	+		+	+	38
Sha'ar Hagolan	+	+	+	+	+		+	+	+	+				+	+	+	+	+	+	39
Umm Meshrat I	+	+	+	+	+		+	+	+					+	+		+	+	+	40

KEY: Column Headings: A. Anvil percussion, B. Bipolar core reduction, C. Pebble core reduction, D1. Scraper retouch, D2. Macrolithic backing/truncation, D3. Microlithic backing/truncation, D4. Burination, D5. Convergent distal retouch, D6. Concave proximal retouch, D7. Flake core reduction, E1. Long core-tool production, E2. Thinned biface production, E3. Tanged biface production, E4. Celt production, G1. Platform core reduction, G2. Blade core reduction, G3. Microblade core reduction, H. Abraded-edge tool reduction, I. Groundstone tool production. Symbols: + = present, r = reported as "rare," ? = report ambiguous.

References: 1. Bar-Yosef (1970), 2. Maher et al. (2014), 3. Nadel (2002), 4. Goring-Morris (1987), 5. Henry (1995), 6. Byrd and Garrard (1992), 7. Simmons (1977), 8. Marks (1976), 9. Valla et al. (2007), 10. Barth (2006), 11. Lechevallier and Ronen (1994), 12. Bar-Yosef and Goren (1973), 13. Crowfoot-Payne (1983) and Dorrell (1983), 14. Ibáñez (2008), 15. Marks and Larson (1977), 16. Henry (1976), 17. Edwards (2012), 18. Moore et al. (2000), 19. Scott (1977), 20. Belfer-Cohen and Grossman (1997), 21. Finlayson, Kuijt, and Goodale (2002), 22. Bar-Yosef, Goring-Morris, and Gopher (2010), 23. Kuijt and Goodale (2006), 24. Bar-Yosef and Gopher (1997), 25. Finlayson and Mithen (2007), 26. Cauvin (1968), 27. Ibáñez (2008), 28. Khalayla and Marder (2003), 29. Rollefson, Simmons, and Kafafi (1992), 30. Gebel et al. (1998), 31. Mortensen (1970), 32. Goring-Morris et al. (1995), 33. Bar-Yosef and Alon (1988), 34. Gopher, Goring-Morris, and Gordon (1994), 35. Garfinkel (1994), 36. Muheisen et al. (1988), 37. Garfinkel and Dag (2008), 38. Gopher (1989), 39. Garfinkel (2002), 40. Cropper (2006).

pieces grade into tanged bifaces, but in most cases residual flake dorsal and ventral surfaces show these tools originated as flakes or blades.

Elongated bifaces take many forms. Long core-tools are often described as "picks." Thinned bifaces, tanged bifaces, and celts occur in many assemblages, though more so in Early Holocene than in Terminal Pleistocene ones.

Blade cores vary widely among Levantine assemblages. Elongated "naviform" (nave/boat-shaped) and "bullet-shaped" blade cores (Figure 8.4 n and o, respectively) show evidence of stereotyped blade core reduction strategies, and, by implication, possible evidence for craft specialization (Quintero 2011).

Abraded-edge tools and groundstone tools include celts and various forms of seed-grinding equipment, stone vessels, and other perforated objects, such as beads (Wright 1991, 1992, 1993, 1994, Bar-Yosef Mayer 2013) (Figure 8.5).

Cutting edges shaped by abrasion occur on both flaked and groundstone celts. Flaked stone celts are usually made of flint and retain evidence of having been shaped by knapping. Groundstone celts are also made of basalt and other tough volcanic rocks. Both flaked and groundstone celts vary widely in size, shape, and in cross-section, and they grade into one another. Some groundstone celts have grooves carved about their circumference perpendicular to their long axis, presumably as aids to hafting. Massive celts weighing up to a kilogram or more were probably used for felling trees and for heavy-duty tasks. Smaller celts, "chisels" and so-called "*herminettes*" (woodworking adzes) appear to have been used for more precise carpentry.

Mortars, pestles, querns, and handstones are the most common forms of groundstone tools. Mortars are stones and bedrock exposures into which a relatively cone-shaped depression has been excavated. Pestles are elongated stones with use-related percussion damage at one or both ends and abrasive wear along their sides. Querns are flat stones on which abrasion has created a relatively wide and shallow concavity. Handstones feature at least one flat or moderately convex use-abraded surface. Mortars and querns are usually made of local rocks and thus vary widely, while pestles and handstones are often made of harder materials, such as basalt. These artifacts were used together (mortars with pestles, querns with handstones) to pulverize seeds, and probably other substances as well, such as mineral pigments. Some querns have small circular depressions carved in them, possibly from reuse as mortars or for grinding using rotary motion.

Stone vessels range from simple hollowed-out hemispheres to pieces with complex pedestals. Many vessels were made from locally available vesicular basalt and limestone, but some were made of alabaster or steatite procured from montane sources and exported to sites at lower elevations. Some of these vessels are damaged from exposure to fire. Some such thermal damage may indicate their use as cooking vessels, while other damage may be accidental. Incised decorations and surface polishing suggest some vessels had symbolic functions.

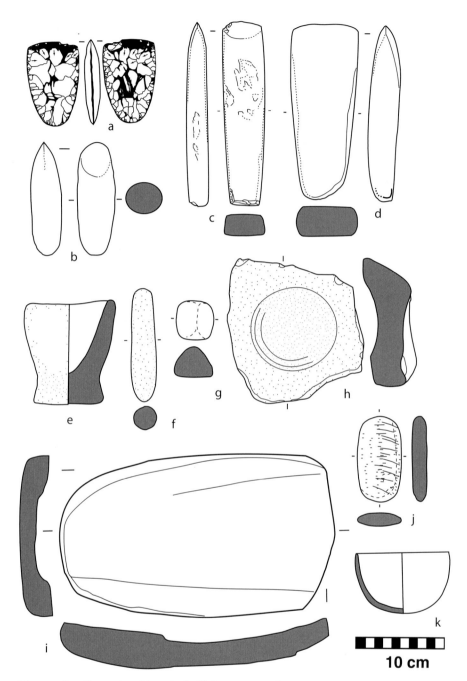

Figure 8.5 Levantine Terminal Pleistocene/Early Holocene groundstone tools. a. abraded-edge flaked stone celt, b–d. groundstone celts, e. mortar, f. pestle, g. rotary handstone, h. rotary quern, i. bidirectional quern, j. bidirectional handstone, k. stone vessel. Sources: Beidha (b), Bouqras (c–d, k), Jayroud 3 (h), Mureybit (i), Netiv Hagdud (g, j), Wadi Hammeh 27 (e–f), Yiftahel (a). Figures adapted from Shea (2013b).

Perforated objects include palettes (flat pieces used to grind pigments or other materials), loom weights, stone beads, pendants, and maces.

RESIDENTIAL SEDENTISM IN THE LEVANT: PREDICTIONS EVALUATED

Table 8.3 summarizes contrasts between Terminal Pleistocene/Early Holocene periods in terms of Modes A–I. Comparing Levantine Terminal Pleistocene and Early Holocene assemblages to one another statistically is far from straightforward. Published descriptions of these assemblages vary widely in how and whether they report hammerstones, bipolar cores, pebble cores (Modes A–C), and cores-on-flakes (Submode D7), but there is no clear pattern in the published evidence. Bifacial hierarchical cores (Mode F) are either absent or classified in such a way that it is difficult to tell if they are present. Thinned bifaces (Submode E2) and edge-abraded tools (Mode H) are only present in the Early Holocene sample. A comparison of these samples omitting these artifact categories and utilizing Submodes D1–D6, E1, E3–E4, G1–G3 and Mode I reveals statistically significant differences (p<.01, chi-square = 47.6 at 12 degrees of freedom).

TABLE 8.3. *Occurrence of Modes A–I among Levantine Terminal Pleistocene and Early Holocene lithic assemblages*

Modes and submodes	Terminal Pleistocene (n = 38)	Early Holocene (n = 29)
A. Anvil percussion	8	18
B. Bipolar core reduction	5	12
C. Pebble core reduction	32	23
D1. Orthogonal retouch	38	28
D2. Macrolithic backing/truncation	38	28
D2. Microlithic backing/truncation	37	13
D4. Burination	35	25
D5. Convergent distal retouch	27	28
D6. Concave proximal retouch	2	23
D7. Flake core reduction	7	14
E1. Long core-tool production	7	11
E2. Thinned biface production	0	5
E3. Tanged biface production	1	5
E4. Celt production	6	21
G1. Platform core reduction	14	20
G2. Blade core reduction	30	25
G3. Microblade core reduction	31	14
H. Abraded-edge tool production	0	15
I. Groundstone tool production	17	24

Matches/Mismatches

The Early Holocene stone tool evidence contrasts with the Terminal Pleistocene evidence in all of the predicted ways.

Non-hierarchical Core Technology: All Levantine Terminal Pleistocene/Early Holocene lithic assemblages feature some hierarchical cores, mostly blade/bladelet cores. However, and where one can tell from published descriptions, non-hierarchical cores usually outnumber hierarchical cores in Early Holocene lithic assemblages (Nishiaki 2000, Shea 2013b: 224). Though frequently selected for illustration, impressively elongated naviform and bullet-shaped blade cores are actually relatively rare in most Early Holocene assemblages (Abbès 2003, Quintero 2011).

Seed-pulverizing Technology: Groundstone seed-pulverizing implements appear in most assemblages. Rare in Late Pleistocene contexts prior to 24 Ka, they become more common in Early Holocene times (Table 8.4). The numbers of Terminal Pleistocene and Early Holocene sites at which various groundstone tools occur differ from one another at a high level of statistical significance (chi-square = 50.6, at 8 degrees of freedom, p<.01). Between Terminal Pleistocene and Early Holocene periods, the numbers of assemblages preserving pestles and mortars (including bedrock mortars) decrease, while those preserving querns and handstones increase. Changes in the actual numbers and upper size ranges of the artifacts themselves parallel these trends (Shea 2013b: 271).

Complex Projectile Technology: Archery experiments and microwear analysis suggest Terminal Pleistocene backed/truncated bladelets and microliths were attached as barbs on spearthrower darts (Yaroshevich et al. 2010)

TABLE 8.4. *Numbers of Levantine Terminal Pleistocene and Early Holocene assemblages in which various kinds of groundstone tools occur*

Artifact type	Terminal Pleistocene (n = 64)		Early Holocene (n = 130)	
	n	%	n	%
Quern	17	27	68	52
Handstone	28	44	84	65
Mortar	39	61	38	29
Bedrock mortar	16	25	15	12
Pestle	29	45	42	32
Stone vessel	20	31	60	46
Grooved stone	14	22	41	32
Perforated stone	6	9	34	26
Celt	2	3	39	30

Sources: Wright (1993: Tables 3–5, 1994: Tables 4–9)

(Figure 8.6). Assemblages dating near the end of this period feature short triangular pieces and "crescents" that were mounted orthogonally (i.e., with the unretouched edge aligned transversely or diagonally with the weapon shaft) (e.g., Figure 8.6a–b, and e–d). Such arrangements are rare among ethnographic

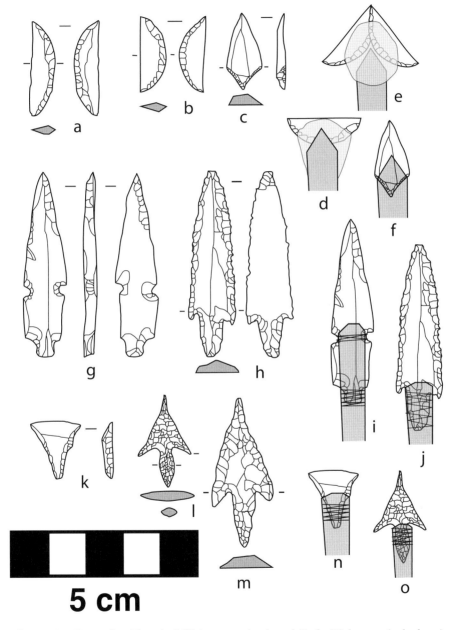

Figure 8.6 Levantine Terminal Pleistocene (a–c) and Early Holocene (g–h, k–m) lithic projectile armatures with conjectural hafting arrangements (e–f, i–j, n–o). Sources: Abu Salem (c), Beidha (g), El Wad Cave (a–b), Givat Haparsa (l), Herzliya (k), Jericho (h), Nahal Seker 81-A (m). Figures adapted from Shea (2013b).

spearthrower dart tips but common among ethnographic and archaeological arrows. Early Holocene assemblages contain a wide range of pointed artifacts whose size, shape, residues, and wear patterns indicate they were used as arrowheads (Gopher 1994). Backed/truncated bladelets and microliths of the sort thought to have been spearthrower dart barbs rarely appear in Early Holocene lithic assemblages, except near the end of the Early Holocene. Their reappearance around 6.5–8.5 Ka coincides with a shift toward smaller tanged points as well. Both developments may indicate a shift from longer bows with heavier arrows to shorter and lighter weapons.

Lithic Anti-personnel Weapons: Microliths embedded in human skeletons confirm that the bow/arrow was in use in the Levant during Terminal Pleistocene times (Bocquentin and Bar-Yosef 2004). Pointed stone tools from Early Holocene contexts have elongated tangs and blades, deep lateral notches, and denticulated edges, features that enhance anti-personnel weapon performance (e.g., Figure 8.6 g–j, l–m, and o). Stone points with these features rarely occur in Terminal Pleistocene assemblages.

Abraded-edge Woodworking Tools/Celts: Celts with abraded working edges are rare in Terminal Pleistocene assemblages, but they become common in Early Holocene ones, particularly at sites located near the Mediterranean Coast (Barkai 2005) (see also Table 8.4). Levantine archaeologists distinguish celts whose edges were used to cut longitudinally (axes) from those used to cut orthogonally (adzes), and those propelled by percussion (chisels) (Figure 8.7). Axes are most common in Terminal Pleistocene assemblages, but adzes are present as well. Adzes and chisels begin to eclipse axes in Early Holocene times. These changes in artifact frequencies may reflect a shift from woodworking focused on clearing forest and cutting firewood to more precise carpentry practices associated with large-scale architecture and, presumably, increasingly scarce lumber (Barkai 2011).

Functionally Specialized Tools: Reflecting conventions of the Industrial Model, Levantine archaeologists give names to some artifact-types implying very specific functions, such as "arrowhead," "knife," and "chisel." Surprisingly little evidence justifies taking these names at face value. Design changes in sickle inserts, perforators, and seed-grinding equipment between Terminal Pleistocene and Early Holocene periods, on the other hand, are congruent with increased functional specialization (Figure 8.8).

"Sickle inserts" include unretouched flakes and blades, backed/truncated pieces, bifacially retouched pieces, and other artifacts. Their defining characteristic is that one or both of their lateral edges exhibit brilliantly reflective "sickle polish" from cutting silica-rich grasses (Unger-Hamilton 1983). Sickle inserts from Terminal Pleistocene assemblages appear in a wide range of sizes and shapes (Cauvin 1983, Gopher, Barkai, and Asaf 2001). Later Early

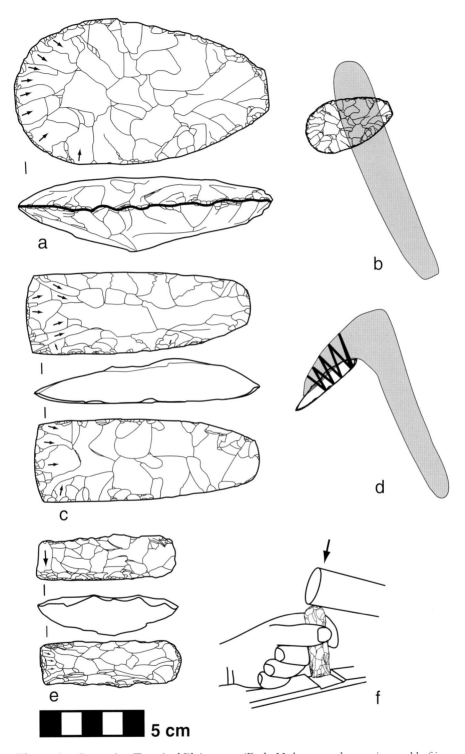

Figure 8.7 Levantine Terminal Pleistocene/Early Holocene celts, conjectural hafting of axes, adzes, and use of chisel. Scale applies to a, c, e only. Sources: Abu Ghosh (a), Byblos (c), Nahal Zehora I (e). Figures adapted from Shea (2013b).

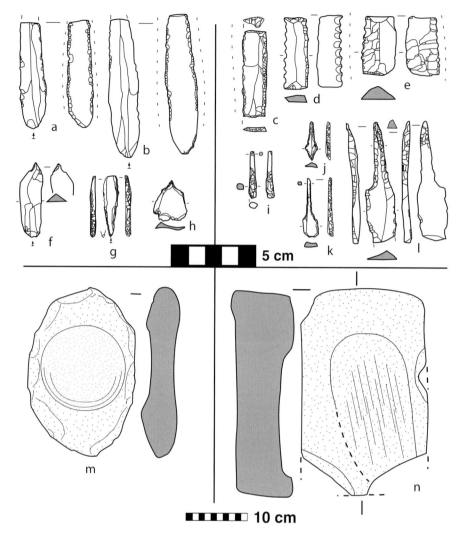

Figure 8.8 Functional specialization among sickle inserts (a–e), perforators (f–l), and seed-grinding equipment (m–n). Artifacts to the left of the vertical line are from Terminal Pleistocene assemblages, those to the right are from Early Holocene ones. Note differences in scale above and below horizontal line. Sources: Ain Ghazal (a–b), Byblos (d), Jayroud (m), Mezraa Teleilat (i–k), Nahal Issaron (l), Netiv Hagdud (n), Qaatif (c), Rosh Zin (g), Saaïde II (h), Tabaqat Fahl (f), and Tel 'Ali (e). Figures adapted from Shea (2013b).

Holocene sickle inserts are shorter and less morphologically variable, suggesting they were employed in more stereotyped ways.

Terminal Pleistocene perforators often feature single or multiple projections on flakes of all sizes and shapes. Early Holocene perforators are increasingly elongated and singular (i.e., one projection per artifact). Some of these elongated perforators might have been weapon tips or knives, but their narrowness makes them vulnerable to bending stress and breakage in such uses. Perforators from later Early Holocene assemblages include cylindrical "drill bits" that preserve heavy abrasive wear from high-speed rotary drilling. Such heavy wear precludes their use for other cutting tasks.

Among seed-pulverizing tools used by ethnographic humans (Kraybill 1977), mortars/pestles are general-purpose tools used with a wide range of movements to crush seeds, nuts, other vegetal matter, and mineral pigments. Querns and handstones are specialized tools mostly used with a narrower range of motions to process small hard seeds. Mortars and pestles become much less common in Early Holocene contexts than in Terminal Pleistocene ones, while querns and handstones become larger and more common. This shift from mortars/pestles to querns/handstones is also consistent with functional specialization (Wright 1991).

Complex and Contingent Patterns of Artifact Design Variation: Both Terminal Pleistocene and Early Holocene lithic records preserve contrasting patterns of lithic design variability. During all but the very final phases of the Terminal Pleistocene, essentially the same rectangular, trapezoidal, and crescent-shaped microliths occur throughout the entire Levant and beyond (Bar-Yosef 1987). There are some minor differences in backing techniques and artifact sizes, but the overall picture of Terminal Pleistocene lithic variation is regional homogeneity. Early Holocene lithic evidence exhibits more complex, spatially and temporally contingent variation. There are both sub-regional patterns of artifact variation as well as correlated turnovers in artifact designs among multiple lines of evidence, such as in ceramics, architecture, personal adornments, and mortuary practices. Perhaps because they are small artifacts used in tasks with intrinsically high breakage/edge-attrition rates, arrowheads and sickle inserts have particularly complex patterns of variability (Gopher 1994, Shea 2013b). Some arrowhead designs occur throughout the Levant, but there are also arrowhead types with sub-regional distributions. Certain arrowhead types are found in the northern Levant but not in the south, and *vice versa*. Arrowhead designs also exhibit patterned changes through time. Around 9.5 Ka, larger elongated and tanged points replace small triangular and side-notched points. Smaller points replace larger ones beginning around 8.3 Ka.

These changes in arrowheads and sickle inserts are correlated with changes in religious iconography, mortuary practices, architecture, exchange networks, ceramics, and personal adornments. Traditional archaeological systematics recognizes the patterned nature of these changes by dividing the Early Holocene into at least two chronological phases, the "Aceramic" and "Ceramic" Neolithic, each of which subsume a variety of named stone tool industries (Gopher and Gophna 1993, Kozlowski and Aurenche 2005). (In older literature, these periods are known as "Pre-Pottery" and "Pottery" Neolithic.)

Lithic Overdesign: Figure 8.9 shows examples of "simple" and "overdesigned" stone artifacts from the Terminal Pleistocene/Early Holocene

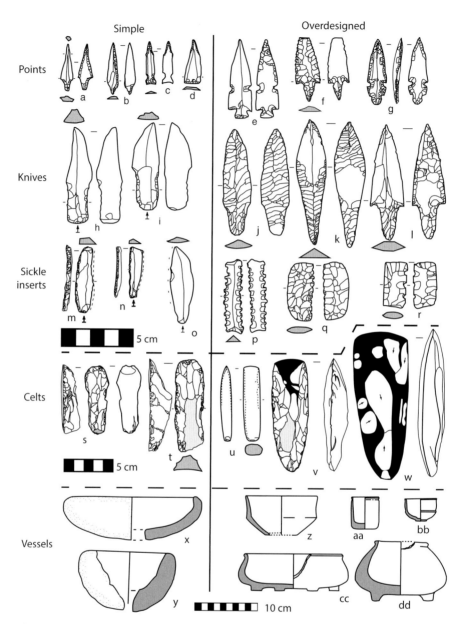

Figure 8.9 "Simple" and "overdesigned" stone points (a–g), knives (h–l), sickle inserts (m–r), celts (s-w), and vessels (x–dd) from the Terminal Pleistocene/Early Holocene Levant. Artifacts in the left column are from Terminal Pleistocene contexts, those to the right from Early Holocene ones. Note differences in scale between rows separated by the dashed lines. Sources: Abu Hureyra (s), Abu Salem (b, m–n), Beidha (g), Bouqras (u, z–dd), Byblos (j–k, v–w), Givat Haesev (y), Mureybit (h–i, t), Munhata (l), Nahal Oren (e), Nahal Seker 81-A (f), Netiv Hagdud (a, c–d, o), Neveh David (x), Nizzanim (q–r), and Sha'ar Hagolan (p). Figures adapted from Shea (2013b).

Levant. Evidence for lithic overdesign is relatively uncommon in Terminal Pleistocene assemblages. The clearest examples of such evidence are rare artifacts made of obsidian. Analysis of these obsidian artifacts' chemical composition links them to sources hundreds of kilometers north of the Levant in Anatolia (modern-day Turkey and Iraqi Kurdistan) (Cann, Dixon, and Renfrew 1969). During Terminal Pleistocene times, Levantine assemblages preserve negligible quantities of obsidian, but these quantities increase markedly during the Early Holocene. Levantine knappers did not use obsidian to make morphologically distinct artifacts. Rather, they made small blades and tanged points essentially identical to those made of flint. This suggests that obsidian was procured at least as much for its potential display value as for any material-specific functional or mechanical quality.

Levantine tanged points (variously described as projectile points, arrowheads, spear points, and daggers) show evidence of overdesign in extensive pressure flaking. These artifacts are relatively uncommon in Terminal Pleistocene assemblages but abundant in Early Holocene ones. Invasive pressure flaking does not improve a tool's piercing or cutting power in obvious ways (quite the opposite, actually), but it is a clear advertisement of effort above and beyond the minimum necessary to create a piercing/cutting implement.

During use, all but sickle inserts' immediate cutting edge was embedded in mastic. This would seem to make sickle inserts an unlikely medium for lithic overdesign. Nevertheless, they exhibit features consistent with lithic overdesign. Terminal Pleistocene sickle inserts are relatively simple, backed pieces or blades, occasionally featuring some basal modification for hafting (Cauvin 1983). Early Holocene sickle inserts show extensive edge modification, including pressure flaking, and denticulation.

Celts show a similar pattern to sickle blades. Terminal Pleistocene flaked stone celts were rarely abraded, and, when so, usually abraded only on their cutting edge (Barkai 2005). Early Holocene celts were often polished and abraded over extensive areas of their surface to the point that production-related flake scars have been obliterated. Such extensive abrasion does not improve tool function, but it does create a bright and visually striking reflective polish.

Stone vessels are overdesigned as well (Wright 1991). Vessels from Terminal Pleistocene contexts are either seed-pulverizing equipment (mortars) or relatively small and shallow bowls. Larger vessels, particularly flat ones (dishes and platters) that could effectively display food or other items, are more common in Early Holocene contexts. Many Early Holocene stone vessels have basal elaborations (legs, pedestals) and exterior decorative carvings. They are also more often made of exotic alabaster and steatite. That these artifacts persist alongside pottery cooking vessels suggests they retained a significant symbolic function even as ceramic alternatives became available. Because stone vessels are less fragile than earthenware, symbolic messages encoded in their designs could have been broadcast for generations.

The Levantine lithic evidence supports the predicted consequences for increased residential sedentism, but how broadly can we extrapolate these findings? As we saw in Chapter 7, humans fine-tune their technology to suit novel ecogeographic circumstances. A point-by-point comparison of the Levantine evidence with that from other regions will inevitably reveal differences. Regionally variable roles for agriculture and pastoralism further complicate such comparisons as well. There are, however, at least two other regions in which residential sedentism became established prior to agriculture: Japan (Habu 2004), and the Pacific Coast of North America (Ames 2003). Similar patterns to those seen in the Levant appear alongside evidence for residential sedentism in both these regions.

Cause vs. Consequence?

Cause and consequence can be difficult to disentangle in the lithic evidence correlated with increased sedentism. For example, reduced residential mobility might have led to more substantial architecture and to improvements in celt design. Alternatively, improved celt design may have allowed the construction of more substantial architecture. Textbook accounts portray Terminal Pleistocene Levantine humans who had depleted local plant food resources as having to rely on backup foods, such as cereal grasses. This is thought to have led them to devise larger and more efficient seed-pulverizing tools to process cereal grasses in bulk. Yet, the reverse might also be true. Mortars designed to recover calories in bulk from formerly marginal-value cereal grasses might have decreased incentives for residential mobility. The ecological niche-stabilizing effects of using bows and arrows can also be cast as either cause for or consequence of sedentism. Lithic overdesign might reflect a symbolic message transmission "arms race" among growing communities. Alternatively, it might signal the emergence of stable, symbolically mediated alliance networks that encouraged people to aggregate and reside together for longer periods. In the nineteenth- and early twentieth-century American West, pinning a badge onto someone and calling them "Sheriff" was a first step in turning lawless frontier settlements into towns.

Contrasts with Traditional Approaches

Technological versatility has served our species well, but it also makes it difficult for archaeologists to infer specific details of prehistoric subsistence strategies from occurrences of particular artifacts. Traditional archaeological accounts of the Terminal Pleistocene/Early Holocene lithic evidence from the East Mediterranean Levant, and similar developments elsewhere, generally view changes in stone tool technology as consequences of the origins of food production, specifically cereal agriculture and pastoralism. There are reasons to be cautious about such interpretations. Just as modern-day homeowners' efforts to fix problems with tools and materials at hand ("hacks") precede trips to the hardware store, the first farmer/herders in the Levant probably tried to solve problems associated with farming and herding with pre-existing hunting and gathering technology. Only later, when those solutions began to fail would one expect selective pressure to push them into devising wholly new technological solutions tailored to food production's novel challenges. It should come as no surprise that in the Levant and elsewhere humans were cultivating plants and herding animals for hundreds or even thousands of years before the lithic archaeological record shows distinctive evidence for agriculture and/or pastoralism (Snir et al. 2015).

That stone tools like those associated with early food production in the Levant are known from pre-agricultural contexts and found among non-agricultural ethnographic humans further supports this hypothesis. Edge-polished axes, for example, were widespread in Australia for tens of thousands of years before Europeans brought agriculture to that continent. In the Americas, bifacially flaked projectile points similar in size and shape to those found in Levantine Early Holocene contexts occur in the portable toolkits of mobile ethnographic hunter-gatherers from the Arctic Circle to the southernmost tip of South America. Stone seed-grinding tools are found in pre-agricultural and non-agricultural contexts worldwide. Even the stone tools most closely linked with agriculture in the Early Holocene Levant, sickle inserts, are little more than backed, truncated, and denticulated pieces like those hominins have been making since Plio-Pleistocene times. As with so many other evolutionary phenomena, what at first glance appear to be "Neolithic novelties" turn out to be exaptations, older technological strategies repurposed to new challenges, a quintessential characteristic of human behavioral variability.

Box 7 *Extreme Flintknapping*

Many stone tool assemblages preserve evidence for lithic overdesign involving "extreme flintknapping," vast expenditures of time and energy without
any clear mechanical functional benefit. Pleistocene examples of these artifacts
are often conspicuously enlarged, symmetrical and elongated (Figure 8.10).

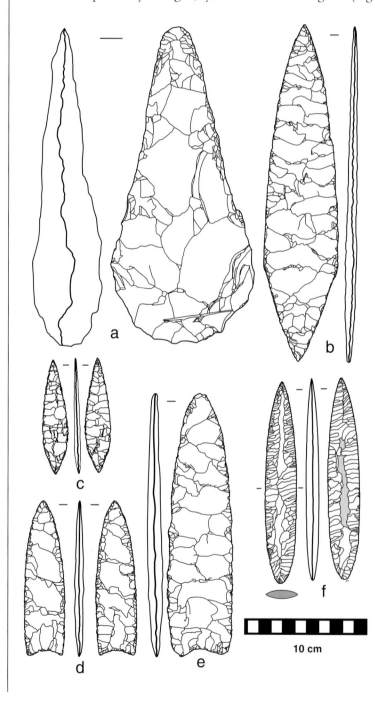

Caption for Figure 8.10   (cont.)

Figure 8.10 Prehistoric examples of extreme flintknapping: a. Middle-
Late Pleistocene long core-tool from Mantes, France, b–c. large thinned bifaces from
Le Volgü and Les Jeans Blancs, France, d–e. fluted point and thinned biface from the
Fenn Cache, western United States, f. thinned biface with parallel-pressure flaking scars
from Byblos, Lebanon. Redrawn after Bordes (1961), Smith (1966), Cauvin (1968),
Frison and Bradley (1999).

Box 7 (*Cont.*)

Most long core-tools are 10–20 cm in length with irregular, curving
edges. Still, some are so large and so symmetrical (Figure 8.10a) that it is
difficult to avoid concluding that there was a symbolic motive for their
design.

Most of the thinned bifaces found in European Later Pleistocene lithic
assemblages are relatively small artifacts less than 10 cm long (Figure 8.10c).
At the cave site of Le Volgü (France), however, excavators working in 1874
uncovered a cache of fourteen very large foliate bifaces (Smith 1966)
(Figure 8.10b). Other caches have been found at additional sites of equivalent
antiquity.

Elongated basally thinned bifaces occur in North America at sites dating
to between 10 and 12 Ka (Meltzer 2009). Most of these "fluted points"
artifacts are less than 10 cm long (Figure 8.10d). Wear patterns suggest use as
spear points. However, nearly every region preserves fluted points far too
long and thin to have been effective projectile points. The Fenn Cache from
the western United States preserves an exceptional sample of these artifacts
(Frison and Bradley 1999) (Figure 8.10e).

Elongated bifaces whose surfaces are covered by parallel pressure-flaking
scars to no obvious functional or mechanical benefit occur in many
Levantine Holocene contexts (Shea 2013b) (Figure 8.10f). Egyptian
Predynastic "ripple-flaked" knives also show such labor-intensive
overdesign (Kelterborn 1984).

Some of these artifacts, such as the long core-tools, may reflect "costly
signaling" (Kohn and Mithen 1999, but see Nowell 2009). Yet, the cache
contexts from which the Volgü and Fenn examples were found suggest they
were involved in more complex patterns of artifact curation (Aubry et al.
2003, Meltzer 2009).

Overdesigned artifacts are often interpreted as evidence for prehistoric
craft specialists. While this hypothesis seems plausible for recent contexts
preserving other evidence for systematic division of labor, there are reasons
to be skeptical about this hypothesis' validity for older contexts. Few

Box 7 (*Cont.*)

modern-day craft/hobby knappers are actually professional craft specialists. They flintknap a lot, but this is rarely their principal source of income. And yet many of them can reproduce the artifacts shown in Figure 8.10 (Whittaker 2004). Doing so is not easy, but, demonstrably, it can be done. Secondly, these "extreme" artifacts are far less common in the archaeological record than their appearance in archaeology textbooks suggests. This scarcity contrasts with gunflints, which are actual products of Industrial Era craft specialist stone tool production. These simple backed/truncated pieces can be found at seventeenth- to nineteenth-century sites worldwide.

One of the common mistakes traditional approaches to the lithic evidence make in dealing with products of "extreme flintknapping" is viewing them in isolation. These artifacts are often shown separately from the other stone tools with which they occur in archaeological contexts. This makes it difficult to tell whether the extreme nature of their designs reflects a systemic increase in tool making effort across-the-board or a more narrowly focused activity. Archaeologists' habitual practice of depicting these rare artifacts as if they were both common and typical finds for one or another group of lithic assemblages creates the illusion that the "across-the-board " hypothesis is true, without actually testing other plausible alternative hypotheses.

CHAPTER 9

CONCLUSION

> The things you own end up owning you.
> Chuck Palahniuk (1996) *Fight Club*

We live in a world our ancestors built with stone tools. To maintain ourselves in that world, we now rely on metal, plastic, and electricity. These energetically expensive technologies "own" us in ways stone tools did not own earlier hominins. This chapter considers the evolutionary origins of our obligatory tool use. First, it summarizes the stone tool evidence for the origins of behavioral differences between hominins and non-human primates. Next, it proposes a model for strategic changes in how ancestral hominins made and used stone tools. Finally, it discusses how comparative analytical approaches and strategic perspectives on lithic technology, such as those used in this book, improve our understanding of human evolution.

OVERVIEW

A comparative analytical approach to the stone tool evidence allowed twenty-five predictions about how the lithic record should have changed along with the evolution of distinctive qualities of human behavior. The stone tool evidence supports twenty-two of the twenty-five predictions (see Table 9.1). Two of the three mismatches involve mixed or equivocal results, rather than outright contradictions.

The oldest stone cutting tools appear in African Plio-Pleistocene contexts (1.7–3.5 Ma). They occur together with hominin fossils that differ from fossils of older hominins, apes, and monkeys in having reduced prognathism and relatively small incisors and canine teeth. Plio-Pleistocene hominins used stone cutting tools for pre-oral food processing and to make tools out of other materials, tasks for which non-human primates use their teeth and fingernails (Schick and Toth 1993). By knapping stone, Plio-Pleistocene hominins created artificial teeth and nails that allowed them to obtain nutrients from resources

TABLE 9.1. *Summary of predictions about stone tool variation.*

Predictions by chapter (time period)	Prediction met?
Ch. 4 Plio-Pleistocene Stone Cutting Tools (>1.7 Ma)	
4.1. Systematic production of small stone cutting tools	+
4.2. Stone cutting tools used for pre-oral food processing	+
4.3. Stone cutting tools used to manufacture tools out of other materials	+
Ch. 5 Early-Middle Pleistocene Logistical Mobility (0.3–1.7 Ma)	
5.1. Increases in raw material transportation distances	+
5.2. Tool designs that enhance portability and increase utility	+
5.3. Non-residential sites provisioned with stone cutting tools	+
5.4. Residential sites featuring stone tools	−
Ch. 6 Middle-Late Pleistocene Language and Symbolic Artifacts (50–300 Ka)	
6.1. Multiple simultaneous solutions to problems	+
6.2. Combinatory technology	+
6.3. Functional variability	+
6.4. "Quasi-linguistic" spatial and temporal variation	+
6.5. Symbolic design variation	m
Ch. 7 Late Pleistocene/Early Holocene Dispersal and Diaspora (9–50 Ka)	
7.1. Specialized hide-working tools, projectile armatures in cold habitats	+
7.2. Heavy-duty carpentry tools, particularly near rivers and coastlines	m
7.3. Patterned artifact style variation, especially among lithic weapon armatures	+
7.4. Differences in artifact designs between donor and recipient regions	+
7.5. Ecogeographically patterned differences between earlier and later stone tools	+
Ch. 8 Late Pleistocene/Early Holocene Residential Sedentism (6.5–24 Ka)	
8.1. Increased emphasis on non-hierarchical core reduction	+
8.2. Larger, more varied, and more substantially modified seed-pulverizing tools	+
8.3. Increased evidence for the use of the bow and arrow	+
8.4. Stone weapon tips designed for use as anti-personnel weapons	+
8.5. Abraded-edge woodworking tools/celts	+
8.6. Functionally specialized tools	+
8.7. Complex and contingent patterns of artifact design variation	+
8.8. Increased lithic artifact overdesign	+

Note: + = prediction matched by evidence, − = prediction mismatch with evidence, m = mixed or equivocal results.

non-human primates largely ignore, such as large mammal carcasses and plant underground storage organs. Doing this widened and stabilized their ecological niches. This strategy evidently worked well. By 1.7 Ma, the archaeological record for much of Africa and temperate-tropical Eurasia contains evidence of stone percussors, pebble cores, flakes, and other stone cutting tools.

The hominin fossil record and non-lithic archaeological evidence for Early-Middle Pleistocene times (0.3–1.7 Ma) preserve evidence for logistical mobility – for hominins systematically gathering and transporting tools, food, and other resources across the landscape for greater distances than non-human primates move such things. Novel features of the Early-Middle Pleistocene lithic evidence include core elongation/long core-tool production, bifacial hierarchical core reduction, and flake curation by retouch. Each of these activities increases not only potential tool utility but also incentives for transporting stone tools while foraging. As such, they seem to be strategic accommodations to logistical mobility. Lithic evidence for logistical mobility varies through time and space. Even at this early point in the evolution of the Genus *Homo*, ancestral hominins possessed derived capacities for behavioral variability different from those of living non-human primates.

Fossil and genetic evidence show the Middle-Late Pleistocene (50–300 Ka) as a crucial period for the origins of spoken language and communication assisted by symbolic artifacts. We will never know what Middle-Late Pleistocene hominins said, or how they phrased it, but we can see that their linguistic behaviors influenced lithic artifact design variability. Middle-Late Pleistocene stone tools show increasing typological variation among major technological strategies, as well as greater geographic and temporal patterning in stone tool design variation. This quasi-linguistic patterning coincides with growing evidence for the use of mineral pigments, personal adornments, mortuary practices, and other activities involving symbolic artifacts whose linguistic bases are beyond serious scientific dispute. The geographic and chronological scope of this patterning across the Middle-Late Pleistocene becomes more fine-grained in recent periods, but it is not clear to what degree this reflects an evolutionary trend in the relationship between technology and language, the winnowing away of older evidence by geological attrition, or other factors.

Humans evolved in Africa prior to 200 Ka, and they began dispersing to Eurasia shortly thereafter, reaching what is now Israel ca. 95–130 Ka. First appearances of *H. sapiens* in southern and eastern Asia prior to 50 Ka do not coincide with major shifts in the stone tool evidence. Later Pleistocene human dispersals do. Evidently these warmer, humid habitats did not challenge dispersing humans to quite the same degree as colder and more arid ones did. From an evolutionary standpoint, this is to be expected. Hominins are tropical primates. Stone tools dating to 9–50 Ka in Sahul, northern Eurasia, and the Americas contrast not only with the Middle-Late Pleistocene lithic evidence but also with one another, and in predictable ways. Dispersals to Sahul and northern Eurasia both evoke the production of abraded-edge tools, but otherwise these regions preserve contrasting patterns of lithic variability. Northern Eurasian stone tools show a high level of typological patterning through time and space that stone tools from Sahul do not. Early American tool makers brought with them toolkits similar to those found after 18–22 Ka in northern Eurasia. Some of the more distinctive components of northern Eurasian lithic technology, namely edge-abraded celts and prismatic blade/microblade core reduction, appear to have been abandoned as humans moved south into warmer American habitats. The lithic records for Sahul, northern Eurasia, and the Americas also preserve evidence for technological "fine-tuning." Over time, the stone tool evidence in each region diverges both from the earliest lithic evidence in that region and internally, along ecogeographically patterned axes of variation.

Humans became residentially sedentary in many parts of the world during Late Pleistocene and Early Holocene times (6.5–24 Ka). The East Mediterranean Levant preserves an especially detailed record for this process. Many of the changes in the stone tool evidence caused by increased residential sedentism in the Levant after 11 Ka involve increased production effort, or "design intensification." Hierarchical cores and microliths continued to be made and used as humans became more sedentary, but over time both declined relative to products of more "expedient" bipolar and non-hierarchical core reduction strategies. Among stone tools from Early Holocene village sites, blade cores and exotic obsidian were increasingly used to make elite goods, large, and/or flashy objects seemingly designed to broadcast messages about social status. Labor-intensive abraded-edge celts became more common, possibly in response to increased forest clearance, demands for firewood, and more substantial architecture. Groundstone tools grew larger and more ubiquitous, too. Pulverizing tools joined use-polished sickles and other evidence for subsistence strategies increasingly focused on seeds and nuts with high processing costs. Larger implements and systematic overdesign may reflect increases in "conspicuous consumption" or "costly signaling" among ever-larger populations of agricultural villages and towns.

Cumulative patterning is one of the most distinctive ways in which human behavior differs from that of living non-human primates (Tomasello 1999). Predictably, the stone tool evidence accompanying human evolution changes mainly by addition. New ways of making stone tools come and go at local and regional scales, but, on a global scale, few are permanently abandoned. Long core-tools and bifacial hierarchical cores (LCTs and BHCs) seem to vanish from the lithic record during Later Pleistocene times, but this is probably an artifact of archaeological systematics, of archaeologists attaching different names to similar artifacts from different time periods. In the Holocene Levant, for example, archaeologists use the terms "picks" and "roughouts" for artifacts that would be called LCTs if they came from Pleistocene contexts.

By taking a comparative and analytical approach to the stone tool evidence for human evolution, this book has explored one path that can bring the stone tool evidence back into major issues in human origins research. This comparative analytical approach also reveals the major strategic changes in how hominins made and used stone tools.

STRATEGIC CHANGES IN HOMININ STONE TOOL USE

Earth's only obligatory tool-using primate, *Homo sapiens*, numbers in the billions. Apes who occasionally use tools are all endangered species. To understand these technological primates' divergent evolutionary fates, we have to consider how occasional tool use became obligatory tool use over the course of hominin evolution. Most primates get along just fine without stone tools, or, indeed, without using tools at all. Tool-using primates are exceptions, not the norm. Non-human primates that use tools are, for the most part, "occasional" tool users. They use tools, but they do so neither constantly nor universally among species. Nor are most of them much inclined to use tools when alternative ways of getting at food are available. Non-human primates bear the costs of tool use reluctantly, whereas humans embrace them enthusiastically.

Recent human tool use has obligatory, habitual, and occasional dimensions (Table 9.2). Marooned on a desert island one would be *obliged* to devise means for securing and transporting potable water. One would *habitually* use a mirror and/or a radio transmitter to signal possible rescuers. One would *occasionally* use a knife to cut firewood and shelter materials from branches otherwise too thick to break by hand. Extracting these qualities of recent human and non-human primate tool use from their contemporary contexts and using them to characterize variation in prehistoric hominin tool use involves a certain risk of oversimplification. Nevertheless, and thus viewed, the major changes in the stone tool evidence over the last three million years seem to reflect earlier hominins' strategies for occasionally making and using stone tools being successively augmented by habitual and obligatory stone tool use. This strategic perspective reveals changes in the "deep structure" of the hominin lithic record that traditional archaeological perspectives on that evidence do not.

Occasional Stone Tool Use

Occasional tool use involves applying tools in a limited range of activities on an irregular schedule and when alternative non-technological solutions are impossible or prohibitively costly. Considered together, non-human primate stone tool use and the occasional dimensions of human stone tool use suggest a long-term lithic record for occasional stone tool use ought to exhibit the following characteristics: (1) large geographic and temporal gaps in the occurrence of

TABLE 9.2. *Characteristics of occasional, habitual, and obligatory stone tool use*

OCCASIONAL TOOL USE: Tools engaged in a limited range of activities on an irregular schedule, and mainly when alternative non-technological solutions are unavailable or prohibitively costly.

- Large geographic and temporal gaps in the occurrence of stone tools that are not explicable by geological attrition.
- Simple least-effort tool designs.
- Spatially and temporally simple operational chains.
- Low artifact discard thresholds, but some larger objects heavily modified.
- Minimally variable artifact variation over wide regions and long (i.e., millennial-scale) time periods.
- A hominin fossil record that varies independently of stone tool evidence (i.e., many sites with hominin fossils unaccompanied by evidence for stone tools).
- Characteristic toolmaking strategies: Modes A, B, C, and Submode G1.

HABITUAL TOOL USE: Tool use focused on a limited range of activities that are near constant in occurrence but with variable degrees of periodicity and intensity.

- Few prolonged (i.e., millennial-scale) gaps in the distribution of stone tools in regions with a hominin fossil record.
- Mostly simple/least-effort technology, but with some stereotyped designs that increase artifact circumference/volume ratios.
- Divergent operational chains for artifacts made/used locally vs. those transported.
- Variable artifact discard thresholds, transported artifacts extensively modified.
- Ecogeographically patterned spatial and temporal variation in tool designs and assemblage composition.
- Lithic and hominin fossil record coterminous at regional scales, but with hominin fossils occurring without stone tools at local scales
- Characteristic toolmaking strategies: Submodes D1–D2, D4–D5, E1–E2, F1–F3, and G2.

OBLIGATORY TOOL USE: Constant and compulsory tool use, fine-tuned to local circumstances and redundant (multiple solutions to same problems deployed simultaneously).

- Few or no gaps in occurrence of stone tools, other than those referable to geological attrition.
- Complex tool designs that emphasize functional versatility.
- Spatially and temporally complex operational chains.
- Widely-variable artifact discard thresholds among which high values are inversely correlated with artifact size.
- Widely variable and cumulative patterns of tool production in small regions and over short time periods.
- Far more archaeological sites with stone tools than sites with hominin fossils.
- Characteristic toolmaking strategies: Submodes D3, D6–D7, E3–E4, G3, Modes H and I.

stone tools that are not explicable in terms of geological attrition or inadequate archaeological survey, (2) simple "least-effort" tool designs, (3) spatially and temporally simple operational chains, (4) low artifact discard thresholds, but with larger and less portable objects heavily modified by repeated use at the same locality, (5) minimally variable artifact variation over wide regions and long (i.e., millennial-scale) time periods, and (6) a hominin fossil record that varies independently of stone tool evidence. That is, there will be many contexts in which hominin fossils are unaccompanied by stone tools, and there will be few correlations between variation in stone tools and variation in the morphology of hominin fossils with which they are stratigraphically associated. Among the products of Modes A–I, those most plausibly referable to occasional tool use include percussors (Mode A), bipolar cores (Mode B), pebble cores (Mode C), and platform cores (Submode G1). All these artifacts appear consistently among stone tools made by novice human knappers (Shea 2015a). They are among the most distinctive products of bonobos that knap stone tools (Toth et al. 1993).

Much of the lithic evidence older than 1.7 Ma is consistent with occasional tool use. Even in areas such as the East African Rift Valley, where Plio-Pleistocene archaeological sites have been assiduously sought for nearly a century, vast amounts of time and space separate occurrences of stone cutting tools. If stone tools were being made constantly throughout Plio-Pleistocene times, the sediments that fill these gaps ought to have lithic artifacts in them. Paleoanthropologists routinely scour exposures of these sediments searching for and finding fragmentary fossils of hominin teeth. If there were flaked stone tools eroding alongside them, paleoanthropologists should have found them. That these gaps persist suggests they accurately reflect long periods of time during which stone tools were neither being made nor used, at least not in ways archaeologists recognize. Also consistent with predictions, stone tools from this period are associated with no fewer than three hominin genera.

How can we test the hypothesis that early stone tool use was occasional rather than obligatory? Teaching is a distinctive hallmark of obligatory human tool use. Our near primate relatives learn by imitation and emulation, but they do not routinely teach one another how to make or use tools. Tostevin (2012) has developed criteria for recognizing teaching, learning, and social intimacy in the Late Pleistocene lithic record. Finding widespread lithic evidence for teaching and learning among Plio-Pleistocene stone tools would challenge the hypothesis that early hominins were only occasional tool users.

What triggered stone cutting tool production among Plio-Pleistocene hominins? Inasmuch as humans have deployed stone tools in every habitat on Earth for purposes ranging from food procurement to making tools out of other materials, a single proximate cause or geographic origin for stone cutting tool production seems unlikely. Occasional stone tool use may have arisen from multiple causes among diverse hominin lineages. At a general level, however, the ultimate causes for stone tool production likely included ancestral hominins' need to procure food and to insulate themselves from their environment, or, put simply, their needs for food and shelter. That stone tool production intensifies along with increasing climatic variability over the Pleistocene suggests a link between these phenomena (Potts 1996). Nevertheless, some habitats and circumstances, namely those least like the regions in which hominins originally evolved, probably encouraged innovative stone tool use more than others.

Can we detect the origins of distinctively hominin occasional stone tool use? Hominins were terrestrial and bipedal for millions of years before the first evidence of knapped stone cutting tools appears, ca. 3.4 Ma. Inasmuch as some arboreal and quadrupedal primates are at least occasional stone tool users, early hominins probably used stone tools long before they modified them. As among recent stone-tool-using non-human primates, early hominin stone tool use was probably anchored close to sources of stone suitable for use as tools without modification, such as pebbles/cobbles and angular rock fragments. If using such rocks as tools occasionally led to improved energy capture and hominin population increases, then one would expect occasional stone tool users to shift from using stone tools where they occur naturally to also moving potential tools to places where they are needed but where they do not occur naturally, and thence onwards to making and using stone tools in places where useful tool materials do not occur naturally. Evidence of this third strategy is found nearly everywhere hominin fossils occur after 1.7 Ma, but only sporadically in older contexts. Stone-tool cut-marks on animal bones such as those identified at Dikika (Ethiopia) and dating to 3.4 Ma that are unaccompanied by knapped lithic artifacts may be evidence of the first strategy. It will be difficult for archaeologists to find evidence for hominins' transporting naturally fractured angular rocks, but by working closely with geoarchaeologists we may be able to detect artificial accumulations of such rocks in contexts where they do not occur independently of human agency.

Habitual Stone Tool Use

A plausible intermediary state between occasional and obligatory tool use, "habitual" tool use, engages tools in a limited range of activities that are near constant in occurrence but with variable degrees of periodicity and intensity. For example, many people light campfires, write scientific papers, and talk/text on "smart" phones, but few of us do these things constantly. When we first do them, we explore a range of alternatives, but eventually we find a few strategies that work for us. Thereafter we do them stereotypically, in one or another chosen way.

Because non-human primates use stone tools occasionally rather than habitually, predictions about what habitual stone tool use ought to look like archaeologically have to be based on the habitual dimension of recent human tool use. This perspective suggests that a long-term lithic record for habitual but non-obligatory stone tool use ought to exhibit the following characteristics: (1) few prolonged (i.e., millennial-scale) gaps in the distribution of stone tools in regions with a hominin fossil record, (2) mostly simple/least-effort technology, but with some stereotyped designs that increase artifact circumference/volume ratios (and, thereby, potential utility), (3) divergent operational chains for artifacts made/used locally vs. those transported as personal gear, (4) variable artifact discard thresholds with transported artifacts being extensively modified, (5) ecogeographically patterned spatial and temporal variation in tool designs and assemblage composition, and (6) lithic and hominin fossil records coterminous at regional scales, but with hominin fossils occurring unaccompanied by stone tools at local scales. Among the lithic products of Modes A–I, those most congruent with habitual tool use are scrapers/notches/denticulates, backed/truncated pieces, microliths, burins, points (Submodes D1–D2, D4–D5), LCTs and thinned bifaces (Submodes E1 and E2), bifacial hierarchical cores (Mode F/Submodes F1–F3), and blade cores (Submode G2). Such artifacts figure prominently in the portable toolkits of recent stone-tool-using humans. They are absent from stone tool assemblages knapped by bonobos and rare among stone tools made by novice flintknappers (Toth et al. 1993, Shea 2015a).

The novel features of lithic evidence dating to 0.3–1.7 Ma are consistent with habitual stone tool use. Lithic assemblages from this period differ from their precursors in featuring elongated non-hierarchical bifacial cores (chiefly LCTs and thinned bifaces), bifacial and unifacial hierarchical cores, and retouched pieces (artifacts referable to Submodes E1–E2, D1–D2, D4–D5, G1–G2, and Modes E, F, and G). These artifacts' qualities fit well with predictions about habitual stone tool use, most notably extensive modification and minimally patterned regional and chronological variation in artifact designs. LCT designs emphasize versatility and service both as a core and as a cutting tool. Retouched flakes reflect prolonged and/or repeated tool use. Hominins' choices of whether to knap LCTs or hierarchical cores may be related to strategic variation in provisioning people vs. provisioning places with tools (Kuhn 1992), but the relationship between these strategies was probably far more complex and situationally variable than a portable toolkit vs. strategic cache dichotomy.

If LCTs, thinned bifaces, hierarchical cores, and retouched flakes were by-products of occasional stone tool use, one would expect them to occur among the stone tools made by novice knappers working without specific instructions and/or by knapping opportunistically. They rarely do so, or at least their occurrence is not well documented (Shea 2015a). If, on the other hand, such artifacts were the products of obligatory tool use, then one would expect to see "linguistically patterned" design variation among them. This prediction is not strongly supported either. LCTs, hierarchical cores, and retouched tools from Europe between 0.3 and 1.6 Ma differ minimally from their African and Asian counterparts other than in ways reflecting lithic raw material variation.

The correlation between evidence for logistical mobility and evidence for more habitual stone tool use is intriguing and worth exploring further. For the present, however, archaeologists should maintain multiple working hypotheses about causes for origins of habitual stone tool use. Gamble and colleagues (2014) have proposed cognitive and social changes as possible causes, but these hypotheses are difficult to test with the lithic evidence in its current state. The two most commonly invoked hypotheses with explicit empirical consequences focus on increased hominin carnivory (Stanford and Bunn 2001, McCall 2014) and geographic dispersal (Fleagle et al. 2010, Shea 2010). Both hypotheses predict that more carnivorous/geographically widespread hominins would have enjoyed more stable ecological niches than less carnivorous/geographically endemic hominins. The hominin fossil record is consistent with this prediction. After 1.7 Ma, geographically "cosmopolitan" species of the Genus *Homo* (i.e., species inhabiting more than one continent simultaneously) are associated with stone tools and with evidence for systematic carnivory focused on large terrestrial mammal prey (McCall 2014). Endemic African hominins, *Australopithecus, Paranthropus*, and *Homo habilis* (the only endemic African species of the Genus *Homo*) last appear in the fossil record around this time. Their extinctions leave no trace in either the stone tool record or in the zooarchaeological evidence for hominin carnivory (Roche, Blumenschine, and Shea 2009).

Obligatory Stone Tool Use

Obligatory tool use is constant, compulsory, fine-tuned to local circumstances, and rich in redundant components (i.e., multiple solutions to the same problems deployed simultaneously). The derived features of ethnographic lithic technology suggest that a long-term record for obligatory stone tool use ought to show the following characteristics: (1) few long-term gaps in occurrences of stone tools, other than those referable to geological attrition, (2) complex tool designs that emphasize functional versatility, (3) spatially and temporally complex operational chains, (4) widely variable artifact discard thresholds among which high values are inversely correlated with artifact size (smaller tools are more extensively modified), (5) widely variable and cumulative patterns of tool production in small regions and over short time periods, and (6) far more archaeological sites with stone tools than sites with hominin fossils. Recent humans deploy all of Modes A–I, but those artifacts most plausibly referable to obligatory tool use include tools that were hafted, such as tanged bifaces, celts, and tanged pieces (Submodes E3–E4, D3 and D6), tools resulting from efforts to recover cutting edge from small source materials, such as cores-on-flakes and microblade cores (Submodes D7 and G3), and tools shaped by abrasion, abraded-edge tools, and groundstone tools (Modes H and I). These ways of shaping stone and their characteristic products are prominent components in the ethnographic lithic record. They are absent from lithic assemblages created by non-human primates.

The newly emergent features of the lithic evidence dating to less than 0.2–0.3 Ma are congruent with obligatory tool use. Microliths, cores-on-flakes, tanged pieces and tanged points, celts, microblade cores, edge-abraded tools, and groundstone tools occur in many lithic assemblages. These stone tools are not ubiquitous; indeed they rarely all occur together in any lithic assemblage. Rather, they appear in a wide range of historically contingent combinations. This patterning is consistent with the hypothesis that the hominins who made them enjoyed capacities for wide behavioral variability similar, if not identical, to living humans. Such artifacts are not found among stone tools attributed to the endemic Indonesian hominin, *Homo floresiensis*, and they are rare among lithic evidence associated with *Homo heidelbergensis* and earlier hominins.

Can we refute the hypothesis that hominins living since 0.2–0.3 Ma were obligatory stone tool users? The archaeological record for such hominins would lack its most visible component, stone tools; but, finding human fossils and/or other unequivocal evidence of human activity, such as hearths and architecture, unaccompanied by stone tools at multiple sites in a given region and over prolonged periods (say, a millennium or more) could be considered such a refutation. The only sites featuring such evidence but lacking stone tools are from recent contexts in which stone tools have been replaced by metal and plastic implements.

How did obligatory stone tool use originate? As with bipedalism and habitual tool use, the correlation between evidence for language and for obligatory tool use is potentially telling, but simple and/or single causes are implausible for so complex an evolutionary phenomenon. More likely, there were multiple "positive feedback" cycles of effective tool use leading to population increase and technological intensification. As hominin populations increased as a consequence of niches stabilized by habitual stone tool use, those populations probably saturated habitats requiring minimal investment of time or energy in stone tools. As hominins dispersed into habitats requiring more technological "insulation," and as the quality of habitats already occupied declined, incentives would have arisen for increasing investments of time and energy in stone tool designs that aided their users in either recovering or conserving energy. Where these intensification efforts were successful, hominin populations increased, leading to further cycles of population increase and technological intensification.

Several derived features of the lithic record after 0.3 Ma are explicable as technological intensification in the service of improved energy capture/ conservation. These include lithic projectile weapon armatures, seed-grinding technology, and abraded-edge tools. Projectile weapons and seed-grinding tools liberate enormous amounts of energy from the environment. Projectile weapons make it possible to hunt fast-moving smaller prey as well as large animals that would be too dangerous to attack at close quarters. Pulverizing circumvents structural defenses plants have evolved to defend their seeds. Abraded-edge tools conserve energetic losses in cutting tasks with high rates of edge attrition both by reducing friction during use and by minimizing the loss of tool mass during resharpening. These ways of using stone tools require enormous outlays of time and energy in advance of tool use. They also entail severe consequences for mechanical failure. Broken in half, an arrowhead, a grinding stone, or an abraded-edge celt can only be restored to a fraction of its former usefulness, if at all, by repairs that severely reduce tool mass, thereby vastly reducing their potential utility. Such risks of catastrophic loss may explain why these tools are not ubiquitous among obligatory tool users. In some circumstances, the risks of such catastrophic failures exceed the benefits of making and using these tools.

That stone projectile points, seed-grinding tools, and abraded-edge tools are virtually unknown prior to 0.3 Ma but common among ethnographic stone tool users supports the hypothesis that hominin stone tool use acquired an increasingly obligatory character during Middle-Late Pleistocene times. Tellingly, these artifacts are especially common in the archaeological record immediately preceding evidence for metallurgy in the Nile Valley, the Mediterranean Basin, Mesopotamia, and eastern Asia. Thus viewed, metal-lurgy, the first pyrotechnic art to "own" those who use it (to the extent that no metal-using society has ever abandoned it), is a predictable outgrowth of lithic intensification and obligatory stone tool use.

The Persistence of Occasional Stone Tool Use Among Non-human Primates

If occasional stone tool use led to habitual and obligatory stone tool use among hominins, why do chimpanzees and other primates remain occasional stone tool users? That one of our nearest primate relatives, common chimpanzees (*Pan troglodytes*), is an adept and facultative stone tool user suggests our last common ancestor with chimpanzees was a stone tool user as well (McGrew 1992, Haslam et al. 2009, Haslam 2014). Nevertheless, there are reasons for skepticism about this hypothesis. First, our other nearest primate relatives, bonobos (*Pan paniscus*), do not make stone tools in the wild, even though they can learn to do so in experimental contexts (Toth et al. 1993). Second, that New World monkeys also use stone percussors to crack open nuts (Spagnoletti et al. 2011) suggests their stone tool use arose independently of hominin stone tool use (Panger et al. 2003). Might chimpanzee stone tool use have developed independently of hominin stone tool use?

Archaeological evidence for chimpanzee stone tool use is known from only a handful of sites in the westernmost portion of that species' former geographic range in equatorial Africa. Thus far, the oldest "percussors-only" archaeological sites located in this area date to a little more than 4 Ka (Mercader et al. 2007). It is not impossible that as the Holocene human population expanded in Sub-Saharan Africa chimpanzees living in habitats circumscribed by human settlement began using stone tools to crack nuts they previously bypassed due to their high processing costs. Thus viewed, chimpanzee stone tool use may be a form of economic intensification brought about indirectly by *Homo sapiens*. The strongest evidence against viewing chimpanzee stone tool use as an evolutionary novelty, evidence that would support viewing it as inherited from our last common ancestor, would be for archaeologists to discover stone tool assemblages in equatorial Africa consisting solely of stone percussors that date to ca. 5–6 Ma, around the time the hominin–panin last common ancestor is thought to have lived (Fleagle 2013).

CONCLUDING THOUGHTS

Few changes in how we humans think about our place in the universe are as profound as the recognition that we evolved. Unfortunately, human evolution is commonly misunderstood as a teleological process, a "march of progress" inevitably resulting in ourselves. Progressive models for human evolution require one to believe in "primitive" humans, people who lacked some essential biological characteristic that made their descendants fully "modern" humans. Recognizing that the strongest evidence for progressive human evolution would be finding living examples of primitive humans, early anthropologists scoured the world for them. For a time, they thought they had found primitive humans in remote regions far away from the European cities where most early anthropologists lived (Sollas 1911). As anthropologists gained linguistic competence with their ethnographic subjects, however, they recognized thoughts and behavior neither less complex nor less variable than their own (Kuper 1988). Anthropologists had better success finding primitive humans in the fossil record. Extinct humans and earlier hominins cannot object to the ways anthropologists characterize them. But being extinct is not the same thing as being mute. In stone tools, prehistoric humans and earlier hominins left behind virtually indestructible evidence of their abilities. Time and again, the stone tool evidence shows that the surest way to be wrong in human origins research is to underestimate Pleistocene hominins' behavioral variability.

Stone tool analysis can contribute meaningfully to research on human evolution, but for it to do so, archaeologists have to change how we think about the sources of change and variability in the lithic evidence. Traditional archaeological approaches to the stone tool evidence for human evolution err when they equate the characteristics of the lithic evidence with intrinsic qualities of hominins themselves, their biological and social identities, or their cognitive abilities. This book treats stone tools as residues of hominins' behavioral strategies. Explaining changes in the stone tool evidence in strategic terms does not require one to invoke any special set of explanatory principles unique to the lithic evidence or to impute unverifiable behavioral qualities of "primitiveness" or "modernity" to Pleistocene hominins. Just as there is neither a quintessentially French way to make a baguette nor an essentially American way to drive a car, different ways of making stone tools are strategies deployed by individuals under variable circumstances. Applying a strategic perspective to the stone tool evidence is simply applied uniformitarianism, the common theoretical touchstone for all natural history (Tooby and DeVore 1987). By requiring us to base our explanations of evidence for past hominin behavior on observations of strategic variation in human and non-human primate behavior today, uniformitarianism is a quiet voice reminding us of the difference between science and science fiction.

In blazing a trail through the woods, it helps to remember that one is building a path, not a superhighway. This book has tried to show a path connecting the stone tool evidence and major issues in human evolution. It is not the only such path, and some of its twists and turns need improvements before they will bear heavy traffic. As paths must, this book ends at a fork in the road. What should archaeologists do next?

The easiest way out of unfamiliar terrain is to backtrack. Having invested much in traditional approaches to the stone tool evidence, some archaeologists will continue "business as usual." Much as archaeologists have done for the last century, they will arrange that evidence in terms of "transitions" and "revolutions" between age-stages and ever more baroquely interconnected named stone tool industries. This is a choice, but choices have consequences. Few paleoanthropologists other than archaeologists have much interest or see much value in "culture history" written about stone tools.

One forward path could be to test some of this work's predictions in greater detail, in more explicitly quantitative terms, and using evidence from different regions. Many archaeologists will find this path familiar, for it articulates well our tendency to specialize in particular geographic regions and/or time periods. Finding, for example, that the predictions for residential sedentism in Chapter 8 are supported in, say, the Upper Nile Valley but not in the Central Andes would lead to more refined hypotheses, or perhaps multiple working hypotheses, about the relationship between residential sedentism and lithic variability. More importantly, if the hypotheses this book proposes about stone tools' roles in human evolution are wrong, they need to be found out, rejected, and replaced with better hypotheses. Such empirical falsifications ought to inform the larger field of human origins research.

A second and somewhat less conventional path would be for archaeologists to focus their attention on particular behaviors and to explore their impacts on the stone tool evidence. Other behavioral differences between humans and non-human primates that need to be explored include the controlled use of fire (Wrangham 2009), correlated shifts in diet and brain enlargement (Aiello and Wheeler 1995), prolonged childhood and post-reproductive survival (Kaplan et al. 2000), cooperative breeding (Burkart et al. 2009, Kramer and Ellison 2010), foraging for dense and predictable resources (Marean 2016), and prolonged co-residence by unrelated individuals (Hill et al. 2011). Working out the predictions for their impacts on the lithic archaeological record will not be easy, but who becomes a scientist only to solve easy problems or an explorer only to follow well-worn paths?

APPENDIX

TRADITIONAL ARCHAEOLOGICAL AGE-STAGES AND INDUSTRIES

The main text of *Stone Tools in Human Evolution* does not use traditional age-stages, or named stone tool industries. Nevertheless, these conventions for describing the stone tool evidence remain in wide use in the professional literature. So that readers encountering that literature for the first time will know what these terms mean, this appendix describes them briefly.

AGE-STAGES

Archaeologists divide Stone Age prehistory in Europe, North Africa, and Asia into Paleolithic, Mesolithic, and Neolithic periods (Scarre 2013). Unlike geological periods, the dates for these archaeological periods vary from region to region depending on the contents of archaeological assemblages.

The Paleolithic encompasses prehistory before the Holocene Epoch, from 12.5 Ka to >3.3 Ma. Lower Paleolithic (>245 Ka) assemblages feature bipolar cores, pebble cores, and platform cores. Long core-tools (LCTs), such as handaxes, cleavers, and picks, appear after 1.7 Ma. The Middle Paleolithic (45–245 Ka) marks the appearance of bifacial hierarchical core technology ("Levallois prepared cores"). Upper Paleolithic (12–45 Ka) stone tool assemblages preserve prismatic blades and blade cores. The Mesolithic (8–12 Ka) sees increasing sedentism and economic intensification. Microliths (backed and/or truncated pieces less than 3 cm long) are this period's signature artifacts. In northern Africa and Southwest Asia the equivalent period is called the Epipaleolithic. In Europe, the Neolithic Period (>6–10 Ka) also sees stone tools shaped by abrasion and evidence for food production involving domesticated plants and animals.

Sub-Saharan African prehistorians use a somewhat different set of age-stages, Earlier, Middle, and Later Stone Age (Barham and Mitchell 2008). The first two of these are essentially the same as the Lower and Middle Paleolithic. The African Later Stone Age differs from the Upper Paleolithic by featuring evidence for microlithic stone tools and by extending further into the Holocene.

From the 1970s onwards Australian archaeologists divided their continent's prehistory into two chronologically sequential technological periods (or "traditions"), a Core-Tool and Scraper Tradition dating ca. 6–45 Ka, and a Small Tool Tradition that lasted until European colonization in the late eighteenth century (Mulvaney and Kamminga 1999). The Core-Tool and Scraper Tradition features tools made by simple hard-hammer percussion of cobbles/pebbles and angular rock fragments, but edge-ground flakes and celts occur as well. Small Tool Tradition assemblages also contain microliths and points and bifaces made by soft-hammer percussion and pressure flaking. Stone seed-grinding equipment is more common. Recent overviews of Australian prehistory make less use of this framework.

Archaeologists use the terms "Paleoindian" and "Archaic" for the earliest periods of New World prehistory (Willey and Phillips 1958). The Paleoindian Period encompasses the final millennia of the Pleistocene and the earliest Holocene, roughly 10–14 Ka. The most distinctive Paleoindian stone tools, "fluted points," are thinned and pointed bifaces with various forms of basal modification. The Archaic Period, whose younger dates vary widely between 5 and 3 Ka, sees reduced residential mobility, increasingly intensified subsistence, and the production of tanged and notched bifacial points. Abraded-edge tools and groundstone tools (celts and seed-grinding equipment) are rare. Terms used for post-Archaic periods in the Americas vary in ways that reflect regional differences in the adoption of agriculture and the development of complex societies. With agriculture, groundstone celts and seed-grinding equipment become common. Reductions in bifacial point size in later time periods herald the introduction of the bow and arrow.

STONE TOOL INDUSTRIES

Stone tool industries group together lithic assemblages from the same age-stages that share evidence for similar ways of making stone tools and similar inventories of artifact-types.

Lower Paleolithic industries include the Oldowan, the Acheulian (also spelled Acheulean), the Developed Oldowan, and various regional industries lacking evidence for LCT production.

Oldowan assemblages date to African contexts older than 1.6 Ma. These assemblages are dominated by evidence for pebble core reduction (Figure 4.5). The term "Oldowan" is occasionally applied to Early Pleistocene assemblages outside of Africa.

Acheulian assemblages contain handaxes, cleavers, picks, and knives and other LCTs (Figures 5.3–5.4, and 5.8). A few Acheulian assemblages date to as much as 1.8 Ma in Africa, but most are younger than 1.6 Ma. African and

Eurasian industries with LCTs dating to between 0.2 and 1.6 Ma are usually called Acheulian and referred to early, middle, or late phases of that industry.

The "Developed Oldowan" industry features elongated discoidal cores, spheroids and subspheroids, and numerous retouched flake tools. Originally thought to be a stage in the development of the Acheulian from the Oldowan, recent research shows that African Developed Oldowan and Early Acheulian overlap chronologically with one another.

Eurasian Lower-Middle Pleistocene stone tool industries lacking LCTs are called by different names within and between regions. Those most commonly cited in the archaeological literature include the Tayacian (mainland Europe and Southwest Asia), the Clactonian (sites in the UK), and the Soan (South Asia).

Middle Paleolithic stone tool industries differ from Lower Paleolithic ones mainly in having regional, rather than continental-scale distributions and shorter duration (tens of thousands of years rather than hundreds of thousands of years).

The Mousterian is the principal Middle Paleolithic stone tool industry in Europe, North Africa, western and southern Asia. Mousterian assemblages contain variable amounts of artifacts referable to Levallois core technology and unifacially retouched flakes (scrapers and points), as well as rare occurrences of long core-tools and thinned bifaces (Figure 6.3–6.6). African prehistorians recognize additional Middle Paleolithic/Middle Stone Age industries, mainly on the basis of a few diagnostic retouched artifact-types. The most-widely recognized of these (and their signature artifact-types) are the Sangoan (core-axes), the Lupemban (elongated pointed bifaces), the Aterian (tanged pieces and points), the Still Bay (thinned bifacial points), and the Howiesons Poort (backed/truncated pieces).

Owing to a recent rapid increase in research activity, the taxonomy of Pleistocene East Asian stone tool industries is somewhat unsettled and defies easy synthesis (Norton and Jin 2009, Bar-Yosef and Wang 2012).

Upper Paleolithic stone tool industries vary widely among major geographic regions. Most archaeology textbooks only describe the longest-known and best-dated sequence of industries from Western Europe. These include (in chronological order) the Aurignacian, Gravettian, Solutrean, and Magdalenian. All of these industries feature prismatic blade technology and various distinctive retouched artifact-types (de Sonneville-Bordes 1963, Demars and Laurent 1992) (Figure 7.6).

Mesolithic and Epipaleolithic stone tool industries typically last for no more than a few thousand years or less and are distributed at regional to sub-regional scales. They are usually defined in terms of shape variation in microliths and ratios of blade vs. non-blade core technology (Figure 8.3). Some of the better-known of these industries include the Azilian, Tardenoisian, and Sauveterrian (Western Europe), the Maglemosian, Ertebølle and *Federmesser* ("feather-knives") cultures (northern Europe), the Kebaran and Natufian (East Mediterranean Levant), and the Capsian and Oranian (North Africa).

Neolithic stone tool industries are rarely given their own names, but rather subsumed into archaeological "cultures" defined on the basis of regional ceramic design variation, architecture, and other evidence. Such combined industries/cultures vary widely in their geographic range and in duration. Few of them exceed a few thousand years or extend to inter-regional scales. Most of them preserve flaked and edge-ground celts as well as bifacially retouched projectile points (Figures 8.4–8.5).

GLOSSARY

Abraded-edge tool Artifact on which a cutting edge has been created by abrasion on one or both intersecting surfaces.

Abraded-edge tool production (Mode H) Creating a cutting edge by abrading one or both of two intersecting surfaces (Figure 3.4).

Age-stages Time periods differentiated from one another by lithic index fossils (e.g., Lower, Middle, Upper Paleolithic).

Anvil percussion (Mode A) Creating a fracture by throwing or striking a core against a hard substrate, such as another rock or a bedrock exposure (Figure 3.3).

Artifact A rock that has been modified by hominin activity.

Artifact-type A grouping of artifacts with similar patterns of retouch, shape, and metric properties.

Assemblage Group of artifacts from the same archaeological context (a site or a level of a site).

Backed/truncated piece Flake/flake fragments steeply retouched (to around 90°) along at least one of their edges.

Backing/truncation (Submodes D2, D3) Steep retouch on either the lateral edges of a flake fragment (backing) or on its distal/proximal ends (truncation) (Figure 3.3).

Basal thinning Retouch that removes material from the proximal end of a flake or an elongated bifacial core.

Behavioral variability Deploying multiple solutions to the same problem simultaneously.

Beringia Easternmost Siberia, Alaska, northwestern Canada, and their continental shelves exposed by lower Pleistocene sea levels.

BHC See bifacial hierarchical core.

Biface Core shaped by flake removals from both sides of one or more working edges.

Bifacial hierarchical core (BHC) Bifacial core with two distinct fracture initiation surfaces: one with relatively short flakes detached from it, and the other with more invasive and extensive flake scars.

Bifacial hierarchical core reduction (Mode F) Obtaining flakes by detaching relatively short flakes from one side of an edge (the fracture initiation surface) and longer flakes from the other side (the flake propagation surface) (Figure 3.4).

Bipolar core Core resulting from bipolar core reduction.

Bipolar core reduction (Mode B) Initiating fracture by striking the uppermost surface of a core or flake that is resting on a hard substrate (Figure 3.3).

Blade An elongated flake (length ≥ 2× width).

Blade core Elongated hemispherical unifacial hierarchical core from which the flakes (blades) detached are relatively long (length ≥ 2× width) and detached parallel to one another. See elongated unifacial hierarchical core.

Blade core reduction (Submode G2) Obtaining blades by detaching them from an elongated unifacial hierarchical core longer than 5 cm (Figure 3.4).

Burin Flake/flake fragment modified by fractures aligned perpendicularly to its upper and lower surfaces and parallel to its edge.

Burin spall A flake, detached by burination, that propagates perpendicular to the ventral surface of the flake from which it has been detached.

Burination (Submode D4) Initiating a fracture that propagates roughly perpendicular to a flake's ventral surface (Figure 3.3).

Celt Elongated core-tool whose distal end has been modified by invasive retouch or abrasion into a cutting edge aligned perpendicularly to its long axis.

Celt production (Submode E4) Knapping a sharp cutting edge on the distal end of an elongated bifacial core (Figure 3.3).

Chaîne opératoire See operational chain.

Clast Rounded rock shaped by geological abrasion.

Comminution Concentrations of small incompletely propagated fractures resulting from repeated percussion.

Concave proximal retouch (Submode D6) Creating one or more symmetrically-positioned concavities near the proximal end of a flake (Figure 3.3).

Convergent distal retouch (Submode D5) Detaching relatively large flakes (>2 cm long) from flake fragments (Figure 3.3).

Core Artifact featuring large-scale (>30 mm long) flake scars on its surfaces (Figure 3.1).

Core reduction A series of acts that result in flakes being detached from a core.

Core-on-flake Flake/flake fragment from which one or more flakes longer than 2 cm have been detached from either ventral or dorsal surfaces and from a prepared striking platform.

Curation Prolonging tool utility by transport, resharpening, or both.

Débitage (1) Flakes, flake fragments, and other fracture by-products (from French term for "waste"). (2) Core reduction strategy intended to create flakes suitable for use as tools. See flake production.

Debris Small (<1–2 cm long) flakes and flake fragments.

Derived Recently evolved.

Distal On flakes, the part most distant from the point of fracture initiation. On cores and retouched tools, usually the thinnest or narrowest part of the tool.

Dorsal surface On flakes, the former exterior surface of the core. On cores, the most convex surface.

Early Holocene Time period, 6.5–11 Ka.

Early-Middle Pleistocene (EMP) Time period, ca. 0.3–1.7 Ma, encompassing later Early Pleistocene and early Middle Pleistocene epochs.

Early Pleistocene Time period, 1.7–2.5 Ma.

Elongated bifacial core-tool Abbreviation for elongated non-hierarchical bifacial core-tool.

Elongated non-hierarchical bifacial core-tool Non-hierarchical bifacial core-tool significantly elongated along at least one of its three major morphological axes.

Elongated non-hierarchical bifacial core-tool reduction (Mode E) A series of non-hierarchical flake detachments from an elongated core-tool (length >width) in such a way that flakes propagate roughly perpendicularly to the core's long axis (Figure 3.3).

Elongated unifacial hierarchical core Core from which the flakes (blades) detached are relatively long (length ≥ 2× width) and detached parallel to one another. See also blade core, microblade core.

EMP See Early-Middle Pleistocene.

Façonnage See shaping.

Flake Piece of stone detached from a core by fracture (Figure 3.1).

Flake core reduction (Submode D7) Detaching one or more flakes longer than 2 cm from a flake (Figure 3.3).

Flake production Tool production strategy aimed at creating flakes suitable for use as tools. See also *débitage*.

Flake retouch/reduction (Mode D) Detaching flakes (hierarchically or non-hierarchically) from the edge of a flake or flake fragment.

Flute A relatively long and wide flake initiated from the proximal end of an elongated bifacial core.

Fracture initiation surface On a core, that side of the worked edge on which a fracture originates (Figure 3.1).

Fracture propagation surface On a core, that side of the worked edge under which a fracture propagates after initiation (Figure 3.1).

Function Artifact variation reflecting mechanical use.

Groundstone tool Artifact featuring convex, planar, or concave surfaces, and/or perforations shaped by cycles of percussion and abrasion.

Groundstone tool production (Mode I) Creating convex, planar, or concave surfaces, and/or perforations on artifacts by cycles of percussion and abrasion (Figure 3.4).

Haft Handle to which a stone tool is attached.

Hammerstone Stone used to initiate fracture in another rock.

Hierarchical core reduction Knapping strategy in which fracture initiation and flake detachment surfaces are not interchangeable.

Holocene Geological epoch, 12.5 Ka to present.

Hominin Bipedal primate.

Human *Homo sapiens*.

Industry/Industries Group of assemblages sharing similar inventories of artifact-types.

Intensification Increasing the amount of time and/or energy devoted to an activity.

Ka Abbreviation, thousands of years ago. Note: in this work, dates less than 45,000 are calibrated radiocarbon years.

Late Pleistocene (LP) Geological period, 12.5–128 Ka.

LCT See long core-tool.

Levant East Mediterranean watershed and adjacent parts of Anatolian Plateau and the Arabian Peninsula.

Lithic Stone.

Lithic raw material Rocks from which lithic artifacts are manufactured. Also known (in other works) as "toolstone."

Long core-tool (LCT) Non-hierarchical bifacial core-tool elongated on at least one axis and having a width/thickness ratio greater than 3 to 1.

Long core-tool production (Submode E1) Obtaining flakes from an elongated bifacial core by detaching them so that they propagate toward one another and relatively far across the core surface (Figure 3.3).

Ma Abbreviation for millions of years ago.

Macrolithic backing/truncation (Submode D2) Backing/truncation applied to flake fragments more than 3 cm long (Figure 3.3).

Manuport An unmodified rock that has been moved into association with other evidence of hominin activity.

Mastic Adhesive substance used to attach stone tools to other objects.

Microblade Blade less than 5 cm long and narrower than 1 cm wide.

Microblade core Blade core less than 5 cm long.

Microblade core reduction (Submode G3) Reduction of a blade core less than 5 cm long (Figure 3.4).

Microlith Backed/truncated flake/flake fragment less than 3 cm long and less than 1 cm wide.

Microlithic backing/truncation (Submode D3) Backing/truncation applied to artifacts ≤3 cm long (Figure 3.3).

Microwear Small-scale fracturing and abrasion (polish and striations) on stone tool edges and surfaces.

Middle-Late Pleistocene (MLP) Time period, ca. 50–300 Ka, encompassing the later part of the Middle Pleistocene and earlier part of the Later Pleistocene.

Middle Pleistocene Time period, 128–730 Ka.

MLP See Middle-Late Pleistocene.

Mode A Anvil percussion (Figure 3.3).

Mode B Bipolar core reduction (Figure 3.3).

Mode C Pebble core reduction (Figure 3.3).

Mode D Flake retouch/reduction (Figure 3.3).

Mode E Elongated non-hierarchical bifacial core reduction (Figure 3.3).

Mode F Bifacial hierarchical core (BHC) reduction (Figure 3.4).

Mode G Unifacial hierarchical core reduction (Figure 3.4).

Mode H Abraded-edge tool production (Figure 3.4).

Mode I Groundstone tool production (Figure 3.4).

Non-hierarchical core reduction Knapping strategy in which fracture initiation and flake propagation surfaces are interchangeable.

Northern Eurasia Europe north of the Alps, Central Asia north of the Himalayan Mountains, northern China and Siberia.

Operational chain (1) The sequence of transformations that occur to materials, stone or otherwise, from raw material procurement, through manufacturing and use to discard. (2) Archaeological reconstructions of those sequences.

Panin African ape (gorillas, chimpanzees, and bonobos).

Pebble core A clast (rounded rock) or angular rock fragment that has had a series of flakes detached by percussion on alternating sides of the same edge. Flake removals are non-hierarchical.

Pebble core reduction (Mode C) Sequential non-hierarchical flake removals from non-elongated clasts (rounded rocks), flakes/flake fragments, or angular rock fragments (Figure 3.3).

Percussor (1) Artifact used to induce fracture. (2) Stone artifacts from which a series of incompletely propagated fractures have been initiated by repeated percussion. Synonym for hammerstone.

Piece Retouched flake/flake fragment.

Platform core Hemispherical unifacial hierarchical core from which the flakes detached are relatively short (length <2× width) and detached parallel to one another.

Platform core reduction (Submode G1) Unifacial hierarchical reduction of a relatively short hemispherical core (Figure 3.4).

Plio–Pleistocene Time period, ca. 1.7–>2.6 Ma, encompassing Later Pliocene and Early Pleistocene geological epochs.

Point Flake/flake fragment on which two retouched edges converge to form a sharp triangular projection.

Preferential bifacial hierarchical core Bifacial hierarchical core from which a single relatively large flake has been detached from the fracture propagation surface.

Preferential bifacial hierarchical core reduction (Submode F1) Bifacial hierarchical core reduction involving the detachment of a single relatively large flake from the fracture propagation surface (Figure 3.4).

Primitive Ancestral.

Prismatic blade An elongated flake (length ≥ 2× width) with parallel lateral edges and dorsal flake scars.

Proximal That part of a flake closest to point of fracture initiation. On cores and retouched tools, orientation conventions/definitions vary, but usually either the thickest or widest part of the tool in plan view.

Recurrent laminar bifacial hierarchical core Bifacial hierarchical core with overlapping series of large flakes detached from the fracture propagation surface.

Recurrent laminar bifacial hierarchical core reduction (Submode F2) Bifacial hierarchical core reduction in which an overlapping series of large flakes are detached parallel to one another from the fracture propagation surface (Figure 3.4).

Recurrent radial/centripetal bifacial hierarchical core Bifacial hierarchical core whose flake scars converge radially from multiple points around its circumference.

Recurrent radial/centripetal bifacial hierarchical core reduction (Submode F3) Bifacial hierarchical core reduction in which overlapping flake scars converge with one another from multiple points around the circumference of the flake detachment surface (Figure 3.4).

Reduction Detaching a series of flakes from a lithic artifact.

Referential model A group of hypotheses based on the holistic observation of an organism's behavior (e.g., "early hominins were like chimpanzees").

Retouch Small-scale fracture scars on the edges of artifacts thought to result from purposeful human activity (Figure 3.1).

Retouched piece Flakes and flake fragments modified by retouch.

Sahul New Guinea, Australia, Tasmania, and such of their continental shelves exposed by lower Pleistocene sea levels.

Scaled pieces See bipolar cores.

Scraper retouch (Submode D1) Removing a series of flakes continuously along a flake's edge in such a way that the resulting edge is relatively acute in cross-section (<70°) (Figure 3.3).

Scrapers, notches, and denticulates (SNDs) Flakes/flake fragments with at least one acute (<90°) retouched edge shaped by orthogonal retouch.

Shaping Tool production strategy intended to impose shape on a core or retouched piece (aka *façonnage*).

SNDs See scrapers, notches, and denticulates.

Stone Aggregate of minerals in a solid state.

Strategic model A group of hypotheses based on the observations of a specific dimension of an organism's behavior (e.g., "Early hominin stone tool transport was different from chimpanzee stone tool transport.").

Strategy A way of accomplishing any particular goal.

Striking platform That part of the dorsal surface of a flake between the point of fracture initiation and the segment of the worked edge detached by fracture propagation.

Style Artifact variation thought to reflect tool makers' social identities.

Submode D1 Scraper retouch (Figure 3.3).

Submode D2 Macrolithic backing/truncation (Figure 3.3).

Submode D3 Microlithic backing/truncation (Figure 3.3).

Submode D4 Burination (Figure 3.3).

Submode D5 Convergent distal retouch (Figure 3.3).

Submode D6 Concave proximal retouch (Figure 3.3).

Submode D7 Flake core reduction (Figure 3.3).

Submode E1 LCT production (Figure 3.3).

Submode E2 Thinned biface production (Figure 3.3).

Submode E3 Tanged biface production (Figure 3.3).

Submode E4 Celt production (Figure 3.3).

Submode F1 Preferential BHC reduction (Figure 3.4).

Submode F2 Recurrent laminar BHC reduction (Figure 3.4).

Submode F3 Recurrent radial/centripetal BHC reduction (Figure 3.4).

Submode G1 Platform core reduction (Figure 3.4).

Submode G2 Blade core reduction (Figure 3.4).

Submode G3 Microblade core reduction (Figure 3.4).

Sundaland Southeast Asia and its continental shelf exposed by lower Pleistocene sea levels.

Tang Projection of the proximal end of a flake or other artifact formed by retouched concavities.

Tanged biface Elongated non-hierarchical bifacial core onto which one or more concavities have been retouched at the proximal end, presumably to aid hafting.

Tanged biface production (Submode E3) Creating one or more symmetrically positioned concavities near the proximal end of an elongated bifacial core (Figure 3.3).

Tanged piece Flake/flake fragment on which one or more retouched concavities form a symmetrical projection, presumably as an aid to hafting.

Tanged point Retouched flake fragment or an elongated non-hierarchical bifacial core with convergent distal retouch and concave proximal retouch.

Technocomplex Group of assemblages with similar technologies but different typological characteristics.

Technology Artifact variation reflecting differences in manufacturing techniques.

Terminal Pleistocene Time period, ca. 11–24 Ka.

Tested stone Stone from which one or two flakes have been detached by percussion.

Thinned biface Elongated non-hierarchical bifacial core with flake scars on one or both sides extending from their edge to either the midline of their long axis or beyond. Width/thickness ratios are usually greater than 2 to 1.

Thinned biface production (Submode E2) Obtaining flakes from an elongated bifacial core by detaching them so that they propagate relatively far across the core surface (Figure 3.3).

Tool Object used by an organism to manipulate other objects or organisms.

Typology Artifact variation reflecting differences in shape and/or retouch.

Unifacial hierarchical core Core with a stable hierarchy of fracture initiation and fracture propagation surfaces intersecting at right angles.

Unifacial hierarchical core reduction (Mode G) Hierarchical core reduction in which the fracture initiation surface is roughly planar and maintained at nearly a right angle to the fracture propagation surface (Figure 3.4).

Ventral surface On flakes, the surface created by the fracture that detached the flake from a core. On cores, the most concave or planar surface.

Worked edge That part of a core's circumference from which flakes have been detached.

BIBLIOGRAPHY

Abbès, F. 2003. *Les outillages néolithique en Syrie du nord: Méthode de débitage et gestion laminaire durant le PPNB.* Oxford, UK: Archaeopress (British Archaeological Reports International Series 1150).

Addington, L. 1986. *Lithic Illustration: Drawing Flaked Stone Artifacts for Publication.* Chicago, IL: University of Chicago Press.

Adler, D. S., K. N. Wilkinson, S. Blockley, D. F. Mark, R. Pinhasi, B. A. Schmidt-Magee, S. Nahapetyan, C. Mallol, F. Berna, P. J. Glauberman, Y. Raczynski-Henk, N. Wales, E. Frahm, O. Jöris, A. MacLeod, V. C. Smith, V. L. Cullen, and B. Gasparian. 2014. Early Levallois technology and the Lower to Middle Paleolithic transition in the southern Caucasus. *Science* 345:1609–1613.

Agusti, J., and M. Antón. 2003. *Mammoths, Sabertooths, and Hominids: 65 Million Years of Mammalian Evolution in Europe.* New York: Columbia University Press.

Ahmad, G. S., and J. J. Shea. 2009. *Reconstructing Late Pleistocene Human Behavior in the Jordan Valley: The Middle Paleolithic Stone Tool Assemblage from Ar Rasfa.* Oxford, UK: Archaeopress (British Archaeological Reports International Series 2042).

Aiello, L. C., and P. Wheeler. 1995. The expensive-tissue hypothesis: The brain and digestive system in human and primate evolution. *Current Anthropology* 36:199–221.

Alemseged, Z. 2014. Early hominins, in *The Cambridge World Prehistory, Volume 1: Africa, South and Southeast Asia and the Pacific.* Edited by C. Renfrew and P. Bahn, pp. 47–64. New York: Cambridge University Press.

Alexander, R. D. 1987. *The Biology of Moral Systems.* New York: Aldine de Gruyter.

Alperson-Afil, N. 2008. Continual fire-making by hominins at Gesher Benot Ya'aqov, Israel. *Quaternary Science Reviews* 27:1733–1739.

Ambrose, S. H. 2001. Paleolithic technology and human evolution. *Science* 291:1748–1753.

Ames, K. M. 2003. The Northwest Coast. *Evolutionary Anthropology* 12:19–33.

Anderson, J. R., E. A. Williamson, and J. Carter. 1983. Chimpanzees of Sapo Forest, Liberia: Density, nests, tools and meat-eating. *Primates* 4:594–601.

Anderson-Gerfaud, P. C. 1990. Aspects of behaviour in the Middle Palaeolithic: Functional analysis of stone tools from Southwest France, in *The Emergence of Modern Humans.* Edited by P. A. Mellars, pp. 389–418. Edinburgh: Edinburgh University Press.

Andrefsky, W. J. 2005. *Lithics: Macroscopic Approaches to Analysis,* Second Edition. New York: Cambridge University Press.

Anikovich, M. V., A. A. Sinitsyn, J. F. Hoffecker, V. T. Holliday, V. V. Popov, S. N. Lisitsyn, S. L. Forman, G. M. Levkovskaya, G. A. Pospelova, I. E. Kuz'mina, N. D. Burova, P. Goldberg, R. I. Macphail, B. Giaccio, and N. D. Praslov. 2007. Early Upper Paleolithic in Eastern Europe and implications for the dispersal of modern humans. *Science* 315:223–226.

Anton, S. C., R. Potts, and L. C. Aiello. 2014. Evolution of early *Homo*: An integrated biological perspective. *Science* 345:40–45.

Aprahamian, G. D. 2001. Le dessin du materiel lithique, in *Beyond Tools: Redefining the PPN*

Lithic Assemblages of the Levant. Edited by I. Caneva, C. Lemorini, D. Zampetti, and P. Biagi, pp. 93–106. Berlin: ex oriente.

Arthur, K. W. 2010. Feminine knowledge and skill reconsidered: Women and flaked stone tools. *American Anthropologist* 112:228–243.

Arzarello, M., F. Marcolini, G. Pavia, M. Pavia, C. Petronio, M. Petrucci, L. Rook, and R. Sardella. 2007. Evidence of earliest human occurrence in Europe: The site of Pirro Nord (Southern Italy). *Naturwissenschaften* 94:107–112.

Aubry, T., M. Almeida, M. J. Neves, and B. Walter. 2003. Solutrean laurel leaf point production and raw material procurement during the Last Glacial Maximum in Southern Europe: Two examples from Central France and Portugal, in *Multiple Approaches to the Study of Bifacial Technologies.* Edited by M. Soressi and H. L. Dibble, pp. 165–182. Philadelphia, PA: University of Pennsylvania Museum.

Audouin-Rouzeau, F., and S. Beyries. Editors. 2002. *Le travail du cuir de la préhistoire à nos jours.* Antibes: Éditions APDCA (Actes des XXIIe Rencontres Internationales d'Archéologie et d'Histoire d'Antibes).

Austin, L. 1994. The life and death of a Boxgrove biface, in *Stories in Stone.* Edited by N. Ashton and A. David, pp. 119–126. Oxford, UK: Lithics Study Society Occasional Paper, No. 4.

Baena, J., D. Lordkipanidze, F. Cuartero, R. Ferring, D. Zhvania, D. Martin, T. Shelia, G. Bidzinashuili, M. Roca, and D. Rubio. 2010. Technical and technological complexity in the beginning: The study of Dmanisi lithic assemblage. *Quaternary International* 223:45–53.

Bailey, G. Editor. 1998. *Klithi: Palaeolithic Settlement and Quaternary Landscapes in Northwest Greece, Volume 1: Excavation and Intra-Site Analysis Klithi.* London: McDonald Institute for Archaeological Research.

Bar-Yosef, O. 2000. The Middle and Early Upper Paleolithic in Southwest Asia and neighboring regions, in *The Geography of Neandertals and Modern Humans in Europe and the Greater Mediterranean.* Edited by O. Bar-Yosef and D. Pilbeam, pp. 107–156. Cambridge, MA: Peabody Museum of Archaeology and Ethnology (Bulletin No. 8).

Bar-Yosef Mayer, D. 2005. The exploitation of shells as beads in the Palaeolithic and Neolithic of the Levant. *Paléorient* 31:176–185.

Bar-Yosef Mayer, D. 2013. Towards a typology of stone beads in the Neolithic Levant. *Journal of Field Archaeology* 38:129–142.

Bar-Yosef, O. 1970. The Epipaleolithic Cultures of Palestine. Ph.D. Dissertation (unpublished), Hebrew University.

Bar-Yosef, O. 1987. The Late Pleistocene in the Levant, in *The Pleistocene Old World: Regional Perspectives.* Edited by O. Soffer, pp. 219–236. New York: Plenum Press.

Bar-Yosef, O. 2011. Climatic fluctuations and early farming in West and East Asia. *Current Anthropology* 52:S175–S193.

Bar-Yosef, O. 2015. Chinese Palaeolithic challenges for interpretations of Palaeolithic archaeology. *Anthropologie* 53:77–92.

Bar-Yosef, O., and D. Alon. 1988. Nahal Hemar Cave. *Atiqot* XVIII.

Bar-Yosef, O., and A. Belfer-Cohen. 1989. The origins of sedentism and farming communities in the Levant. *Journal of World Prehistory* 3:447–498.

Bar-Yosef, O., and A. Gopher. Editors. 1997. *An Early Neolithic Village in the Jordan Valley. Part 1: The Archaeology of Netiv Hagdud.* Cambridge, MA: Peabody Museum of Archaeology and Ethnology.

Bar-Yosef, O., and N. Goren. 1973. Natufian remains from Hayonim Cave. *Paléorient* 1:49–68.

Bar-Yosef, O., and N. Goren-Inbar. 1993. *The Lithic Assemblages of 'Ubeidiya. Qedem 34.* Jerusalem: Hebrew University Institute of Archaeology.

Bar-Yosef, O., A. N. Goring-Morris, and A. Gopher. Editors. 2010. *Gilgal: Early Neolithic Occupations in the Lower Jordan Valley: The Excavations of Tamar Noy.* Oakville, CT: Oxbow Books.

Bar-Yosef, O., and S. L. Kuhn. 1999. The big deal about blades: Laminar technologies and human evolution. *American Anthropologist* 101:322–338.

Bar-Yosef, O., and Y. Wang. 2012. Paleolithic archaeology in China. *Annual Review of Anthropology* 41:319–335.

Barham, L. Editor. 2000. *The Middle Stone Age of Zambia, South Central Africa.* Bristol, UK: Western Academic and Specialist Press.

Barham, L. 2010. A technological fix for "Dunbar's dilemma." *Proceedings of the British Academy* 158:367–389.

Barham, L. 2013. *From Hand to Handle: The First Industrial Revolution.* New York, NY: Oxford University Press.

Barham, L., and P. Mitchell. 2008. *The First Africans: African Archaeology from the Earliest Toolmakers to Most Recent Foragers*. New York: Cambridge University Press.

Barkai, R. 2005. *Flint and Stone Axes as Cultural Markers. Socio-Economic Changes as Reflected in Holocene Flint Tool Industries of the Southern Levant*. Berlin: ex oriente.

Barkai, R. 2011. The evolution of Neolithic and Chalcolithic woodworking tools and the intensification of human production: Axes, adzes, and chisels from the Southern Levant, in *Stone Axe Studies III*. Edited by V. Davis and M. Edmonds, pp. 39–54. Oxford, UK: Oxbow Books.

Barkai, R., A. Gopher, and R. Shimelmitz. 2006. Middle Pleistocene blade production in the Levant: An Amudian assemblage from Qesem Cave, Israel. *Eurasian Prehistory* 3:39–74.

Barth, M. 2006. The lithic artifacts from Baaz Rockshelter, in *Tübingen-Damascus Excavation and Survey Project, 1999–2005*. Edited by N. J. Conard, pp. 25–109. Tübingen: Kerns Verlag.

Basell, L. S. 2008. Middle Stone Age (MSA) site distributions in eastern Africa and their relationship to Quaternary environmental change, refugia and the evolution of *Homo sapiens*. *Quaternary Science Reviews* 27:2484–2498.

Baumler, M. F., and J. D. Speth. 1993. A Middle Paleolithic assemblage from Kunji Cave, Iran, in *The Paleolithic Prehistory of the Zagros-Taurus*. Edited by D. Olzewski and H. L. Dibble, pp. 1–73. Philadelphia, PA: University of Pennsylvania Museum (Monograph No. 83).

Belfer-Cohen, A., and A. N. Goring-Morris. 2011. Becoming farmers: The inside story. *Current Anthropology* 52:S209–S220.

Belfer-Cohen, A., and L. Grossman. 1997. The lithic assemblage of Salibiya I. *Journal of the Israel Prehistoric Society* 27:19–41.

Bell, R. E. 2000. *Archaeological Investigations at the Site of El Inga, Ecuador. Noble Museum of Natural History Monograph No. 1*. Norman, OK: University of Oklahoma Press.

Bender, B. 1978. From gatherer–hunter to farmer: A social perspective. *World Archaeology* 10:204–222.

Berna, F., P. Goldberg, L. K. Horwitz, J. Brink, S. Holt, M. Bamford, and M. Chazan. 2012. Microstratigraphic evidence of in situ fire in the Acheulean strata of Wonderwerk Cave, Northern Cape province, South Africa.

Proceedings of the National Academy of Sciences 109:E1215–E1220.

Beyene, Y., S. Katoh, G. WoldeGabriel, W. K. Hart, K. Uto, M. Sudo, M. Kondo, M. Hyodo, P. R. Renne, G. Suwa, and B. Asfaw. 2013. The characteristics and chronology of the earliest Acheulean at Konso, Ethiopia. *Proceedings of the National Academy of Sciences* 110:1584–1591.

Béyries, S. 1988. Functional variability of lithic sets in the Middle Paleolithic, in *The Upper Pleistocene Prehistory of Western Eurasia, Volume 1, University of Pennsylvania Museum Monograph No. 54*. Edited by H. L. Dibble and A. Montet-White, pp. 213–223. Philadelphia: University of Pennsylvania Press.

Binford, L. R. 1962. Archaeology as anthropology. *American Antiquity* 28:217–225.

Binford, L. R. 1978. *Nunamuit Ethnoarchaeology*. New York: Academic Press.

Binford, L. R. 1979. Organization and formation processes: Looking at curated technologies. *Journal of Anthropological Research* 35:255–273.

Binford, L. R. 1980. Willow smoke and dogs' tails: Hunter-gatherer settlement systems and archaeological site formation. *American Antiquity* 45:4–20.

Binford, L. R. 1983. *In Pursuit of the Past: Decoding the Archaeological Record*. New York: Thames & Hudson.

Binford, L. R. 1985. Human ancestors: Changing views of their behavior. *Journal of Anthropological Archaeology* 4:292–327.

Binford, L. R. 1986. An Alyawara day: Making men's knives and beyond. *American Antiquity* 51:547–562.

Bingham, P. M. 2000. Human evolution and human history: A complete theory. *Evolutionary Anthropology* 9:248–257.

Bingham, P. M., and M. Souza. 2009. *Death at a Distance and the Birth of a Humane Universe*. Charleston, NC: Booksurge.

Bird, J. 1988. *Travels and Archaeology in South Chile*. Iowa City, IO: University of Iowa Press.

Blumenschine, R. J. 1986. *Early Hominid Scavenging Opportunities: Implications of Carcass Availability in the Serengeti and Ngorongoro Ecosystems*. Oxford, UK: Archaeopress (British Archaeological Reports International Series 283).

Blumenschine, R. J., and B. L. Pobiner. 2007. Zooarchaeology and the ecology of early hominin carnivory, in *Evolution of the Human*

Diet: The Known, the Unknown, and the Unknowable. Edited by P. Ungar, pp. 167–190. Oxford, UK: Oxford University Press.

Bocquentin, F., and O. Bar-Yosef. 2004. Early Natufian remains: Evidence for physical conflict from Mt. Carmel, Israel. *Journal of Human Evolution* 47:19–23.

Boëda, E., J.-M. Geneste, and L. Meignen. 1990. Identification de chaines opératoires lithiques du Paléolithique ancien et moyen. *Paléo* 2:43–80.

Boëda, E., A. Lordeau, C. Lahaye, G. D. Felice, S. Viana, I. Clemente-Conte, M. Pino, M. Fontugne, S. Hoeltz, N. Guidon, A.-M. Pessis, A. Da Costa, and M. Pagli. 2013. The Late-Pleistocene industries of Piauí, Brazil: New data, in *Paleoamerican Odyssey.* Edited by K. E. Graf, C. V. Ketron, and M. R. Waters, pp. 445–467. College Station, TX: Center for the Study of the First Americans, Texas A&M University.

Boesch, C., and H. Boesch. 1982. Optimisation of nut-cracking with natural hammers by wild chimpanzees. *Behaviour* 83:265–286.

Boesch, C., and H. Boesch. 1984a. Mental map in wild chimpanzees: An analysis of hammer transports for nut cracking. *Primates* 25:160–170.

Boesch, C., and H. Boesch. 1984b. Possible causes of sex differences in the use of natural hammers by wild chimpanzees. *Journal of Human Evolution* 13:415–440.

Boesch-Aschermann, H., and C. Boesch. 1994. Hominization in the rainforest: The chimpanzee's piece of the puzzle. *Evolutionary Anthropology* 3:9–16.

Bohmers, A. 1951. Die Höhlen von Mauern. *Palaeohistoria* 1:1–107.

Bordes, F. 1961. *Typologie du Paléolithique ancien et moyen.* Bordeaux: Delmas.

Bordes, F. 1968. *The Old Stone Age.* New York: McGraw-Hill.

Bordes, F. 1969. Reflections on technology and techniques in the Paleolithic. *Arctic Anthropology* 6:1–29.

Bordes, F. 1972. *A Tale of Two Caves.* New York: Harper and Row.

Bordes, F., and D. de Sonneville-Bordes. 1970. The significance of variability in Palaeolithic assemblages. *World Archaeology* 2:61–73.

Boutié, P., and S. Rosen. 1989. Des gisements Moustériens dans le Neguev central: Resultats preliminaires de prospections, in *Investigations in South Levantine Prehistory/Préhistoire du Sud-Levant.* Edited by O. Bar-Yosef and B. Vandermeersch, pp. 169–185. Oxford, UK: Archaeopress (British Archaeological Reports International Series 497).

Bouzouggar, A., N. Barton, M. Vanhaeren, F. d'Errico, S. Collcutt, T. Higham, E. Hodge, S. Parfitt, E. Rhodes, J.-L. Schwenninger, C. Stringer, E. Turner, S. Ward, A. Moutmir, and A. Stambouli. 2007. 82,000-year-old shell beads from North Africa and implications for the origins of modern human behavior. *Proceedings of the National Academy of Sciences* 104:9964–9969.

Bowdler, S., and R. Jones. 1984. *Hunter Hill, Hunter Island. Archaeological Investigations of a Prehistoric Tasmanian Site.* Canberra: Australian National Museum (Terra Australis Volume 8).

Bowdler, S., R. Jones, H. Allen, and A. G. Thorne. 1970. Pleistocene human remains from Australia: A living site and human cremation from Lake Mungo, Western New South Wales. *World Archaeology* 2:39–60.

Bower, B. 2015. Reading the stones: There is more than one way to tell the story of human evolution via ancient tools. *Science News* 187:16–21.

Bowler, P. J. 1986. *Theories of Human Evolution: A Century of Debate, 1844–1944.* Baltimore: Johns Hopkins University Press.

Bowles, S. 2006. Group competition, reproductive leveling, and the evolution of human altruism. *Science* 314:1569–1572.

Brain, C. K., and P. Shipman. 1993. The Swartkrans bone tools. *Transvaal Museum Monograph* 8.

Bramble, D. M., and D. E. Lieberman. 2004. Endurance running and the evolution of *Homo. Nature* 432:345–352.

Brandt, S., and K. J. Weedman. 1997. The ethnoarchaeology of hide working and flaked stone tool use in Southern Ethiopia, in *Ethiopia in Broader Perspective: Papers of the 12th International Conference on Ethiopian Studies.* Edited by K. Fukui, E. Kuimoto, and M. Shigeta, pp. 351–361. Kyoto: Shokado Book Sellers.

Brandt, S. A., E. C. Fisher, E. A. Hildebrand, R. Vogelsang, S. H. Ambrose, J. Lesur, and H. Wang. 2012. Early MIS 3 occupation of

Mochena Borago Rockshelter, Southwest Ethiopian Highlands: Implications for Late Pleistocene archaeology, paleoenvironments and modern human dispersals. *Quaternary International* 274:38–54.

Brantingham, P. J., S. L. Kuhn, and K. W. Kerry. Editors. 2004. *The Early Upper Paleolithic Beyond Western Europe*. Berkeley, CA: University of California Press.

Braun, D. R. 2014. Earliest stone tool industries, in *The Cambridge World Prehistory, Volume 1: Africa, South and Southeast Asia and the Pacific*. Edited by C. Renfrew and P. Bahn, pp. 65–79. New York: Cambridge University Press.

Bril, B., J. Smaers, J. Steele, R. Rein, T. Nonaka, G. Dietrich, E. Biryukova, S. Hirata, and V. Roux. 2012. Functional mastery of percussive technology in nut-cracking and stone-flaking actions: Experimental comparison and implications for the evolution of the human brain. *Philosophical Transactions of the Royal Society of London B: Biological Sciences* 367:59–74.

Brink, J. 1978. *An Experimental Study of Microwear Formation on Endscrapers*. Ottawa: National Museum of Canada, National Museum of Man Mercury Series.

Brown, K. S., C. W. Marean, A. I. R. Herries, Z. Jacobs, C. Tribolo, D. Braun, D. L. Roberts, M. C. Meyer, and J. Bernatchez. 2009. Fire as an engineering tool of early modern humans. *Science* 325:859–862.

Brumm, A., F. Aziz, G. van den Bergh, M. J. Morwood, M. W. Moore, I. Kurniawan, D. Hobbs, and R. Fullagar. 2006. Early stone technology on Flores and its implications for *Homo floresiensis*. *Nature* 441:624–628.

Brumm, A., M. W. Moore, G. D. van den Bergh, I. Kurniawan, M. J. Morwood, and F. Aziz. 2010. Stone technology at the Middle Pleistocene site of Mata Menge, Flores, Indonesia. *Journal of Archaeological Science* 37:451–473.

Bunn, H. T., J. W. K. Harris, Z. Kaufulu, E. Kroll, K. Schick, N. Toth, and A. K. Behrensmeyer. 1980. FxJj 50: An early Pleistocene site in northern Kenya. *World Archaeology* 12:109–136.

Burger, J. M., N. Messian, S. Patel, A. del Prado, and C. Anderson. 2004. What a coincidence! The effects of incidental similarity on compliance. *Personality and Social Psychology Bulletin* 30:35–43.

Burkart, J. M., S. B. Hrdy, and C. P. Van Schaik. 2009. Cooperative breeding and human cognitive evolution. *Evolutionary Anthropology* 18:175–186.

Burroughs, W. J. 2005. *Climate Change in Prehistory: The End of the Reign of Chaos*. Cambridge, UK: Cambridge University Press.

Byrd, B. F., and A. N. Garrard. 1992. New dimensions to the Epipalaeolithic of the Wadi el-Jilat in Central Jordan. *Paléorient* 18:47–62.

Callahan, E. 1979. The basics of biface knapping in the Eastern Fluted Point Tradition. *Archaeology of Eastern North America* 7:1–180.

Callow, P., and J. M. Cornford. Editors. 1986. *La Cotte de St. Brelade 1961–1978, Excavations of C.B.M. McBurney*. Norwich, UK: Geo Books.

Cann, J. R., J. E. Dixon, and C. Renfrew. 1969. Obsidian analysis and the obsidian trade, in *Science in Archaeology. A Survey of Progress and Research*. Edited by D. Brothwell and E. Higgs, pp. 578–591. London: Thames & Hudson.

Carbonell, E., J. M. Bermudez de Castro, J. M. Pares, A. Perez-Gonzalez, G. Cuenca-Bescos, A. Olle, M. Mosquera, R. Huguet, J. van der Made, A. Rosas, R. Sala, J. Vallverdu, N. Garcia, D. E. Granger, M. Martinon-Torres, X. P. Rodriguez, G. M. Stock, J. M. Verges, E. Allue, F. Burjachs, I. Caceres, A. Canals, A. Benito, C. Diez, M. Lozano, A. Mateos, M. Navazo, J. Rodriguez, J. Rosell, and J. L. Arsuaga. 2008. The first hominin of Europe. *Nature* 452:465–469.

Carr, C. 1995. A unified middle-range theory of artifact design, in *Style, Society, and Person: Archaeological and Ethnological Perspectives*. Edited by C. Carr and J. Neitzel, pp. 171–258. New York, NY: Plenum.

Carvalho, S., D. Biro, E. Cunha, K. Hockings, W. C. McGrew, B. G. Richmond, and T. Matsuzawa. 2012. Chimpanzee carrying behaviour and the origins of human bipedality. *Current Biology* 22:180–181.

Carvalho, S., E. Cunha, C. Sousa, and T. Matsuzawa. 2008. *Chaînes opèratoires* and resource-exploitation strategies in chimpanzee (*Pan troglodytes*) nut cracking. *Journal of Human Evolution* 55:148–163.

Caspari, R., and M. Wolpoff. 2013. The process of modern human origins: The evolutionary and demographic changes giving rise to modern humans, in *The Origins of Modern Humans: Biology Reconsidered*. Edited by F. H. Smith and

J. C. Ahern, pp. 355–391. New York: John Wiley and Sons.

Cauvin, J. 1968. *Fouilles de Byblos IV: Les outillages néolithiques de Byblos et du littoral libanais*. Paris: Librairie d'Amérique et d'Orient, Adrien Maisonneuve.

Cauvin, J. 2000. *The Birth of the Gods and the Origin of Agriculture*. Cambridge, UK: Cambridge University Press.

Cauvin, M.-C. 1983. Les faucilles préhistoriques du Proche-Orient données morphologiques et fonctionelles. *Paléorient* 9:63–79.

Cavallo, J. A., and R. J. Blumenschine. 1989. Tree-stored leopard kills: Expanding the hominid scavenging niche. *Journal of Human Evolution* 18:393–399.

Chavaillon, J., N. Chavaillon, F. Hours, and M. Piperno. 1979. From the Oldowan to the Middle Stone Age at Melka-Kunture (Ethiopia). Understanding cultural changes. *Quaternaria* 21:87–114.

Chazan, M. 1997. Redefining Levallois. *Journal of Human Evolution* 33:719–735.

Chiotti, L. 2005. *Les industries lithiques aurignaciennes de l'abri Pataud, Dordogne, France: Les fouilles de Hallam L. Movius Jr*. Oxford, UK: Archaeopress (British Archaeological Reports International Series 1392).

Chomsky, N. 2002. *Syntactic Structures*, Second Edition. The Hague: Mouton.

Churchill, S. E. 1993. Weapon technology, prey size selection, and hunting methods in modern hunter-gatherers: Implications for hunting in the Palaeolithic and Mesolithic, in *Hunting and Animal Exploitation in the Later Paleolithic and Mesolithic of Eurasia*. Edited by G. L. Peterkin, H. Bricker, and P. A. Mellars, pp.11–24. Washington, D.C.: American Anthropological Association (Archaeological Paper 4).

Churchill, S. E. 2006. Bioenergetic perspectives on Neanderthal thermoregulatory and activity budgets, in *Neanderthals Revisited: New Approaches and Perspectives*. Edited by K. Harvarti and T. Harrison, pp. 113–134. Dordrecht: Springer.

Churchill, S. E. 2014. *Thin on the Ground: Neandertal Biology, Archaeology and Ecology*. New York: Wiley-Blackwell.

Cieri, R. L., S. E. Churchill, R. G. Franciscus, J. Tan, and B. Hare. 2014. Craniofacial feminization, social tolerance, and the origins of behavioral modernity. *Current Anthropology* 55:419–443.

Clark, G. 1954. *Excavations at Star Carr*. Cambridge: Cambridge University Press.

Clark, G. 1977. *World Prehistory in New Perspective*, Third Edition. Cambridge, UK: Cambridge University Press.

Clark, G. A., and J. Riel-Salvatore. 2006. Observations on systematics in Paleolithic archaeology, in *Transitions before the Transition*. Edited by E. Hovers and S. L. Kuhn, pp. 29–57. New York: Plenum/Kluwer.

Clark, J. D. 1967. The Middle Acheulian occupation site at Latamne, northern Syria. *Quaternaria* 9:1–68.

Clark, J. D. 1984. The cultures of the Middle Palaeolithic/Middle Stone Age, in *The Cambridge History of Africa, Volume 1*. Edited by J. D. Clark, pp. 248–341. Cambridge, UK: Cambridge University Press.

Clark, J. D. Editor. 2001. *Kalambo Falls Prehistoric Site, Volume III, The Earlier Cultures: Middle and Earlier Stone Age*. Cambridge, UK: Cambridge University Press.

Clark, J. D., Y. Beyene, G. WoldeGabriel, W. K. Hart, P. R. Renne, H. Gilbert, A. Defleur, G. Suwa, S. Katoh, K. R. Ludwig, J.-R. Boisserie, B. Asfaw, and T. D. White. 2003. Stratigraphic, chronological and behavioural contexts of Pleistocene *Homo sapiens* from Middle Awash, Ethiopia. *Nature* 423:747–752.

Clark, J. D., and H. Kurashina. 1981. A study of the work of a modern tanner in Ethiopia and its relevance for archaeological interpretation, in *Modern Material Culture: the Archaeology of Us*. Edited by R. A. Gould and M. B. Schiffer, pp. 303–320. New York: Academic Press.

Clark, P. U., A. S. Dyke, J. D. Shakun, A. E. Carlson, J. Clark, B. Wohlfarth, J. X. Mitrovica, S. W. Hostetler, and A. M. McCabe. 2009. The Last Glacial Maximum. *Science* 325:710–714.

Clarke, D. L. 1978. *Analytical Archaeology*, Second Edition. New York: Columbia University Press.

Clarke, R. 1935. The flint-knapping industry at Brandon. *Antiquity* 9:38–56.

Clarkson, C., M. Smith, B. Marwick, R. Fullagar, L. A. Wallis, P. Faulkner, T. Manne, E. Hayes, R. G. Roberts, and Z. Jacobs. 2015. The archaeology, chronology and stratigraphy of Madjedbebe (Malakunanja II): A site in northern Australia with early occupation. *Journal of Human Evolution* 83:46–64.

Collard, M., B. Buchanan, and M. J. O'Brien. 2013. Population size as an explanation for patterns in the paleolithic archaeological record: More caution is needed. *Current Anthropology* 54:S388–S396.

Collard, M., M. D. Kemery, and S. J. Banks. 2005. Causes of toolkit variation among hunter-gatherers: A test of four competing hypotheses. *Canadian Journal of Archaeology* 29:1–19.

Collins, M. B. 1997. The lithics from Monte Verde, a descriptive-morphological analysis, in *Monte Verde: A Late Pleistocene Site in Chile.* Edited by T. D. Dillehay, pp. 383–506. Washington, D.C.: Smithsonian Institution Press.

Collins, M. B. 1999. *Clovis Blade Technology.* Dallas, TX: University of Texas Press.

Collins, M. B. 2014. Initial peopling of the Americas: Context, findings and issues, in *The Cambridge World Prehistory, Volume 2: East Asia and the Americas.* Edited by C. Renfrew and P. Bahn, pp. 903–922. New York: Cambridge University Press.

Combier, J., and A. Montet-White. Editors. 2002. *Solutré, 1968–1998. Mémoire de la Société Préhistorique française XXX.* Paris: Société préhistorique française.

Conard, N. J. Editor. 2006. *When Neanderthals and Modern Humans Met.* Tübingen: Kerns Verlag.

Conard, N. J., and D. S. Adler. 1997. Lithic reduction and hominid behavior in the Middle Paleolithic of the Rhineland. *Journal of Archaeological Science* 53:147–175.

Conard, N. J., J. Serangeli, U. Böhner, B. M. Starkovich, C. E. Miller, B. Urban, and T. Van Kolfschoten. 2015. Excavations at Schöningen and paradigm shifts in human evolution. *Journal of Human Evolution* 89:1–17.

Corbey, R., A. Jagich, M. Collard, and K. Vaesne. 2016. The Acheulean handaxe: More like bird song than a Beatles' tune? *Evolutionary Anthropology* 25:6–19.

Cornelissen, E. 1992. *Site GNJH-17 and Its Implications for the Archaeology of the Kapthurin Formation, Baringo, Kenya.* Tervuren, Belgium: Annals du Musée Royal de l'Afrique Centrale (Volume 133).

Cosgrove, R. 1995. Late Pleistocene behavioural variation and time trends: The case from Tasmania. *Archaeology in Oceania* 30:83–104.

Cotterell, B., and J. Kamminga. 1987. The formation of flakes. *American Antiquity* 52:675–708.

Coward, F. 2010. Small worlds, material culture and ancient Near Eastern social networks, in *Social Brain and Distributed Mind.* Edited by R. I. M. Dunbar, C. Gamble, and J. A. J. Gowlett, pp. 449–480. Oxford, UK: Oxford University Press (Proceedings of the British Academy 158).

Crabtree, D. 1972. *An Introduction to Flintworking.* Pocatello, ID: Idaho State Museum (Occasional Paper No. 28).

Crew, H. L. 1976. The Mousterian site of Rosh Ein Mor, in *Prehistory and Paleoenvironments of the Central Negev, Israel, Volume 1.* Edited by A. E. Marks, pp. 75–112. Dallas, TX: Southern Methodist University Press.

Crompton, R. H., and J. A. J. Gowlett. 1993. Multidimensional form in Acheulian bifaces from Kilombe, Kenya. *Journal of Human Evolution* 25:175–199.

Cropper, D. 2006. Chipped stone polyhedrons from Late Neolithic Umm Meshrat I, Jordan. *Paléorient* 32:85–97.

Crosby, A. W. 1986. *Ecological Imperialism: The Biological Expansion of Europe, 900–1900.* Cambridge, UK: Cambridge University Press.

Crowfoot-Payne, J. 1983. The flint industries of Jericho, in *Excavations at Jericho, Volume 5.* Edited by K. M. Kenyon and T. A. Holland, pp. 622–759. London: The British School of Archaeology in Jerusalem.

Cziesla, E. 1990. On refitting stone artefacts, in *The Big Puzzle: International Symposium on Refitting Stone Implements.* Edited by E. Cziesla, S. Eickhoff, N. Arts, and D. Winter, pp. 9–44. Bonn: Holos Press.

Derev'anko, A. P., D. B. Shimkin, and W. R. Powers. 1998. *The Paleolithic of Siberia: New Discoveries and Interpretations.* Chicago, IL: University of Illinois Press.

d'Errico, F. 2003. The invisible frontier. A multiple species model for the origin of behavioral modernity. *Evolutionary Anthropology* 12:188–202.

d'Errico, F. 2007. The origin of humanity and modern cultures: Archaeology's view. *Diogenes* 54:122–133.

d'Errico, F., and L. Backwell. 2003. Possible evidence of bone tool shaping by Swartkrans early hominids. *Journal of Archaeological Science* 30:1559–1576.

d'Errico, F., C. Henshilwood, M. Vanhaeren, and K. van Niekerk. 2005. *Nassarius kraussianus* shell beads from Blombos Cave: Evidence for symbolic behaviour in the Middle Stone Age. *Journal of Human Evolution* 48:3–24.

de la Torre, I. 2004. Omo revisited: Evaluating the technological skills of Pliocene hominids. *Current Anthropology* 45:439–467.

de la Torre, I., and R. Mora. 2005. *Technological Strategies in the Lower Pleistocene at Olduvai Beds I & II*. Liège, Belgium: Université de Liège (ERAUL 112).

de la Torre, I., and R. Mora. 2009. The technology of the ST site complex, in *Peninj: A Research Project on Human Origins 1995–2005*. Edited by M. Domínguez-Rodrigo, L. Alcala, and L. Luque, pp. 145–189. Cambridge, MA: Oxbow Books (American School of Prehistoric Research).

de Lumley, H., D. Barsky, and D. Cauche. 2009. Archaic stone industries from East Africa and Southern Europe: Pre-Oldowan and Oldowan, in *The Cutting Edge: New Approaches to the Archaeology of Human Origins*. Edited by K. Schick and N. Toth, pp. 55–92. Gosport, IN: Stone Age Institute Press.

de Mortillet, G. 1883. *La Préhistorique: Antiquité de l'homme*. Paris: C. Reinwald.

de Sonneville-Bordes, D. 1960. *Le Paléolithique supérieur en Périgord*. Bordeaux, France: Delmas.

de Sonneville-Bordes, D. 1963. Upper Paleolithic cultures in Western Europe. *Science* 142:347–355.

Debénath, A., and H. L. Dibble. 1994. *Handbook of Paleolithic Typology, Volume 1: Lower and Middle Paleolithic of Europe*. Philadelphia: University of Pennsylvania Press.

deFrance, S. D., D. K. Keefer, J. B. Richardson, and A. U. Alvarez. 2001. Late Paleo-Indian coastal foragers: Specialized extractive behavior at Quebrada Tacahuay, Peru. *Latin American Antiquity* 12:413–426.

Delagnes, A., J.-R. Boisserie, Y. Beyene, K. Chuniaud, C. Guillemot, and M. Schuster. 2011. Archaeological investigations in the Lower Omo Valley (Shungura Formation, Ethiopia): New data and perspectives. *Journal of Human Evolution* 61:215–222.

Delagnes, A., A. Lenoble, S. Harmand, J.-P. Brugal, S. Prat, J.-J. Tiercelin, and H. Roche. 2006. Interpreting pachyderm single carcass sites in the African Lower and Early Middle Pleistocene record: A multidisciplinary approach to the site of Nadung'a 4 (Kenya). *Journal of Anthropological Archaeology* 25:448–465.

Delagnes, A., and H. Roche. 2005. Late Pliocene hominid knapping skills: The case of Lokalalei 2 C, West Turkana, Kenya. *Journal of Human Evolution* 48:435–472.

Deller, D. B., and C. J. Ellis. 2011. *Crowfield (AfHj-31): A Unique Paleoindian Fluted Point Site from Southwestern Ontario*. Ann Arbor, MI: University of Michigan Museum.

Delporte, H. 1968a. L'abri du facteur à Tursac: Étude generale. *Gallia Préhistoire* 11:1–112.

Delporte, H. Editor. 1968b. *Le Grand Abri de La Ferrassie: Fouilles 1968–1973. Études Quaternaires 7, Université de Provence*. Paris: Institut de Paléontologie Humaine.

Demars, P.-Y., and P. Laurent. 1992. *Types d'outils du Paléolithique Supérieur en Europe*. Paris: Presses du CNRS.

Dennell, R. 2009. *The Palaeolithic Settlement of Asia*. Cambridge, UK: Cambridge University Press.

Dibble, H., and M. Lenoir. Editors. 1995. *The Middle Paleolithic of Combe Capelle Bas (France). University Museum Monograph 91*. Philadelphia, PA: University Museum, University of Pennsylvania.

Dibble, H. L. 1995. Middle Paleolithic scraper reduction: Background, clarification, and review of the evidence to date. *Journal of Archaeological Method and Theory* 2:299–368.

Dibble, H. L., V. Aldeias, Z. Jacobs, D. I. Olszewski, Z. Rezek, S. C. Lin, E. Alvarez-Fernandez, C. C. Barshay-Szmidt, E. Hallett-Desguez, D. Reed, K. Reed, D. Richter, T. E. Steele, A. Skinner, B. Blackwell, E. Doronicheva, and M. El-Hajraoui. 2013. On the industrial attributions of the Aterian and Mousterian of the Maghreb. *Journal of Human Evolution* 64:194–210.

Dibble, H. L., M. A. Hajraoui, and D. I. Olszewski. 2012. Grotte des contrebandiers: Les industries lithiques, in *La Préhistoire de la région de Rabat-Témara*. Edited by M. A. Hajraoui, R. Nespoulet, A. Debénath, and H. L. Dibble, pp. 253–263. Rabat, Morocco: Institut National des Sciences de l'Archéologie et du Patrimoine.

Dibble, H. L., and S. P. McPherron. 2006. The missing Mousterian. *Current Anthropology* 47:777–803.

Dibble, H. L., and Z. Rezek. 2009. Introducing a new experimental design for controlled studies of flake formation: Results for exterior platform angle, platform depth, angle of blow, velocity, and force. *Journal of Archaeological Science* 36:1945–1954.

Dillehay, T. D. 2013. Entangled knowledge: Old trends and new thoughts in First South American Studies, in *Paleoamerican Odyssey*. Edited by K. Graf, pp. 377–396. College Station, TX: Texas A&M University Press.

Disotell, T. 2013. Genetic perspectives on ape and human evolution, in *A Companion to Paleoanthropology*. Edited by D. Begun. Hoboken, NJ: Blackwell.

Dixon, E. J. 1999. *Bones, Boats and Bison: Archeology and the First Colonization of Western North America*. Albuquerque, NM: University of New Mexico Press.

Dixon, E. J. 2013. Late Pleistocene colonization of North America from Northeast Asia: New insights from large-scale paleogeographic reconstructions. *Quaternary International* 285:57–67.

Domínguez-Rodrigo, M., L. Alcala, and L. Luque. Editors. 2009. *Peninj: A Research Project on Human Origins 1995–2005*. Cambridge, MA: Oxbow Books (American School of Prehistoric Research).

Domínguez-Rodrigo, M., R. Barba, and C. P. Egeland. Editors. 2007. *Deconstructing Olduvai*. New York: Springer.

Domínguez-Rodrigo, M., and T. R. Pickering. 2003. Early hominid hunting and scavenging: A zooarchaeological review. *Evolutionary Anthropology* 12:275–282.

Dorrell, P. G. 1983. Appendix A: Stone vessels, tools, and objects, in *Excavations at Jericho*, Volume 5. Edited by K. M. Kenyon and T. A. Holland, pp. 487–575. London: The British School of Archaeology in Jerusalem.

Dortch, J. 2004. Late Quaternary vegetation change and the extinction of Black-flanked Rock-wallaby (*Petrogale lateralis*) at Tunnel Cave, southwestern Australia. *Palaeogeography, Palaeoclimatology, Palaeoecology* 211:185–204.

Dubreuil, L., and D. Savage. 2014. Ground stones: A synthesis of the use-wear approach. *Journal of Archaeological Science* 48:139–153.

Dunbar, R. I. M. 1992. Neocortex size as a constraint on group size in primates. *Journal of Human Evolution* 20:469–493.

Edwards, P. C. Editor. 2012. *Wadi Hammeh 27: An early Natufian site at Pella, Jordan*. Leiden: Koninklijke Brill NV.

Ellis, C. J. 1997. Factors influencing the use of stone projectile tips: An ethnographic perspective, in *Projectile Technology*. Edited by H. Knecht, pp. 37–78. New York: Plenum.

Enard, W., M. Przeworski, S. E. Fisher, C. S. L. Lai, V. Wiebe, T. Kitano, A. P. Monaco, and S. Pääbo. 2002. Molecular evolution of FOXP2, a gene involved in speech and language. *Nature* 418:869–872.

Eren, M. I., F. Diez-Martin, and M. Domínguez-Rodrigo. 2013. An empirical test of the relative frequency of bipolar reduction in Beds VI, V, and III at Mumba Rockshelter, Tanzania: Implications for the East African Middle to Late Stone Age transition. *Journal of Archaeological Science* 40:248–256.

Eren, M. I., A. Greenspan, and C. G. Sampson. 2008. Are Upper Paleolithic blade cores more productive than Middle Paleolithic discoidal cores? A replication experiment. *Journal of Human Evolution* 55:952–961.

Eren, M. I., S. J. Lycett, R. J. Patten, B. Buchanan, J. Pargeter, and M. J. O'Brien. 2016. Test, model, and method validation: The role of experimental stone artifact replication in hypothesis-driven archaeology. *Ethnoarchaeology* 8:103–136.

Feblot-Augustins, J. 1997. *La Circulation des matières premières au Paléolithique: Synthèse de données, perspectives comportementales*. Liège: Etudes et Recherches Archéologiques de l'Université de Liège, No. 75.

Finlayson, B., I. Kuijt, and N. B. Goodale. 2002. Results from the 2001 excavations at Dhra', Jordan: Chipped stone technology, typology, and intra-assemblage variability. *Paléorient* 28:125–140.

Finlayson, B., and S. Mithen. Editors. 2007. *The Early Prehistory of Wadi Faynan, Southern Jordan: Archaeological Survey of Wadis Faynan, Ghuwayr and al-Bustan and Evaluation of the Pre-Pottery Neolithic A Site of WF16*. Oxford, UK: Council for British Research in the Levant (Levant Supplementary Series, Volume 4).

Fisher, S. E., and M. Ridley. 2013. Culture, genes, and the human revolution. *Science* 340:929–930.

Fleagle, J. G. 2013. *Primate Adaptation and Evolution*, Third Edition. Waltham, MA: Academic Press.

Fleagle, J. G., and F. E. Grine. 2014. The genus *Homo* in Africa, in *The Cambridge World Prehistory, Volume 1: Africa, South and Southeast Asia and the Pacific*. Edited by C. Renfrew and P. Bahn, pp. 85–105. New York: Cambridge University Press.

Fleagle, J. G., and D. E. Lieberman. 2015. Major transformations in the evolution of primate locomotion, in *Great Transformations in Vertebrate Evolution*. Edited by K. P. Dial, N. Shubin, and E. Brainard, pp. 257–278. Chicago, IL: University of Chicago Press.

Fleagle, J. G., J. J. Shea, F. E. Grine, A. L. Baden, and R. Leakey. Editors. 2010. *Out of Africa 1: The First Hominin Colonization of Eurasia*. New York: Springer.

Foley, R. A. 1987. Hominid species and stone-tool assemblages: How are they related? *Antiquity* 61:380–392.

Foley, R.A. 2002. Adaptive radiations and dispersals in hominin evolutionary ecology. *Evolutionary Anthropology* 11:32–37.

Foley, R.A., and M. M. Lahr. 1997. Mode 3 technologies and the evolution of modern humans. *Cambridge Archaeological Journal* 7:3–36.

Frison, G. C., and B. A. Bradley. 1980. *Folsom Tools and Technology of the Hanson Site, Wyoming*. Albuquerque, NM: University of New Mexico Press.

Frison, G. C., and B. A. Bradley. 1999. *The Fenn Cache: Clovis Weapons & Tools*. Santa Fe, NM: One Horse Land and Cattle Company.

Gabunia, L., S. C. Antón, D. Lordkipanidze, A. Vekua, A. Justus, and C. C. Swisher, III. 2001. Dmanisi and dispersal. *Evolutionary Anthropology* 10:158–170.

Gallagher, J. P. 1977. Contemporary stone tools in Ethiopia: Implications for archaeology. *Journal of Field Archaeology* 4:406–414.

Gamble, C. 1999. *The Palaeolithic Societies of Europe*. New York: Cambridge University Press.

Gamble, C. 2013. *Settling the Earth: The Archaeology of Deep Human History*. New York: Cambridge University Press.

Gamble, C., J. Gowlett, and R. Dunbar. 2014. *Thinking Big: How the Evolution of Social Life Shaped the Human Mind*. New York: Thames & Hudson.

Gamble, C., and R. Kruszynski. 2009. John Evans, Joseph Prestwich and the stone that shattered the time barrier. *Antiquity* 83:461–475.

Garcea, E. A. A. Editor. 2010. *South-Eastern Mediterranean Peoples Between 130,000 and 10,000 Years Ago*. Oxford, UK: Oxbow.

Garfinkel, Y. 1994. The PPNC Flint Assemblage from Tel 'Ali, in *Neolithic Chipped Stone Industries of the Fertile Crescent: Proceedings of the First Workshop on PPN Chipped Lithic Industries*. Edited by H. G. Gebel and S. K. Kozlowski, pp. 543–565. Berlin: ex oriente.

Garfinkel, Y. Editor. 2002. *Sha'ar Hagolan Vol 1. Neolithic Art in Context*. Oxford, UK: Oxbow Books.

Garfinkel, Y., and D. Dag. Editors. 2008. *Neolithic Ashkelon*. Jerusalem: Institute of Archaeology, Hebrew University.

Garrod, D. A. E. 1937. Et-Tabun: Description and archaeology, in *The Stone Age of Mount Carmel, Volume 1: Excavations in the Wady el-Mughara*. Edited by D. A. E. Garrod and D. Bate, pp. 57–70. Oxford, UK: Clarendon Press.

Gebel, H. G., M. Muheisen, H. J. Nissen, and N. Qadi. 1998. Late PPNB Basta: Results of 1992, in *Central Settlements in Neolithic Jordan*. Edited by H.-D. Beinert, H. G. Gebel, and R. Neef, pp. 71–104. Berlin: ex oriente.

Geneste, J.-M. 1988. Systèmes d'approvisionnement en matières premières au Paléolithique moyen et supérieur en Aquitaine, in *L'Homme de Néandertal: Volume 8*. Edited by M. Otte, pp. 61–70. Liège: Université de Liège.

Gero, J. M. 1991. Genderlithics: Women's roles in stone tool production, in *Engendering Archaeology: Women in Prehistory*. Edited by J. M. Gero and M. W. Conkey, pp. 163–193. Oxford, UK: Blackwell.

Gillespie, R., D. R. Horton, P. Ladd, P. G. Macumber, T. H. Rich, R. Thorne, and R. V. S. Wright. 1978. Lancefield Swamp and the extinction of the Australian megafauna. *Science* 200:1044–1048.

Gladyshev, S. A., J. W. Olsen, A. V. Tabarev, and A. J. T. Jull. 2012. The Upper Paleolithic of Mongolia: Recent finds and new perspectives. *Quaternary International* 281:36–46.

Goebel, T., and I. Buvit. Editors. 2011. *From the Yenisei to the Yukon*. College Station, TX: Texas A&M University Press.

Goebel, T., M. R. Waters, and D. H. O'Rourke. 2008. The Late Pleistocene dispersal of modern humans in the Americas. *Science* 319:1497–1501.

González Echegaray, J., and L. G. Freeman. 1978. *Vida y muerte en Cueva Morín*. Santander, Spain: Institución Cultural de Cantabria.

Goodall, J. 1986. *The Chimpanzees of Gombe: Patterns of Behavior*. Cambridge, MA: Harvard University Press.

Gopher, A. 1989. *The Flint Assemblages of Munhata (Israel).* Paris: Association Paléorient (Les Cahiers du Centre de Recherche Français de Jérusalem 4).

Gopher, A. 1994. *Arrowheads from the Neolithic Levant: A Seriation Analysis.* Winona Lake, IN: Eisenbrauns.

Gopher, A., R. Barkai, and A. Asaf. 2001. Trends in sickle blade production in the Neolithic of the Hula Valley, Israel, in *Beyond Tools: Redefining the PPN Lithic Assemblages of the Levant.* Edited by I. Caneva, C. Lemorini, D. Zampetti, and P. Biagi, pp. 411–424. Berlin: ex oriente.

Gopher, A., R. Barkai, R. Shimelmitz, M. Khalaidy, C. Lemorini, I. Hershkovitz, and M. Stiner. 2005. Qesem Cave: An Amudian site in central Israel. *Journal of the Israel Prehistoric Society* 35:62–92.

Gopher, A., and R. Gophna. 1993. Cultures of the Eighth and Seventh Millennia BP in the Southern Levant: A review for the 1990s. *Journal of World Prehistory* 7:297–353.

Gopher, A., A. N. Goring-Morris, and D. Gordon. 1994. Nahal Issaron. The lithics of the Late PPNB Occupation, in *Neolithic Chipped Stone Industries of the Fertile Crescent: Proceedings of the First Workshop on PPN Chipped Lithic Industries.* Edited by H. G. Gebel and S. K. Kozlowski, pp. 479–494. Berlin: ex oriente.

Goren-Inbar, N. 1985. The lithic assemblage of the Berekhat Ram Acheulian site, Golan Heights. *Paléorient* 11:7–28.

Goren-Inbar, N. 1990. The lithic assemblages, in *Quneitra: A Mousterian Site on the Golan Heights.* Edited by N. Goren-Inbar, pp. 61–149. Jerusalem: Hebrew University Institute of Archaeology (Qedem 31).

Goren-Inbar, N., S. Belitzky, Y. Goren, R. Rabinovich, and I. Saragusti. 1992. Gesher Benot Ya'aqov - the "Bar": An Acheulian assemblage. *Geoarchaeology* 7:27–40.

Goren-Inbar, N., C. S. Feibel, K. L. Verosub, Y. Melamed, M. E. Kislev, E. Tchernov, and I. Saragusti. 2000. Pleistocene milestones on the Out-of-Africa Corridor at Gesher Benot Ya'aqov, Israel. *Science* 289:944–947.

Goren-Inbar, N., and I. Saragusti. 1996. An Acheulian biface assemblage from Gesher Benot Ya'acov, Israel: Indications of African affinities. *Journal of Field Archaeology* 23:15–30.

Goring-Morris, A. N. 1987. *At the Edge: Terminal Pleistocene Hunter-Gatherers in the Negev and Sinai.* Oxford, UK: Archaeopress (British Archaeological Reports International Series 361).

Goring-Morris, A. N., E. Hovers, and A. Belfer-Cohen. 2009. The dynamics of Pleistocene and Early Holocene settlement patterns and human adaptations in the Levant: An overview, in *Transitions in Prehistory: Essays in Honor of Ofer Bar-Yosef.* Edited by J. J. Shea and D. E. Lieberman, pp. 185–252. Oakville, CT: Oxbow.

Goring-Morris, N., Y. Goren, L. K. Horwitz, I. Hershkovitz, R. Lieberman, J. Sarel, and D. Bar-Yosef. 1995. The 1992 season of excavations at the Pre-Pottery Neolithic B settlement of Kfar Hahoresh. *Mitekufat Haeven, Journal of the Israel Prehistoric Society* 26:74–121.

Gould, R. A. 1980. *Living Archaeology.* Cambridge, UK: Cambridge University Press.

Grabowski, M., K. G. Hatala, W. L. Jungers, and B. G. Richmond. 2015. Body mass estimates of hominin fossils and the evolution of human body size. *Journal of Human Evolution* 85:75–93.

Graf, K. E. 2013. Siberian Odyssey, in *Paleoamerican Odyssey.* Edited by K. E. Graf, C. V. Ketron, and M. R. Waters, pp. 65–80. College Station, TX: Center for the Study of the First Americans, Texas A&M University.

Graf, K. E., C. V. Ketron, and M. R. Waters. Editors. 2013. *Paleoamerican Odyssey.* College Station, TX: Center for the Study of the First Americans, Texas A&M University.

Gramley, R. M. 1982. *The Vail Site: A Paleoindian Encampment in Maine. Bulletin of the Buffalo Society of Natural Sciences 30.* Buffalo, NY.

Grayson, D. K. 1986. Eoliths, archaeological ambiguity, and the generation of "middle-range" research, in *American Archaeology Past and Future.* Edited by D. J. Meltzer, D. D. Fowler, and J. A. Sabloff, pp. 77–133. Washington, D.C.: Smithsonian Institution Press.

Grimaldi, S. 1998. Torre in Pietra (Rome, Italy). Technological analysis, *chaîne opératoire* and technical objectives. *Paléo* 10:109–122.

Grine, F. E., R. M. Bailey, K. Harvati, R. P. Nathan, A. G. Morris, G. M. Henderson, I. Ribot, and A. W. G. Pike. 2007. Late Pleistocene human skull from Hofmeyr, South

Africa, and modern human origins. *Science* 315:226–229.

Groube, L., J. Chappell, J. Muke, and D. Price. 1986. A 40,000 year-old human occupation site at Huon Peninsula, Papua New Guinea. *Nature* 324:453–455.

Habgood, P. J., and N. R. Franklin. 2008. The revolution that didn't arrive: A review of Pleistocene Sahul. *Journal of Human Evolution* 55:187–222.

Habu, J. 2004. *The Ancient Jomon of Japan.* New York: Cambridge University Press.

Hahn, J. 1977. *Aurignacien: Das ältere Jungpaläolithikum in Mittel- und Osteuropa. Fundamenta A9.* Cologne: Herman Bohlau.

Hahn, J. 1988. *Die Geißenklösterle-Höhle im Achtal bei Blaubeuren, Volume 1.* Stuttgart: Konrad Theiss Verlag.

Hardy, B. L., M. Kay, A. E. Marks, and K. Monigal. 2001. Stone tool function at the Paleolithic sites of Starosele and Buran Kaya III, Crimea: Behavioral implications. *Proceedings of the National Academy of Sciences* 98:10,972–10,977.

Harmand, S. 2007. Variability in raw material selectivity at the Late Pliocene sites of Lokalalei, West Turkana, Kenya, in *Interdisciplinary Approaches to the Oldowan.* Edited by E. Hovers and D. Braun. Dordrecht: Springer (Vertebrate Paleobiology and Paleoanthropology Series).

Harmand, S., J. E. Lewis, C. S. Feibel, C. J. Lepre, S. Prat, A. Lenoble, X. Boes, R. L. Quinn, M. Brenet, A. Arroyo, N. Taylor, S. Clement, G. Daver, J.-P. Brugal, L. Leakey, R. A. Mortlock, J. D. Wright, S. Lokorodi, C. Kirwa, D. V. Kent, and H. Roche. 2015. 3.3-million-year-old stone tools from Lomekwi 3, West Turkana, Kenya. *Nature* 521:310–315.

Haslam, M. 2014. On the tool use behavior of the bonobo-chimpanzee last common ancestor, and the origins of hominine stone tool use. *American Journal of Primatology* 76:910–918.

Haslam, M., A. Hernandez-Aguilar, V. Ling, S. Carvalho, I. de la Torre, A. DeStefano, A. Du, B. Hardy, J. Harris, L. Marchant, T. Matsuzawa, W. McGrew, J. Mercader, R. Mora, M. Petraglia, H. Roche, E. Visalberghi, and R. Warren. 2009. Primate archaeology. *Nature* 460:339–344.

Hawks, J. 2013. Evolutionary biology: Twisting the tale of human evolution. *Nature* 495:172.

Hayden, B. 1979. *Palaeolithic Reflections: Lithic Technology and Ethnographic Excavations among Australian Aborigines.* Canberra: Australian Institute of Aboriginal Studies.

Hayden, B. 1989. From chopper to celt: The evolution of resharpening techniques, in *Time, Energy and Stone Tools.* Edited by R. Torrence. Cambridge, UK: Cambridge University Press.

Hayden, B. 1994. Competition, labor, and complex hunter-gatherers, in *Key Issues in Hunter-Gatherer Research.* Edited by E. S. Burch, Jr. and L. J. Ellanna, pp. 223–239. Oxford, UK: Berg.

Hayden, B., and M. W. Nelson. 1981. The use of chipped lithic material in the contemporary Maya Highlands. *American Antiquity* 46:885–898.

Haynes, C. V., Jr., and B. B. Huckell. 2007. *Murray Springs: A Clovis Site with Multiple Activity Areas in the San Pedro Valley, Arizona.* Tucson, AZ: University of Arizona Press.

Haynes, G. 2002. *The Early Settlement of North America: The Clovis Era.* Cambridge, UK: Cambridge University Press.

Henry, D. O. 1976. Rosh Zin: A Natufian settlement near Ein Avdat, in *Prehistory and Paleoenvironments of the Central Negev, Israel, Volume 1.* Edited by A. E. Marks, pp. 317–348. Dallas, TX: Southern Methodist University Press.

Henry, D. O. 1989. *From Foraging to Agriculture: The Levant at the End of the Ice Age.* Philadelphia: University of Pennsylvania Press.

Henry, D. O. Editor. 1995. *Prehistoric Cultural Ecology and Evolution: Insights from Southern Jordan.* New York: Plenum.

Henry, D. O. Editor. 2003. *Neanderthals in the Levant: Behavioral Organization and the Beginnings of Human Modernity.* New York: Continuum.

Henshilwood, C., and M. Lombard. 2014. Becoming human: Archaeology of the Sub-Saharan Middle Stone Age, in *The Cambridge World Prehistory, Volume 1: Africa, South and Southeast Asia and the Pacific.* Edited by C. Renfrew and P. Bahn, pp. 106–130. Cambridge: Cambridge University Press.

Henshilwood, C. S., and C. W. Marean. 2003. The origin of modern human behavior. *Current Anthropology* 44:627–651.

Higham, C. 2002. *The Early Cultures of Mainland Southeast Asia.* Bangkok: River Books.

Hill, K., and H. Kaplan. 1993. On why male foragers hunt and share food. *Current Anthropology* 34:701–706.

Hill, K. R., R. S. Walker, M. Božičevića, J. Eder, T. Headland, B. Hewlett, A. M. Hurtado, F. Marlowe, P. Wiessner, and B. Wood. 2011. Co-residence patterns in hunter-gatherer societies show unique human social structure. *Science* 331:1286–1289.

Hillix, W. A., and D. P. Rumbaugh. 2004. *Animal Bodies, Human Minds: Ape, Dolphin, and Parrot Language Skills*. Berlin: Springer.

Hiscock, P. 2002. Pattern and context in the Holocene proliferation of backed artifacts in Australia, in *Thinking Small: Global Perspectives on Microlithization*. Edited by R. G. Elston and S. L. Kuhn, pp. 163–178. Washington, D.C.: American Anthropological Association (Archaeological Paper 12).

Hiscock, P. 2008. *Archaeology of Ancient Australia*. London: Routledge.

Hiscock, P., and H. Allen. 2000. Assemblage variability in the Willandra Lakes. *Archaeology in Oceania* 35:97–103.

Hiscock, P., and C. Clarkson. 2009. The construction of morphological diversity: A study of Mousterian implement retouching at Combe Grenal, in *Lithic Technology: Measures of Production, Use and Curation*. Edited by W. Andrefsky, Jr., pp. 106–135. Cambridge, UK: Cambridge University Press.

Hodder, I. 1982. *Symbols in Action: Ethnoarchaeological Studies of Material Culture*. Cambridge, UK: Cambridge University Press.

Hoffecker, J. F. 2001. Late Pleistocene and early Holocene sites in the Nenana River valley, Central Alaska. *Arctic Anthropology*:139–153.

Hoffecker, J. F. 2004. *A Prehistory of the North: Human Settlement of the Higher Latitudes*. Piscataway, NJ: Rutgers University Press.

Hoffecker, J. F. 2011. The early Upper Paleolithic of Eastern Europe reconsidered. *Evolutionary Anthropology* 20:24–39.

Hoffecker, J. F., and S. A. Elias. 2003. Environment and archeology in Beringia. *Evolutionary Anthropology* 12:34–49.

Hoffecker, J. F., and S. A. Elias. 2007. *Human Ecology of Beringia*. New York: Columbia University Press.

Holdaway, S. J. 2004. *Continuity and Change: An Investigation of the Flaked Stone Artefacts from the Pleistocene Deposits at Bone Cave, Southwest Tasmania, Australia*: Archaeology Program, School of Historical and European Studies, La Trobe University.

Holdaway, S. J., and M. Douglas. 2012. A twenty-first century archaeology of stone artifacts. *Journal of Archaeological Method and Theory* 19:101–131.

Holdaway, S. J., and N. Stern. 2004. *A Record in Stone: The Study of Australia's Flaked Stone Artifacts*. Melbourne, Australia: Museum Victoria/Aboriginal Studies Press.

Holmes, C. E. 2001. Tanana River Valley archaeology circa 14,000 to 9000 BP. *Arctic Anthropology*:154–170.

Horowitz, A. 1979. *The Quaternary of Israel*. New York: Academic Press.

Hovers, E. 2009a. Learning from mistakes: Flaking accidents and knapping skills in the assemblage of A.L. 894 (Hadar, Ethiopia), in *The Cutting Edge: New Approaches to the Archaeology of Human Origins*. Edited by K. Schick and N. Toth, pp. 151–170. Gosport, IN: Stone Age Institute Press.

Hovers, E. 2009b. *The Lithic Assemblages of Qafzeh Cave*. Oxford, UK: Oxford University Press.

Hovers, E., S. Iliani, O. Bar-Yosef, and B. Vandermeersch. 2003. An early case of color symbolism: Ochre use by modern humans in Qafzeh Cave. *Current Anthropology* 44:491–522.

Howell, F. C., K. W. Butzer, L. G. Freeman, and R. G. Klein. 1995. Observations on the Acheulean Occupation Site of Ambrona (Soria Province, Spain). *Jahrbuch des Römisch-Germanischen Zentralmuseums Mainz* 38:33–82.

Howells, W. W. 1989. *Skull Shapes and the Map: Craniometric Analysis of Modern Homo*. Cambridge, MA: Harvard University Press.

Ibàñez, J. J. Editor. 2008. *Le site néolithique de Tel Mureybit (Syrie du Nord): En hommage à Jacques Cauvin*. Oxford, UK: Archaeopress (British Archaeological Reports International Series 1843 [2 volumes]).

Inizan, M.-L., M. Reduron-Ballinger, H. Roche, and J. Tixier. 1999. *Technology and Terminology of Knapped Stone* (translated by J. Féblot-Augustins from *Préhistoire de la Pierre Taillée*, Tome 5, 1994). Meudon: Cercle de Recherches et d'Etudes Préhistoriques (CNRS).

Isaac, G. L. 1977. *Olorgesailie: Archaeological Studies of a Middle Pleistocene Lake Basin in Kenya*. Chicago, IL: University of Chicago Press.

Isaac, G. L. 1978. The food sharing behavior of protohuman hominids. *Scientific American* 238:90–109.

Isaac, G. L., and B. Isaac. Editors. 1997. *Koobi Fora Research Project Series, Volume 5: Plio-Pleistocene Archaeology.* Oxford, UK: Clarendon.

Isaac, G. L., J. W. K. Harris, Z. M. Kaufulu, and K. D. Schick. 1997. Site formation processes: Application of the observations and experiments to Koobi Fora, in *Koobi Fora Research Project Series, Volume 5: Plio-Pleistocene Archaeology.* Edited by G. Isaac and assisted by B. Isaac, pp. 256–261. Oxford, UK: Clarendon.

Izuho, M. 2013. Human technological and behavioral adaptation to landscape changes around the Last Glacial Maximum in Japan: Focus on Hokkaido, in *Paleoamerican Odyssey.* Edited by K. E. Graf, C. V. Ketron, and M. R. Waters, pp. 45–64. College Station, TX: Center for the Study of the First Americans, Texas A&M University.

Jelinek, A. J. Editor. 2013. *Neandertal Lithic Industries at La Quina.* Tucson, AZ: University of Arizona Press.

Jochim, M. A. 1988. Optimal foraging and the division of labor. *American Anthropologist* 90:130–136.

Johnson, C. R., and S. McBrearty. 2010. 500,000 year old blades from the Kapthurin Formation, Kenya. *Journal of Human Evolution* 58:193–200.

Johnson, L. L. 1978. A history of flint-knapping experimentation, 1838–1976. *Current Anthropology* 19:337–372.

Jones, M. L., A. E. Marks, and D. Kaufman. 1983. Boker: The artifacts, in *Prehistory and Paleoenvironments in the Central Negev, Israel. Volume III: the Avdat/Aqev Area, Part 3.* Edited by A. Marks, pp. 283–332. Dallas, TX: Southern Methodist University Press.

Jones, P. R. 1979. Effects of raw materials on biface manufacture. *Science* 204:835–836.

Jones, P. R. 1980. Experimental butchery with modern stone tools and its relevance for Palaeolithic archaeology. *World Archaeology* 12:153–165.

Jones, P. R. 1981. Experimental implement manufacture and use: A case study from Olduvai Gorge. *Philosophical Transactions of the Royal Society of London B: Biological Sciences* 292:189–195.

Jöris, O. 2014. Early Palaeolithic Europe, in *The Cambridge World Prehistory, Volume 3: West and Central Asia and Europe.* Edited by C. Renfrew and P. Bahn, pp. 1703–1747. New York: Cambridge University Press.

Justice, N. D. 1987. *Stone Age Spear and Arrow Points of the Midcontinental and Eastern United States: A Modern Survey and Reference.* Bloomington, IN: Indiana University Press.

Justice, N. D. 2002a. *Stone Age Spear and Arrow Points of California and the Great Basin.* Indianapolis, IN: University of Indiana Press.

Justice, N. D. 2002b. *Stone Age Spear and Arrow Points of the Southwestern United States.* Indianapolis, IN: University of Indiana Press.

Kaifu, Y., M. Izuho, T. Goebel, H. Sato, and A. Ono. Editors. 2015. *Emergence and Diversity of Modern Human Behavior in Paleolithic Asia.* College Station, TX: Texas A&M University Press.

Kaplan, H., K. Hill, J. Lancaster, and A. M. Hurtado. 2000. A theory of human life history evolution: Diet, intelligence, and longevity. *Evolutionary Anthropology* 9:156–184.

Keates, S. G. 2000. *Early and Middle Pleistocene Hominid Behaviour in Northern China.* Oxford, UK: Archaeopress (British Archaeological Reports International Series 863).

Keeley, L. H. 1980. *Experimental Determination of Stone Tool Uses: A Microwear Analysis.* Chicago, IL: University of Chicago Press.

Keeley, L. H. 1982. Hafting and retooling: Effects on the archaeological record. *American Antiquity* 47:798–809.

Keeley, L. H. 1996. *War Before Civilization.* New York: Oxford University Press.

Keeley, L. H., and N. P. Toth. 1981. Microwear polishes on early stone tools from Koobi Fora, Kenya. *Nature* 293:464–465.

Kelly, R. L. 1995. *The Foraging Spectrum: Diversity in Hunter-Gatherer Lifeways.* Washington, D.C.: Smithsonian Institution Press.

Kelterborn, P. 1984. Towards replicating Egyptian predynastic flint knives. *Journal of Archaeological Science* 11:433–453.

Khalayla, H., and O. Marder. 2003. *The Neolithic Site of Abu Ghosh, the 1995 Excavations.* Jerusalem: Oxbow Books.

Kibunjia, M. 1994. Pliocene archaeological occurrences in the Lake Turkana basin. *Journal of Human Evolution* 27:159–171.

Kiernan, K., R. Jones, and D. Ranson. 1983. New evidence from Fraser Cave for glacial age man in south-west Tasmania. *Nature* 301:28–32.

Kinzey, W. G. Editor. 1986. *The Evolution of Human Behavior: Primate Models.* Albany, NY: State University of New York Press.

Klein, R. G. 2009. *The Human Career*, Third Edition. Chicago, IL: University of Chicago Press.

Kleindienst, M. 1967. Questions of terminology in regard to the study of Stone Age industries in eastern Africa: "Cultural Stratigraphic Units," in *Background to Evolution in Africa*. Edited by W. W. Bishop and J. G. D. Clark, pp. 861–878. Chicago, IL: University of Chicago Press.

Klíma, B. 1995. *Dolní Vestonice II. Ein Mammutjägerplatz und seine Bestattungen*. Liège, Belgium: Université de Liège (ERAUL 73).

Köhler, W. 1925. *The Mentality of Apes*. New York, NY: Harcourt Brace & World.

Kohn, M., and S. Mithen. 1999. Handaxes: products of sexual selection? *Antiquity* 73:518–526.

Kozlowski, J. K. 2000. The problem of cultural continuity between the Middle and Upper Paleolithic in Central and Eastern Europe, in *The Geography of Neandertals and Modern Humans in Europe and the Greater Mediterranean*. Edited by O. Bar-Yosef and D. Pilbeam, pp. 77–106. Cambridge, MA: Peabody Museum of Archaeology and Ethnology (Bulletin No. 8).

Kozlowski, S., and O. Aurenche. 2005. *Territories, Boundaries and Cultures in the Neolithic Near East*. Oxford, UK: Archaeopress (British Archaeological Reports International Series 1362).

Kramer, K. 2005. *Maya Children: Helpers at the Farm*. Cambridge, MA: Harvard University Press.

Kramer, K. L., and P. T. Ellison. 2010. Pooled energy budgets: Resituating human energy allocation tradeoffs. *Evolutionary Anthropology* 19:136–147.

Kramer, K. L., and A. F. Russell. 2015. Was monogamy a key step on the hominin road? Reevaluating the monogamy hypothesis in the evolution of cooperative breeding. *Evolutionary Anthropology* 24:73–83.

Kraybill, N. 1977. Pre-agricultural tools for the preparation of foods in the Old World, in *Origins of Agriculture*. Edited by C. Reed, pp. 485–521. The Hague: Mouton.

Kuhn, S., and R. G. Elston. 2002. Introduction: Thinking small globally, in *Thinking Small: Global Perspectives on Microlithization*. Edited by R. G. Elston and S. L. Kuhn, pp. 1–8. Washington, D.C.: American Anthropological Association (Archaeological Paper 12).

Kuhn, S. L. 1992. On planning and curated technologies in the Middle Paleolithic. *Journal of Anthropological Research* 48:185–214.

Kuhn, S. L. 1993. Mousterian technology as adaptive response: A case study, in *Hunting and Animal Exploitation in the Later Paleolithic and Mesolithic of Eurasia*. Edited by G. L. Peterkin, H. Bricker, and P. A. Mellars, pp. 25–48. Washington, D.C.: American Anthropological Association (Archaeological Paper 4).

Kuhn, S. L. 1995. *Mousterian Lithic Technology: An Ecological Perspective*. Princeton, NJ: Princeton University Press.

Kuijt, I. Editor. 2002. *Life in Neolithic Farming Communities: Social Organization, Identity, and Differentiation*. New York, NY: Springer.

Kuijt, I., and N. Goodale. 2006. Chronological frameworks and disparate technology: An exploration of chipped stone variability and the forager to farmer transition at 'Iraq ed-Dubb, Jordan. *Paléorient* 32:27–45.

Kuman, K., and A. S. Field. 2009. The Oldowan Industry from Sterkfontein Caves, South Africa, in *The Cutting Edge: New Approaches to the Archaeology of Human Origins*. Edited by K. Schick and N. Toth, pp. 151–170. Gosport, IN: Stone Age Institute Press.

Kunz, M. L., and R. E. Reanier. 1995. The Mesa site: A Paleoindian hunting lookout in Arctic Alaska. *Arctic Anthropology*:5–30.

Kuper, A. 1988. *The Invention of Primitive Society: Transformations of an Illusion*. London: Routledge.

Lamb, L. 1996. Investigating changing stone technologies, site use and occupational intensities at Fern Cave, north Queensland. *Australian Archaeology*:1–7.

Landau, M. L. 1991. *Narratives of Human Evolution*. New Haven, CT: Yale University Press.

Langbroek, M. 2004. *Out of Africa: An Investigation into the Earliest Occupation of the Old World*. Oxford, UK: Archaeopress (British Archaeological Reports International Series 1244).

Larsen-Peterkin, G. 1993. Lithic and organic hunting technology in the French Upper Paleolithic, in *Hunting and Animal Exploitation in the Later Paleolithic and Mesolithic of Eurasia*. Edited by G. L. Peterkin, H. Bricker, and P. A. Mellars, pp. 49–68. Washington, D.C.: American Anthropological Association (Archaeological Paper No. 4).

Laughlin, J. P., and R. L. Kelly. 2010. Experimental analysis of the practical limits of lithic refitting. *Journal of Archaeological Science* 37:427–433.

Lavallée, D. 2000. *The First South Americans.* Salt Lake City, UT: University of Utah Press.

Leakey, L. S. B. 1926. A new classification of the bow and arrow in Africa. *Journal of the Royal Anthropological Institute of Great Britain and Ireland* 56:259–299.

Leakey, L. S. B. 1936. *Stone Age Africa.* London: Oxford University Press.

Leakey, L. S. B. 1954. *Adam's Ancestors.* London: Methuen.

Leakey, L. S. B., P. V. Tobias, and J. R. Napier. 1964. A new species of the genus *Homo* from Olduvai Gorge. *Nature* 202:7–9.

Leakey, M., P. V. Tobias, J. E. Martyn, and R. E. F. Leakey. 1969. An Acheulean industry with prepared core technique and the discovery of a contemporary hominid mandible at Lake Baringo, Kenya. *Proceedings of the Prehistoric Society* 35:48–76.

Leakey, M. D. 1966. A review of the Oldowan Culture from Olduvai Gorge, Tanzania. *Nature* 210:462–466.

Leakey, M. D. 1971. *Olduvai Gorge, Volume 3: Excavations in Beds I and II, 1960–1963.* Cambridge: Cambridge University Press.

Leakey, M. D., and D. A. Roe. Editors. 1994. *Olduvai Gorge, Volume 5: Excavations in Beds III, IV and the Masek Beds, 1968–1971.* Cambridge: Cambridge University Press.

Lechevallier, M., and A. Ronen. Editors. 1994. *Le Gisement de Hatoula en Judée occidentale, Israël: Rapport de fouilles 1980–1988.* Jerusalem: Centre de Recherches Préhistoriques Français de Jérusalem.

Lee, G. 2013. The characteristics of Upper Paleolithic industries in Korea: Innovation, continuity, and interaction, in *Paleoamerican Odyssey.* Edited by K. E. Graf, C. V. Ketron, and M. R. Waters, pp. 270–288. College Station, TX: Center for the Study of the First Americans, Texas A&M University.

Lemmonier, P. 1992. *Elements for an Anthropology of Technology.* Ann Arbor, MI: University of Michigan Museum of Anthropology (Paper No. 88).

Lemorini, C., T. W. Plummer, D. R. Braun, A. N. Crittenden, P. W. Ditchfield, L. C. Bishop, F. Hertel, J. S. Oliver, F. W. Marlowe, M. J. Schoeninger, and R. Potts. 2014. Old stones' song: Use-wear experiments and analysis of the Oldowan quartz and quartzite assemblage from Kanjera South (Kenya). *Journal of Human Evolution* 72:10–25.

Lepre, C. J., H. Roche, D. V. Kent, S. Harmand, R. L. Quinn, J.-P. Brugal, P.-J. Texier, A. Lenoble, and C. S. Feibel. 2011. An earlier origin for the Acheulian. *Nature* 477:82–85.

Levi-Sala, I. 1996. *A Study of Microscopic Polish on Flint Implements.* Oxford, UK: Archaeopress (British Archaeological Reports International Series 629).

Lewis-Williams, D. 2002. *The Mind in the Cave.* New York, NY: Thames & Hudson.

Lieberman, D. E. 2011. *The Evolution of the Human Head.* Cambridge, MA: Belknap/Harvard University Press.

Lieberman, D. E. 2013. *The Story of the Human Body: Evolution, Health and Disease.* New York, NY: Pantheon Books.

Lieberman, D. E., D. M. Bramble, D. A. Raichlen, and J. J. Shea. 2008. Brains, brawn and the evolution of endurance running capabilities, in *The First Humans: Origin of the Genus Homo.* Edited by F. Grine, J. G. Fleagle, and R. E. F. Leakey, pp. 77–98. New York, NY: Springer.

Lieberman, P. 2006. *Toward an Evolutionary Biology of Language.* Cambridge, MA: Harvard University Press.

Lieberman, P. 2015. Language did not spring forth 100,000 years ago. *PLOS Biology* 13: e10002064.

Lieberman, P., and R. C. McCarthy. 2014. The evolution of speech and language, in *Handbook of Paleoanthropology.* Edited by W. Henke and I. Tattersall, pp. 1–33. Berlin: Springer.

Lieberman, P. E., E. S. Crelin, and D. S. Klatt. 1974. Phonetic ability and related anatomy of the newborn, adult human, Neanderthal Man and chimpanzee. *American Anthropologist* 74:287–307.

Lin, S., Z. Rezek, D. Braun, and H. Dibble. 2013. On the utility and economization of unretouched flakes: The effects of exterior platform angle and platform depth. *American Antiquity* 78:724–745.

Lourandos, H. 1997. *Continent of Hunter-Gatherers.* Cambridge, UK: Cambridge University Press.

Lubbock, J. 1865. *Pre-Historic Times, as Illustrated by Ancient Remains and the Manners and Customs of Modern Savages.* London: Williams and Norgate.

Lundin, C. 2003. *98.6 Degrees: The Art of Keeping Your Ass Alive.* Salt Lake City, UT: Gibbs Smith.

Lycett, S. J., and C. J. Bae. 2010. The Movius Line controversy: The state of the debate. *World Archaeology* 42:521–544.

Lynch, T. F. 1983. The Paleo-Indians, in *Ancient South Americans*. Edited by J. D. Jennings, pp. 87–138. San Francisco, CA: W. H. Freeman & Co.

Lynch, T. F. 1985. *Guitarrero Cave: Early Man in the Andes*. New York, NY: Academic Press.

MacDonald, G. F. 1985. *Debert: A Paleo-Indian Site in Central Nova Scotia*. Buffalo, NY: Persimmon Press.

Machin, A. J., R. T. Hosfield, and S. J. Mithen. 2007. Why are some handaxes symmetrical? Testing the influence of handaxe morphology on butchery effectiveness. *Journal of Archaeological Science* 34:883–893.

MacKay, A. 2014. Coalescence and fragmentation in the Late Pleistocene archaeology of southernmost Africa. *Journal of Human Evolution* 72:26–51.

Madsen, B., and N. Goren-Inbar. 2004. Acheulian giant core technology and beyond: An archaeological and experimental case study. *Eurasian Prehistory* 2:3–52.

Madsen, D. B., D. N. Schmitt, and D. Page. Editors. 2015. *The Paleoarchaic Occupation of the Old River Bed Delta*. Salt Lake City, UT: University of Utah Press.

Maher, L., T. Richter, J. T. Stock, and M. Jones. 2014. Preliminary results from recent excavations at the Epipalaeolithic site of Kharaneh IV, in *Jordan's Prehistory: Past and Future Research*. Edited by F. Khraysheh and G. Rollefson, pp. 81–92. Amman: Department of Antiquities of Jordan.

Mania, D. 1995. The earliest occupation of Europe: The Elbe-Saale region (Germany), in *The Earliest Occupation of Europe*. Edited by W. Roebroeks and T. Van Kolfschoten, pp. 85–102. Leiden: University of Leiden.

Marean, C. W. 2007. Heading north: An Africanist perspective on the replacement of Neanderthals by modern humans, in *Rethinking the Human Revolution*. Edited by P. Mellars, K. Boyle, O. Bar-Yosef, and C. Stringer, pp. 367–382. Cambridge, UK: McDonald Institute for Archaeological Research Monographs.

Marean, C. W. 2015. The most invasive species of all. *Scientific American* 313:32–39.

Marean, C. W. 2016. The transition to foraging for dense and predictable resources and its impact on the evolution of modern humans. *Philosophical Transactions of the Royal Society of London B: Biological Sciences* 371: 20150239.

Marean, C. W., M. Bar-Matthews, J. Bernatchez, E. Fisher, P. Goldberg, A. I. R. Herries, Z. Jacobs, A. Jerardino, P. Karkanas, T. Minichillo, P. J. Nilssen, E. Thompson, I. Watts, and H. M. Williams. 2007. Early human use of marine resources and pigment in South Africa during the Middle Pleistocene. *Nature* 449:905–908.

Marks, A. E. 1976. Site D5: A geometric Kebaran "A" occupation in the Nahal Zin, in *Prehistory and Paleoenvironments of the Central Negev, Israel, Volume 1*. Edited by A. E. Marks, pp. 293–316. Dallas, TX: Southern Methodist University Press.

Marks, A. E., and V. P. Chabai. Editors. 1998. *The Middle Paleolithic of Western Crimea, Volume 1*. Liège, Belgium: Université de Liège (ERAUL 84).

Marks, A. E, and D. Kaufman. 1983. Boker Tachtit: The artifacts, in *Prehistory and Paleoenvironments in the Central Negev, Israel, Volume 3*. Edited by A. Marks, pp. 69–126. Dallas, TX: Southern Methodist University Press.

Marks, A. E., and P. A. Larson, Jr. 1977. Test excavations at the Natufian site of Rosh Horesha, in *Prehistory and Paleoenvironments in the Central Negev, Israel, Volume 2*. Edited by A. E. Marks, pp. 191–232. Dallas: Southern Methodist University Press.

Marlowe, F. W. 2005. Hunter-gatherers and human evolution. *Evolutionary Anthropology* 14:54–67.

Marzke, M. W. 1997. Precision grips, hand morphology, and tools. *American Journal of Physical Anthropology* 102: 91–110.

Marzke, M. W. 2013. Tool making, hand morphology and fossil hominins. *Philosophical Transactions of the Royal Society of London B: Biological Sciences* 368: 20120414.

McBrearty, S., L. Bishop, T. Plummer, R. Dewar, and N. Conard. 1998. Tools underfoot: Human trampling as an agent of lithic artifact edge modification. *American Antiquity* 63:108–130.

McBrearty, S., and A. S. Brooks. 2000. The revolution that wasn't: A new interpretation of the origin of modern human behavior. *Journal of Human Evolution* 39:453–563.

McBurney, C. B. M. 1967. *The Haua Fteah (Cyrenaica) and the Stone Age of the South-East Mediterranean*. Cambridge: Cambridge University Press.

McCall, G. 2012. Ethnoarchaeology and the organization of lithic technology. *Journal of Archaeological Research* 20:157–203.

McCall, G. S. 2014. *Before Modern Humans: New Perspectives on the African Stone Age*. Walnut Creek, CA: Left Coast Press.

McCown, T. D. 1937. Mugharet es-Skhul. Description and excavations, in *The Stone Age of Mount Carmel, Volume 1: Excavations in the Wady el-Mughara*. Edited by D. Garrod and D. M. A. Bate, pp. 91–112. Oxford, UK: Clarendon Press.

McGrail, S. 2001. *Boats of the World: From the Stone Age to Medieval Times*. Oxford, UK: Oxford University Press.

McGrew, W. C. 1992. *Chimpanzee Material Culture: Implications for Human Evolution*. Cambridge, UK: Cambridge University Press.

McNett, C. W. Editor. 1985. *Shawnee-Minisink: A Stratified Paleoindian-Archaic Site in the Upper Delaware Valley of Pennsylvania*. Orlando, FL: Academic Press.

McNiven, I. J. 2000. Backed into the Pleistocene. *Archaeology in Oceania* 35:48–52.

McPherron, S. 2006. What typology can tell us about Acheulian handaxe production, in *Axe Age: Acheulian Toolmaking from Quarry to Discard*. Edited by N. Goren-Inbar and G. Sharon, pp. 267–286. London: Equinox.

McPherron, S., Z. Alemseged, C. W. Marean, J. G. Wynn, D. Reed, D. Geraads, R. Bobé, and H. Béarat. 2010. Evidence for stone tool-assisted consumption of animal tissues before 3.39 million years ago at Dikika, Ethiopia. *Nature* 466: 857–860.

McPherron, S. P. 1999. Ovate and pointed handaxe assemblages: two points make a line. *Préhistoire Européenne* 14:9–32.

Meignen, L. 2011. The contribution of Hayonim Cave assemblages to the understanding of the so-called Early Levantine Mousterian, in *The Lower and Middle Palaeolithic in the Middle East and Neighbouring Regions*. Edited by J.-M. Le Tensorer, R. Jagher, and M. Otte, pp. 85–100. Liège, Belgium: Université de Liège.

Mellars, P., and J. C. French. 2011. Tenfold population increase in Western Europe at the Neandertal-to-modern human transition. *Science* 333:623–627.

Mellars, P. A. 1991. Cognitive changes and the emergence of modern humans in Europe. *Cambridge Archaeological Journal* 1:63–76.

Mellars, P. A. 1996. *The Neanderthal Legacy: An Archaeological Perspective from Western Europe*. Princeton, NY: Princeton University Press.

Meltzer, D. J. 2009. *First Peoples in a New World*. Berkeley, CA: University of California Press.

Mercader, J., H. Barton, J. Gillespie, J. Harris, S. Kuhn, R. Tyler, and C. Boesch. 2007. 4,300-year-old chimpanzee sites and the origins of percussive stone technology. *Proceedings of the National Academy of Sciences* 104:3043–3048.

Mercader, J., M. Panger, and C. Boesch. 2002. Excavation of a chimpanzee stone tool site in the African rain forest. *Science* 296:1452–1455.

Merrick, H. V. 1975. Change in Later Pleistocene Lithic Industries in Eastern Africa. Ph.D. Dissertation (unpublished), University of California at Berkeley.

Miller, T. O., Jr. 1979. Stonework of the Xêtá Indians of Brazil, in *Lithic Use-Wear Analysis*. Edited by B. Hayden, pp. 401–407. New York, NY: Academic Press.

Minichillo, T. 2006. Raw material use and behavioral modernity: Howiesons Poort lithic foraging strategies. *Journal of Human Evolution* 50:359–364.

Mitchell, P. 2002. *The Archaeology of Southern Africa*. Cambridge, UK: Cambridge University Press.

Mithen, S. J. 1996. *The Prehistory of the Mind*. New York, NY: Thames & Hudson.

Mithen, S. J. 1998. A creative explosion? Theory of mind, language, and the disembodied mind of the Upper Paleolithic, in *Creativity in Human Evolution and Prehistory*. Edited by S. Mithen, pp. 165–191. London: Routledge.

Mithen, S. J. 2004. *After the Ice: A Global Human History, 20,000–5000 BC*. Cambridge, MA: Harvard University Press.

Mithen, S. J. 2005. *The Singing Neanderthal: The Origins of Music, Language, Mind and Body*. London: Weidenfeld & Nicholson.

Molleson, T. 1994. The eloquent bones of Abu Hureyra. *Scientific American* 271:70–75.

Molleson, T., and K. Jones. 1991. Dental evidence for dietary change at Abu Hureyra. *Journal of Archaeological Science* 18:525–539.

Molleson, T., and K. Jones. 1993. Dietary change and the effects of food preparation on microwear patterns in the Late Neolithic of Abu Hureyra, Northern Syria. *Journal of Human Evolution* 24:455–468.

Monnier, G. F., J. L. Ladwig, and S. T. Porter. 2012. Swept under the rug: The problem of unacknowledged ambiguity in lithic residue identification. *Journal of Archaeological Science* 39:3284–3300.

Moore, A. M. T., G. C. Hillman, and A. J. Legge. Editors. 2000. *Village on the Euphrates: From Foraging to Farming at Abu Hureyra.* Oxford, UK: Oxford University Press.

Moore, J. D. 2014. *A Prehistory of South America.* Denver, CO: University Press of Colorado.

Moore, M. W., T. Sutikna, M. J. Morwood, and A. Brumm. 2009. Continuities in stone flaking technology at Liang Bua, Flores, Indonesia. *Journal of Human Evolution* 57:503–526.

Mora, R., and I. de la Torre. 2005. Percussion tools in Olduvai Beds I and II (Tanzania): Implications for early human activities. *Journal of Anthropological Archaeology* 24:179–192.

Morgan, B. J., and E. E. Abwe. 2006. Chimpanzees use stone hammers in Cameroon. *Current Biology* 16:R632–R633.

Morrow, J. E., and A. M. Toby. 1999. Geographic variation in fluted projectile points: A hemispheric perspective. *American Antiquity* 64:215–230.

Morse, D. F. Editor. 1997. *Sloan: A Paleoindian Dalton Cemetery in Arkansas.* Washington, D.C.: Smithsonian Institution Press.

Morse, K. 1988. Mandu Mandu Creek rockshelter: Pleistocene human coastal occupation of North West Cape, Western Australia. *Archaeology in Oceania* 23:81–88.

Mortensen, P. 1970. A preliminary study of the chipped stone industry from Beidha, an Early Neolithic village in southern Jordan. *Acta Archaeologica* 41:1–54.

Morwood, M. J., and W. L. Jungers. 2009. Conclusions: Implications of the Liang Bua excavations for hominin evolution and biogeography. *Journal of Human Evolution* 57:640–648.

Movius, H. L., Jr. 1948. The Lower Paleolithic Cultures of Southern and Eastern Asia. *Transactions of the American Philosophical Society (n.s.)* 38.

Muheisen, M., H. G. Gebel, C. Hannss, and R. Neef. 1988. 'Ain Rahub, a new Final Natufian and Yarmoukian site near Irbid, in *The Prehistory of Jordan.* Edited by A. Garrard and H. G. Gebel, pp. 472–502. Oxford, UK: Archaeopress (British Archaeological Reports International Series 396).

Mulvaney, D. J. 1975. *The Prehistory of Australia*, Second edition. London: Penguin.

Mulvaney, J., and J. Kamminga. 1999. *Prehistory of Australia.* Washington, D.C.: Smithsonian Institution Press.

Nadel, D. Editor. 2002. *Ohalo II, A 23,000-Year-Old Fisher-Hunter-Gatherers' Camp on the Shore of the Sea of Galilee.* Haifa, Israel: Reuben and Edith Hecht Museum, University of Haifa.

Nash, S. E. 1996. Is curation a useful heuristic?, in *Stone Tools: Theoretical Insights into Human Prehistory.* Edited by G. H. Odell, pp. 81–100. New York, NY: Plenum.

Nelson, N. 1916. Flint-working by Ishi, in *William Henry Holmes Anniversary Volume.* Edited by F. W. Hodge, pp. 397–402. Washington, D.C.: Smithsonian Institution.

Nishiaki, Y. 2000. *Lithic Technology of Neolithic Syria.* Oxford, UK: Archaeopress (British Archaeological Reports International Series 840).

Nishiaki, Y., and K. Nagai. 2011. Obsidian knappers at the Late PPNB "consumer" settlement of Tell Seker Al-Aheimar, Northeast Syria. *Paléorient* 37:91–105.

Norton, C. J., and J. J. H. Jin. 2009. The evolution of modern human behavior in East Asia: Current perspectives. *Evolutionary Anthropology* 18:247–260.

Nowell, A. 2009. The case against sexual selection as an explanation of handaxe morphology. *PaleoAnthropology* 2009:77–88.

Nowell, A. 2010. Defining behavioral modernity in the context of Neandertal and anatomically modern human populations. *Annual Review of Anthropology* 39:437–452.

O'Connell, J. F., and J. Allen. 2004. Dating the colonization of Sahul (Pleistocene Australia-New Guinea): A review of recent research. *Journal of Archaeological Science* 31:835–853.

O'Connell, J. F., and J. Allen. 2012. The restaurant at the end of the universe: Modelling the colonization of Sahul. *Australian Archaeology* 74:5–17.

O'Connor, S., T. Maloney, D. Vannieuwenhuyse, J. Balme, and R. Wood. 2014. Occupation at Carpenter's Gap 3, Windjana Gorge, Kimberly, Western Australia. *Australian Archaeology* 78:10–23.

Odell, G. H. 1981. The mechanics of use-breakage of stone tools: Some testable hypotheses. *Journal of Field Archaeology* 37:197–210.

Odell, G. H. 1996. Economizing behavior and the concept of "curation," in *Stone Tools: Theoretical Insights into Human Prehistory*. Edited by G. H. Odell, pp. 51–80. New York, NY: Plenum.

Odell, G. H. 2004. *Lithic Analysis*. New York, NY: Kluwer.

Oliver, P. 1987. *Dwellings: The House Across the World*. Dallas: University of Texas Press.

Oppenheimer, S. 2004. *The Real Eve: Modern Man's Journey out of Africa*. New York, NY: Carroll & Graf Publishers.

Oswalt, W. 1976. *An Anthropological Analysis of Food-Getting Technology*. New York, NY: John Wiley.

Oswalt, W. H. 1973. *Habitat and Technology: The Evolution of Hunting*. New York, NY: Holt, Rinehart, and Winston.

Panger, M., A. S. Brooks, B. G. Richmond, and B. Wood. 2003. Older than the Oldowan? Rethinking the emergence of hominin tool use. *Evolutionary Anthropology* 11:226–234.

Pappu, S., Y. Gunnell, J.-P. Brugal, and Y. Touchard. 2003. Excavations at the Palaeolithic site of Attirampakkam, South India: Preliminary findings. *Current Anthropology* 44:591–597.

Pargeter, J., and J. Bradfield. 2012. The effects of Class I and II sized bovids on macrofracture formation and tool displacement: Results of a trampling experiment in a southern African Stone Age context. *Journal of Field Archaeology* 37:238–251.

Parry, W. A., and R. L. Kelly. 1987. Expedient core technology and sedentism, in *The Organization of Core Technology*. Edited by J. K. Johnson and C. A. Morrow, pp. 285–304. Boulder, CO: Westview Press.

Patten, B. 2009. *Old Tools – New Eyes: A Primal Primer of Flintknapping*, Second Edition. Denver, CO: Stone Dagger Publications.

Peretto, C. Editor. 1994. *Le industrie litiche del giacimento paleolitico di Isernia la Pineta*. Campobasso, Italy: Cosmo Iannone.

Petraglia, M. D. 2007. Mind the gap: Factoring the Arabian Peninsula and the Indian Subcontinent into Out of Africa models, in *Rethinking the Human Revolution*. Edited by P. Mellars, K. Boyle, O. Bar-Yosef, and C. Stringer, pp. 383–394. Cambridge, UK: McDonald Institute for Archaeological Research Monographs.

Pettitt, P. 2010. *The Palaeolithic Origins of Human Burial*. New York, NY: Routledge.

Pitulko, V., P. Nikolskiy, A. Basilyan, and E. Pavlova. 2013. Human habitation in Arctic Western Beringia prior to the LGM, in *Paleoamerican Odyssey*. Edited by K. E. Graf, C. V. Ketron, and M. R. Waters, pp. 13–44. College Station, TX: Center for the Study of the First Americans, Texas A&M University.

Pleurdeau, D. 2005. Human technical behavior in the African Middle Stone Age: The lithic assemblage of Porc-Epic Cave (Dire-Dawa, Ethiopia). *African Archaeological Review* 22:177–197.

Plummer, T. 2004. Flaked stone and old bones: Biological and cultural evolution at the dawn of technology. *Yearbook of Physical Anthropology* 47:118–164.

Plummer, T., L. C. Bishop, P. Ditchfield, and J. Hicks. 1999. Research on Late Pliocene Oldowan sites at Kanjera South, Kenya. *Journal of Human Evolution* 36:151–170.

Potts, R. 1987. Reconstructions of early hominid socioecology: A critique of primate models, in *The Evolution of Human Behavior: Primate Models*. Edited by W. G. Kinzey, pp. 28–50. Albany, NY: State University of New York Press.

Potts, R. 1988. *Early Hominid Activities at Olduvai*. New York, NY: Aldine de Gruyter.

Potts, R. 1996. *Humanity's Descent: The Consequences of Ecological Instability*. New York, NY: William Morrow and Co.

Potts, R. 1998. Variability selection and hominid evolution. *Evolutionary Anthropology* 7:81–96.

Powell, A., S. Shennan, and M. G. Thomas. 2009. Late Pleistocene demography and the appearance of modern human behavior. *Science* 324:1298–1301.

Pruetz, J. D., and P. Bertolani. 2007. Savanna chimpanzees, *Pan troglodytes verus*, hunt with tools. *Current Biology* 17:412–417.

Quintero, L. A. 2011. *Evolution of Lithic Economies in the Levantine Neolithic: Development and Demise of Naviform Core Technology, as Seen at 'Ain Ghazal ('Ain Ghazal Excavation Reports 2)*. Berlin: ex oriente.

Reitz, E. J., and E. S. Wing. 2008. *Zooarchaeology*, Second Edition. New York, NY: Cambridge University Press.

Renfrew, C. 1996. The sapient behaviour paradox: How to test for potential? in *Modelling the Early Human Mind*. Edited by P. Mellars and K. Gibson, pp. 11–14. Cambridge, UK: MacDonald Institute for Archaeological Research.

Rhodes, J. A., and S. E. Churchill. 2009. Throwing in the Middle and Upper Paleolithic: Inferences from an analysis of humeral retroversion. *Journal of Human Evolution* 56:1–10.

Richerson, P., R. Boyd, and R. L. Bettinger. 2001. Was agriculture impossible during the Pleistocene but mandatory during the Holocene? A climate change hypothesis. *American Antiquity* 66:387–411.

Rigaud, J.-P. Editor. 1989. *La Grotte Vaufrey à Cenac et Saint-Julien (Dordogne): Paléoenvironnements, chronologie et activités humaines*. Châlons et Marne: Paquez et Fils.

Rindos, D. 1984. *The Origins of Agriculture: An Evolutionary Perspective*. New York, NY: Academic Press.

Roberts, M. B., S. A. Parfitt, M. I. Pope, and F. F. Wenban-Smith. 1997. Boxgrove, West Sussex: Rescue excavations of a Lower Palaeolithic landsurface (Boxgrove Project B, 1989–1991). *Proceedings of the Prehistoric Society* 63:303–358.

Roche, H., R. Blumenschine, and J. J. Shea. 2009. Origins and adaptations of early Genus *Homo*: What archaeology tells us, in *The First Humans: Origin of the Genus Homo*. Edited by F. Grine, R. Leakey, and J. Fleagle, pp. 135–147. New York, NY: Springer.

Roche, H., J.-P. Brugal, A. Delagnes, C. Feibel, S. Harmand, M. Kibunjia, S. Prat, and P.-J. Texier. 2003. Les sites archéologiques plio-pleistocènes de la formation de Nachukui, Ouest-Turkana, Kenya: bilan synthetique 1997–2001. *Comptes Rendus Palevol* 2:663–673.

Roe, D. 2003. An overview, with some thoughts on the study of bifaces, in *Multiple Approaches to the Study of Bifacial Technologies*. Edited by M. Soressi and H. L. Dibble, pp. 273–285. Philadelphia, PA: University of Pennsylvania Museum.

Roebroeks, W., and P. Villa. 2011. On the earliest evidence for habitual use of fire in Europe. *Proceedings of the National Academy of Sciences* 108:5209–5214.

Rolian, C., and A. D. Gordon. 2013. Reassessing manual proportions in *Australopithecus afarensis*. *American Journal of Physical Anthropology* 152:393–406.

Rolland, N., and H. L. Dibble. 1990. A new synthesis of Middle Paleolithic variability. *American Antiquity* 55:480–499.

Rollefson, G., A. H. Simmons, and Z. Kafafi. 1992. Neolithic cultures at 'Ain Ghazal, Jordan. *Journal of Field Archaeology* 19:443–470.

Rosen, S. A. 1997. *Lithics after the Stone Age: A Handbook of Stone Tools from the Levant*. Walnut Creek, CA.: Altamira Press.

Sackett, J. 1982. Approaches to style in lithic archaeology. *Journal of Anthropological Archaeology* 1:59–112.

Sahnouni, M. 2006. The North African Early Stone Age and the sites at Ain Hanech, Algeria, in *The Oldowan: Case Studies Into the Earliest Stone Age*. Edited by N. P. Toth and K. Schick, pp. 77–112. Bloomington, IN: Stone Age Institute Press.

Sandweiss, D. H., H. McInnis, R. L. Burger, A. Cano, B. Ojeda, and R. Paredes, M. Sandweiss, and M. D. Glascock. 1998. Quebrada Jaguay: Early South American maritime adaptations. *Science* 281:1830–1832.

Scarre, C. Editor. 2013. *The Human Past: World Prehistory and the Development of Human Societies*, Third Edition. New York, NY: Thames & Hudson.

Schick, K. D., and N. P. Toth. 1993. *Making Silent Stones Speak: Human Evolution and the Dawn of Technology*. New York, NY: Simon & Schuster.

Schiffer, M. B. 1987. *Formation Processes of the Archaeological Record*. Albuquerque, NM: University of New Mexico Press.

Scott, B. 2011. *Becoming Neanderthals: The Earlier British Middle Palaeolithic*. Oakville, CT: David Brown Book Company.

Scott, T. R. 1977. The Harifian of the Central Negev, in *Prehistory and Paleoenvironments in the Central Negev, Israel, Volume 2: The Avdat/Aqev Area, Part 2 and the Har Harif*. Edited by A. E. Marks, pp. 271–322. Dallas: Southern Methodist University Press.

Searcy, M. T. 2011. *The Life-Giving Stone: Ethnoarchaeology of Maya Metates*. Tucson: University of Arizona Press.

Sellet, F. 1993. *Châine opératoire*: The concept and its applications. *Lithic Technology* 18:106–112.

Semaw, S., M. J. Rogers, J. Quade, P. R. Renne, R. F. Butler, M. Domínguez-Rodrigo, D. Stout, W. S. Hart, T. Pickering, and S. W. Simpson. 2003. 2.6-Million-year-old stone tools and associated bones from OGS-6 and OGS-7, Gona, Afar, Ethiopia. *Journal of Human Evolution* 45:169–177.

Semaw, S., M. J. Rogers, and D. Stout. 2009. Insights into Late Pliocene lithic assemblage variability: The East Gona and Ounda Gona South Oldowan archaeology (2.6 million years ago) Afar, Ethiopia, in *The Cutting Edge: New Approaches to the Archaeology of Human Origins.* Edited by K. Schick and N. Toth, pp. 211–246. Gosport, IN: Stone Age Institute Press.

Semenov, S. A. 1964. *Prehistoric Technology.* London: Corey Adams Mackay.

Sept, J. M. 1994. Beyond bones: Archaeological sites, early hominid subsistence, and the costs and benefits of exploiting wild plant foods in east African riverine landscapes. *Journal of Human Evolution* 27:295–320.

Sharon, G. 2007. *Acheulian Large Flake Industries: Technology, Chronology, and Significance.* Oxford, UK: Archaeopress (British Archaeological Reports International Series 1701).

Shea, J. J. 1992. Lithic microwear analysis in archaeology. *Evolutionary Anthropology* 1:143–150.

Shea, J. J. 1997. Middle Paleolithic spear point technology, in *Projectile Technology.* Edited by H. Knecht, pp. 79–106. New York, NY: Plenum.

Shea, J. J. 2003. The Middle Paleolithic of the East Mediterranean Levant. *Journal of World Prehistory* 17:313–394.

Shea, J. J. 2006a. Child's play: Reflections on the invisibility of children in the Paleolithic record. *Evolutionary Anthropology* 15:212–216.

Shea, J. J. 2006b. The origins of lithic projectile point technology: Evidence from Africa, the Levant, and Europe. *Journal of Archaeological Science* 33:823–846.

Shea, J. J. 2007. Behavioral differences between Middle and Upper Paleolithic *Homo sapiens* in the East Mediterranean Levant: The roles of interspecific competition and dispersal from Africa. *Journal of Anthropological Research* 64:449–488.

Shea, J. J. 2008. The Middle Stone Age archaeology of the Lower Omo Valley Kibish Formation: Excavations, lithic assemblages, and inferred patterns of early *Homo sapiens* behavior. *Journal of Human Evolution (Special Issue: Paleoanthropology of the Kibish Formation, Southern Ethiopia)* 55:448–485.

Shea, J. J. 2010. Stone Age visiting cards revisited: A strategic perspective on the lithic technology of early hominin dispersal, in *Out of Africa 1: The First Hominin Colonization of Eurasia.* Edited by J. G. Fleagle, J. J. Shea, F. E. Grine, A. L. Baden, and R. Leakey, pp. 47–64. New York, NY: Springer.

Shea, J. J. 2011a. *Homo sapiens* is as *Homo sapiens* was: Behavioral variability vs. "behavioral modernity" in Paleolithic Archaeology. *Current Anthropology* 52:1–35.

Shea, J. J. 2011b. Refuting a myth of human origins. *American Scientist* 99:128–135.

Shea, J. J. 2011c. Stone tool analysis and human evolution: Some advice from Uncle Screwtape. *Evolutionary Anthropology* 20:48–53.

Shea, J. J. 2013a. Lithic Modes A–I: A new framework for describing global-scale variation in stone tool technology illustrated with evidence from the East Mediterranean Levant. *Journal of Archaeological Method and Theory* 20:151–186.

Shea, J. J. 2013b. *Stone Tools in the Paleolithic and Neolithic of the Near East: A Guide.* New York, NY: Cambridge University Press.

Shea, J. J. 2014. Sink the Mousterian? Named stone tool industries (NASTIES) as obstacles to investigating hominin evolutionary relationships in the Later Middle Paleolithic Levant. *Quaternary International* 350:169–179.

Shea, J. J. 2015a. Making and using stone tools: Advice for learners and teachers and insights for archaeologists. *Lithic Technology* 40:231–248.

Shea, J. J. 2015b. Timescales and variability in hominin technological strategies in the Jordan Rift Valley: What difference does 1.3 million years make?, in *Works in Stone: Contemporary Perspectives on Lithic Analysis.* Edited by M. Shott, pp. 33–45. Salt Lake City, UT: University of Utah Press.

Shea, J. J., and O. Bar-Yosef. 1999. Lithic assemblages from the new (1988–1994) excavations at 'Ubeidiya: A preliminary report. *Mitekufat HaEven* (Journal of the Israel Prehistoric Society) 28:5–20.

Shea, J. J., K. Brown, and Z. Davis. 2002. Controlled experiments with Middle Paleolithic spear points: Levallois points, in *Experimental Archaeology: Replicating Past*

Objects, Behaviors, and Processes. Edited by J. R. Mathieu, pp. 55–72. Oxford, UK: Archaeopress (British Archaeological Reports International Series 1035).

Shea, J. J., Z. Davis, and K. Brown. 2001. Experimental tests of Middle Paleolithic spear points using a calibrated crossbow. *Journal of Archaeological Science* 28:807–816.

Shea, J. J., and J. D. Klenck. 1993. An experimental investigation of the effects of trampling on the results of lithic microwear analysis. *Journal of Archaeological Science* 20:175–194.

Shennan, S. 2001. Demography and cultural innovation: A model and its implications for the emergence of modern human culture. *Cambridge Archaeological Journal* 11:5–16.

Shimelmitz, R., R. Barkai, and A. Gopher. 2011. Systematic blade production at late Lower Paleolithic (400–200 kyr) Qesem Cave, Israel. *Journal of Human Evolution* 61:458–479.

Shimelmitz, R., and S. L. Kuhn. 2013. Early Mousterian Levallois technology in Unit IX of Tabun Cave. *PaleoAnthropology* 2013:1–27.

Shipman, P. 1981. *The Life History of a Fossil: An Introduction to Taphonomy and Paleoecology.* Cambridge, MA: Harvard University Press.

Shipman, P. 2015. *The Invaders: How Humans and Their Dogs Drove Neanderthals to Extinction.* Cambridge, MA: Belknap/Harvard University Press.

Shipton, C. 2013. *A Million Years of Hominin Sociality and Cognition: Acheulean Bifaces in the Hunsgi-Baichbal Valley, India.* Oxford, UK: Archaeopress (British Archaeological Reports International Series 2468).

Shott, M. J. 1996. An exegesis of the curation concept. *Journal of Anthropological Research* 52:259–280.

Shott, M. J. 2003. *Chaîne opératoire* and reduction sequence. *Lithic Technology* 28:95–105.

Simmons, A. H. 1977. The Geometric Kebaran "A" Camp Site of D101 C, in *Prehistory and Paleoenvironments in the Central Negev, Israel, Volume 2: The Avdat/Aqev Area, Part 2 and the Har Harif.* Edited by A. E. Marks, pp. 119–130. Dallas: Southern Methodist University Press.

Simmons, A. H. 2007. *The Neolithic Revolution in the Near East: Transforming the Human Landscape.* Tucson, AZ: University of Arizona Press.

Singer, R., B. Gladfelter, and J. Wymer. 1993. *The Lower Paleolithic Site at Hoxne, England.* Chicago, IL: University of Chicago Press.

Singer, R., and J. Wymer. 1982. *The Middle Stone Age at Klasies River Mouth in South Africa.* Chicago, IL: University of Chicago Press.

Skertchly, S. B. J. 1879. *On the Manufacture of Gun-Flints, the Methods of Excavating for Flint, the Age of Palaeolithic Man, and the Connection Between Neolithic Art and the Gun-Flint Trade. Memoirs of the Geological Survey.* London: Royal Stationery Office.

Slack, M. J., R. L. Fullagar, J. H. Field, and A. Border. 2004. New Pleistocene ages for backed artefact technology in Australia. *Archaeology in Oceania* 39:131–137.

Slimak, L. Editor. 2007. *Artisanats & territoires de chasseurs moustériens de Champ Grand.* Quercy-Mercuès, France: Maison Méditerranéenne des Sciences de l'Homme.

Smallwood, A. M., D. S. Miller, and D. Sain. 2013. Topper Site, South Carolina: An overview of the Clovis lithic assemblage from the Topper Hillside, in *In the Eastern Fluted Point Tradition.* Edited by J. A. M. Gingerich, pp. 280–298. Salt Lake City, UT: University of Utah Press.

Smith, M. A. 2006. Characterizing Late Pleistocene and Holocene stone artefact assemblages from Puritjarra Rock Shelter: A long sequence from the Australian desert. *Records of the Australian Museum* 58:371–410.

Smith, P. E. L. 1966. *Le Solutréen en France.* Bordeaux: Université de Bordeaux Institut de Préhistoire (Mémoire 5).

Snarskis, M. J. 1979. Turrialba: A Paleo-Indian quarry and workshop site in eastern Costa Rica. *American Antiquity* 44:125–138.

Snir, A., D. Nadel, I. Groman-Yaroslavski, Y. Melamed, M. Sternberg, O. Bar-Yosef, and E. Weiss. 2015. The origin of cultivation and proto-weeds, long before Neolithic farming. *PLoS ONE* 10:e0131422.

Sockol, M. D., D. A. Raichlen, and H. Pontzer. 2007. Chimpanzee locomotor energetics and the origin of human bipedalism. *Proceedings of the National Academy of Sciences* 104:12265–12269.

Soffer, O. 1985. *The Upper Paleolithic of the Central Russian Plain.* Orlando, FL: Academic Press.

Soffer, O., and M. W. Conkey. 1997. Studying ancient visual cultures, in *Beyond Art: Pleistocene Image and Symbol.* Edited by M. W. Conkey, O. Soffer, D. Stratmann, and N. G. Jablonski, pp. 1–16. San Francisco, CA: California Academy of Sciences.

Solecki, R. S., and R. L. Solecki. 1993. The pointed tools from the Mousterian Occupations of Shanidar Cave, northern Iraq, in *The Paleolithic Prehistory of the Zagros-Taurus*. Edited by D. Olzewski and H. L. Dibble, pp. 119–146. Philadelphia, PA: University of Pennsylvania Museum (Monograph No. 83).

Sollas, W. J. 1911. *Ancient Hunters and Their Modern Representatives*. London: Macmillan.

Soressi, M., and M. A. Hays. 2003. Manufacture, transport, and use of Mousterian bifaces: A case study from the Perigord (France), in *Multiple Approaches to the Study of Bifacial Technologies*. Edited by M. Soressi and H. L. Dibble, pp. 125–145. Philadelphia, PA: University of Pennsylvania Museum.

Spagnoletti, N., E. Visalberghi, E. Ottoni, P. Izar, and D. Fragaszy. 2011. Stone tool use by adult wild bearded capuchin monkeys (*Cebus libidinosus*). Frequency, efficiency and tool selectivity. *Journal of Human Evolution* 61:97–107.

Speth, J. D. 1990. Seasonality, resource stress, and food sharing in so-called "egalitarian" foraging societies. *Journal of Anthropological Archaeology* 9:148–188.

Speth, J. D. 2010. *The Paleoanthropology and Archaeology of Big-Game Hunting: Protein, Fat or Politics?* New York, NY: Springer.

Stanford, C. B., and H. T. Bunn. Editors. 2001. *Meat Eating and Human Evolution*. New York, NY: Oxford University Press.

Stanford, D. J., and B. A. Bradley. 2012. *Across Atlantic Ice: The Origins of America's Clovis Culture*. Berkeley, CA: University of California Press.

Stout, D. 2011. Stone toolmaking and the evolution of human culture and cognition. *Philosophical Transactions of the Royal Society of London B: Biological Sciences* 366:1050–1059.

Stout, D., E. E. Hecht, N. Khreisheh, B. Bradley, and T. Chaminade. 2015. Cognitive demands of Lower Paleolithic toolmaking. *PLoS ONE* 10:e0121804.

Straus, L. G. 1995. The Upper Paleolithic of Europe: An overview. *Evolutionary Anthropology* 4:4–16.

Straus, L. G., and G. A. Clark. Editors. 1987. *La Riera Cave: Stone Age Hunter-Gatherer Adaptations in Northern Spain. Arizona State University Anthropological Research Papers*. Tempe, AZ: Arizona State University.

Straus, L. G., and T. Goebel. 2011. Humans and Younger Dryas: Dead end, short detour, or open road to the Holocene? *Quaternary International* 242:259–261.

Stringer, C. 2012. The status of *Homo heidelbergensis* (Schoetensack 1908). *Evolutionary Anthropology: Issues, News, and Reviews* 21:101–107.

Summerhayes, G. R., M. Leavesley, A. Fairbairn, H. Mandui, J. Field, A. Ford, and R. Fullagar. 2010. Human adaptation and plant use in Highland New Guinea 49,000 to 44,000 Years Ago. *Science* 330:78–81.

Susman, R. L. 1994. Fossil evidence for early hominid tool use. *Science* 265:1570–1573.

Susman, R. L. 1998. Hand function and tool behavior in early hominids. *Journal of Human Evolution* 35:23–46.

Svoboda, J. Editor. 1994. *Pavlov I, excavations 1952–1953. Études et recherches de l'Université de Liège, No. 66*. Liège, Belgium: Université de Liège (ERAUL 66).

Svoboda, J., and O. Bar-Yosef. Editors. 2003. *Stránská skála. Origins of the Upper Paleolithic in the Brno Basin, Moravia, Czech Republic*. Cambridge, MA: Peabody Museum of Archaeology and Ethnology, Harvard University (American School of Prehistoric Research Bulletin 47).

Takashi, T. 2012. MIS3 edge-ground axes and the arrival of the first *Homo sapiens* in the Japanese Archipelago. *Quaternary International* 248:70–78.

Taylor, W. W. 1948. *A Study of Archaeology*. Washington, D.C.: American Anthropological Association (Memoir 69).

Tchernov, E. 1997. Are Late Pleistocene environmental factors, faunal changes, and cultural transformations causally connected? The case of the Southern Levant. *Paléorient* 23:209–228.

Testart, A. 1982. The significance of food storage among hunter-gatherers: Residence patterns, population densities and social inequalities. *Current Anthropology* 23:523–537.

Tixier, J. 1970. L'abri sous roche de Kasr Aqil. *Bulletin du Musée de Beyrouth* 23:171–191.

Tomasello, M. 1999. *The Cultural Origins of Human Cognition*. Cambridge, MA: Harvard University Press.

Tomasello, M. 2005. *Constructing a Language: A Usage-Based Theory of Language Acquisition*. Cambridge, MA: Harvard University Press.

Tooby, J. M., and I. DeVore. 1987. The reconstruction of hominid behavioral evolution through strategic modeling, in *The Evolution of Hominid Behavior: Primate Models*. Edited by W. G. Kinzey, pp.

183–237. Albany, NY: State University of New York Press.

Tostevin, G. B. 2012. *Seeing Lithics: A Middle-Range Theory for Testing for Cultural Transmission in the Pleistocene.* American School of Prehistoric Research Publications, Peabody Museum, Harvard University. Oakville, CT: Oxbow.

Toth, N., J. D. Clark, and G. Ligabue. 1992. The last stone axe makers. *Scientific American* 263:88–93.

Toth, N. P., and K. Schick. Editors. 2006. *The Oldowan: Case Studies Into the Earliest Stone Age.* Bloomington, IN: Stone Age Institute Press.

Toth, N., and K. Schick. 2009. The Oldowan: The tool making of early hominins and chimpanzees compared. *Annual Review of Anthropology* 38:289–305.

Toth, N., K. D. Schick, E. S. Savage-Rumbaugh, R. Sevcik, and D. Rumbaugh. 1993. Pan the tool-maker: Investigations into the stone tool-making and tool-using abilities of a bonobo (*Pan paniscus*). *Journal of Archaeological Science* 20:81–91.

Toth, N. P. 1985. The Oldowan reassessed: A close look at early stone artifacts. *Journal of Archaeological Science* 12:101–120.

Toth, N. P., and K. Schick. Editors. 2006. *The Oldowan: Case Studies Into the Earliest Stone Age.* Bloomington, IN: Stone Age Institute Press.

Trinkaus, E. 2005. Early modern humans. *Annual Review of Anthropology* 34:207–230.

Trinkaus, E., and W. W. Howells. 1979. The Neandertals. *Scientific American* 241:118–133.

Trinkaus, E., and P. Shipman. 1993. *The Neandertals: Changing the Image of Mankind.* New York, NY: Knopf.

Tryon, C. A., and J. T. Faith. 2013. Variability in the Middle Stone Age of Eastern Africa. *Current Anthropology* 54:S234–S254.

Tryon, C. A., S. McBrearty, and P.-J. Texier. 2005. Levallois lithic technology from the Kapthurin Formation, Kenya: Acheulian origin and Middle Stone Age diversity. *African Archaeological Review* 22:199–229.

Tsirk, A. 2014. *Fractures in Knapping.* Oxford, UK: Archaeopress Archaeology.

Tuffreau, A. 1992. Middle Paleolithic settlement in northern France, in *The Middle Paleolithic: Adaptation, Behavior, and Variability.* Edited by H. L. Dibble and P. A. Mellars, pp. 59–74. Philadelphia, PA: University of Pennsylvania Museum (Monograph No. 72).

Turner, A., and M. Antón. 2004. *Evolving Eden: An Illustrated Guide to the Evolution of the African Large-Mammal Fauna.* New York, NY: Columbia University Press.

Twiss, K. C. 2007. The Neolithic of the Southern Levant. *Evolutionary Anthropology* 16:24–35.

Ungar, P. Editor. 2007. *Evolution of the Human Diet: The Known, the Unknown, and the Unknowable.* New York, NY: Oxford University Press.

Ungar, P. S., and M. Sponheimer. 2011. The diets of early hominins. *Science* 334:190–193.

Unger-Hamilton, R. 1983. An investigation into the variables affecting the development and the appearance of plant polish on the blades, in *Traces d'utilization sur les outiles Néolithiques du Proche Orient.* Edited by J. Cauvin, pp. 243–250. Lyon: Travaux de la maison de l'Orient 5.

Valla, F., et al. 2007. Les fouilles de Ain Mallaha (Eynan) de 2003–2005: Quatrième rapport préliminaire. *Journal of the Israel Prehistoric Society* 2007:135–379.

Valoch, K. 1993. Vedrovice V, eine Siedlung des Szeletien in Südmähren. *Quartär* 43/44:7–93.

van Schaik, C. P., and G. R. Pradhan. 2003. A model for tool-use traditions in primates: Implications for the coevolution of culture and cognition. *Journal of Human Evolution* 44:645–664.

Van Valkenburgh, B. 2001. The dog-eat-dog world of carnivores: A review of past and present carnivore community dynamics, in *Meat Eating and Human Evolution.* Edited by C. B. Stanford and H. T. Bunn, pp. 101–121. New York, NY: Oxford University Press.

Vanhaeren, M., and F. d'Errico. 2006. Aurignacian ethno-linguistic geography of Europe revealed by personal ornaments. *Journal of Archaeological Science* 33:1105–1128.

Veblen, T. 1899. *Theory of the Leisure Class.* New York, NY: Macmillan.

Veth, P., M. Smith, J. Bowler, K. Fitzsimmons, A. N. Williams, and P. Hiscock. 2009. Excavations at Parnkupirti, Lake Gregory, Great Sandy Desert: OSL ages for occupation before the Last Glacial Maximum. *Australian Archaeology* 69:1–10.

Villa, P. 1983. *Terra Amata and the Middle Pleistocene Archaeological Record of Southern France.* Berkeley, CA: University of California Press.

Villa, P., A. Delagnes, and L. Wadley. 2005. A late Middle Stone Age artifact assemblage from Sibudu (KwaZulu-Natal). Comparisons with the European Middle Paleolithic. *Journal of Archaeological Science* 32:399–422.

Volman, T. 1984. Early prehistory of southern Africa, in *South African Prehistory and Paleoenvironments*. Edited by R. G. Klein, pp. 169–220. Boston: A. A. Balkema.

Wadley, L. 2010. Compound adhesive manufacture as a behavioral proxy for complex cognition in the Middle Stone Age. *Current Anthropology* 51:S111–S119.

Wadley, L. 2015. Those marvellous millennia: The Middle Stone Age of Southern Africa. *Azania: Archaeological Research in Africa* 50:155–226.

Waguespack, N. M. 2007. Why we're still arguing about the Pleistocene occupation of the Americas. *Evolutionary Anthropology* 16:63–74.

Waters, M. D., and C. D. Pevney. Editors. 2011. *Clovis Lithic Technology: Investigation of a Stratified Workshop at the Gault Site, Texas*. Peopling of the Americas Publications. College Station, TX: Texas A&M University Press.

Weedman, K. 2006. An ethnoarchaeological study of hafting and stone tool diversity among the Gamo of Ethiopia. *Journal of Archaeological Method and Theory* 13:188–237.

Wells, S. 2009. *Deep Ancestry: Inside the Genographic Project*. Washington, D.C.: National Geographic Society.

Wendorf, F., and R. Schild. 1974. *A Middle Stone Age Sequence from the Central Rift Valley, Ethiopia*. Warsaw, Poland: Polska Akademia Nauk.

West, F. H. Editor. 1996. *American Beginnings: The Prehistory and Paleoecology of Beringia*. Chicago, IL: University of Chicago Press.

White, J. P. 1968. Ston Naip Bilong Tumbuna: The living Stone Age in New Guinea, in *La Préhistoire: Problèmes et tendances*. Edited by F. Bordes and D. de Sonneville-Bordes, pp. 511–516. Paris: CNRS.

White, J. P., and R. Lampert. 1987. Creation and discovery, in *Australians to 1788*. Edited by D. J. Mulvaney and J. P. White, pp. 3–23. Broadway (NSW), Australia: Fairfax, Syme & Weldon Associates.

White, M. J. 2001. Out of Abbeville: Sir John Evans, Paleolithic patriarch and handaxe pioneer, in *A Very Remote Period Indeed: Papers on the Palaeolithic Presented to Derek Roe*. Edited by S. Milliken and J. Cook, pp. 242–248. Oxford, UK: Oxbow Books.

White, P. 2014. Sahul and Near Oceania in the Pleistocene, in *The Cambridge World Prehistory, Volume 1: Africa, South and Southeast Asia and the Pacific*. Edited by C. Renfrew and P. Bahn, pp. 566–578. New York, NY: Cambridge University Press.

Whiten, A., and C. Boesch. 2001. The cultures of chimpanzees. *Scientific American* 284:61–67.

Whittaker, J. C. 1994. *Flintknapping: Making and Understanding Stone Tools*. Austin, TX: University of Texas Press.

Whittaker, J. C. 2004. *American Flintknappers: Stone Age Art in the Age of Computers*. Austin: University of Texas Press.

Whittaker, J. C., and M. Stafford. 1999. Replicas, fakes and art: The Twentieth-Century Stone Age and its effects on archaeology. *American Antiquity* 64:203–214.

Wiessner, P. 1983. Style and social information in Kalahari San projectile points. *American Antiquity* 48:253–276.

Wilkins, J., and M. Chazan. 2012. Blade production ~500 thousand years ago at Kathu Pan 1, South Africa: Support for a multiple origins hypothesis for early Middle Pleistocene blade technologies. *Journal of Archaeological Science* 39:1883–1900.

Wilkins, J., B. Schoville, and K. Brown. 2014. An experimental investigation of the functional hypothesis and evolutionary advantage of stone-tipped spears. *PLoS ONE* 9:e104514.

Wilkins, J., B. J. Schoville, K. S. Brown, and M. Chazan. 2012. Evidence for early hafted hunting technology. *Science* 338:942–946.

Willey, G. R., and P. Phillips. 1958. *Method and Theory in American Archaeology*. Chicago, IL: University of Chicago Press.

Willoughby, P. R. 2007. *The Evolution of Modern Humans in Africa: A Comprehensive Guide*. New York, NY: Altamira.

Wilmsen, E. N., and F. H. H. Roberts. 1978. *Lindenmeier, 1934–1974: Concluding Report on Excavations*. Washington, D.C.: Smithsonian Institution.

Winterhalder, B. 1986. Diet choice, risk, and food sharing in a stochastic environment. *Journal of Anthropological Archaeology* 5:369–392.

Winterhalder, B. 2001. The behavioural ecology of hunter-gatherers, in *Hunter-Gatherers: An Interdisciplinary Perspective*. Edited by C. Panter-Brick, R. H. Layton, and P. Rowley-Conwy, pp. 12–38. Cambridge, UK: Cambridge University Press.

Witthoft, J. 1967. Glazed polish on flint tools. *American Antiquity* 32:383–388.

Wobst, M. H. 1977. Stylistic behavior and information exchange, in *For the Director, Research Essays in Honor of James B. Griffin*. Edited by C. Cleland, pp. 317–342. Ann Arbor: Museum of Anthropology, University of Michigan (Anthropology Paper 61).

Wood, B. A. 2006. *Human Evolution: A Very Short Introduction*. Oxford, UK: Oxford University Press.

Wrangham, R. W. 1999. Evolution of coalitionary killing. *Yearbook of Physical Anthropology* 42:1–30.

Wrangham, R. W. 2009. *Catching Fire: How Cooking Made Us Human*. New York, NY: Basic Books.

Wright, K. 1991. The origins and development of ground stone assemblages in Late Pleistocene Southwest Asia. *Paléorient* 17:19–45.

Wright, K. 1992. A classification system for ground stone tools from the prehistoric Levant. *Paléorient* 18:53–81.

Wright, K. 1993. Early Holocene ground stone assemblages in the Levant. *Levant* 25:93–111.

Wright, K. 1994. Ground-stone tools and hunter-gatherer subsistence in Southwest Asia: Implications for the transition to farming. *American Antiquity* 59:238–263.

Wynn, T. 1995. Handaxe enigmas. *World Archaeology* 27:10–24.

Wynn, T. 2002. Archaeology and cognitive evolution. *Behavioral and Brain Sciences* 25:389–402.

Yaroshevich, A., D. Kaufman, D. Nuzhnyy, O. Bar-Yosef, and M. Weinstein-Evron. 2010. Design and performance of microlith implemented projectiles during the Middle and the Late Epipaleolithic of the Levant: Experimental and archaeological evidence. *Journal of Archaeological Science* 37:368–388.

Yellen, J. 1977. *Archaeological Approaches to the Present: Models for Reconstructing the Past*. New York, NY: Academic Press.

Yellen, J., A. Brooks, D. Helgren, M. Tappen, S. Ambrose, R. Bonnefille, J. Feathers, G. Goodfriend, K. Ludwig, P. Renne, and K. Stewart. 2005. The archaeology of the Aduma Middle Stone Age sites in the Awash Valley, Ethiopia. *PaleoAnthropology* 10:25–100.

Yu, P.-L. 2006. From atlatl to bow and arrow: Implicating projectile technology in changing systems of hunter-gatherer mobility, in *Archaeology and Ethnoarchaeology of Mobility*. Edited by F. Sellet, R. Greaves, and P.-L. Yu, pp. 201–220. Gainesville, FL: University Press of Florida.

Zachos, J., M. Pagani, L. Sloan, E. Thomas, and K. Billups. 2001. Trends, rhythms, and aberrations in global climate 65 Ma to present. *Science* 292:686–693.

Zahavi, A., and A. Zahavi. 1997. *The Handicap Principle: A Missing Piece of Darwin's Puzzle*. Oxford, UK: Oxford University Press.

Zeder, M. A. 2011. The origins of agriculture in the Near East. *Current Anthropology* 52:S221–S235.

Zilhao, J. 2014. The Upper Paleolithic of Europe, in *The Cambridge World Prehistory, Volume 3: West and Central Asia and Europe*. Edited by C. Renfrew and P. Bahn, pp. 1703–1747. New York, NY: Cambridge University Press.

Zink, K. D., and D. E. Lieberman. 2016. Impact of meat and Lower Paleolithic food processing techniques on chewing in humans. *Nature* 531: 500–503.

Zohary, M. 1973. *Geobotanical Foundations of the Middle East*. Stuttgart: Gustav Fischer Verlag.

INDEX